TIMBER DESIGN

for the
Civil Professional
Engineering Examination

Third Edition

Robert L. Brungraber, Ph.D., P.E.

PROFESSIONAL PUBLICATIONS, INC.
Belmont, CA 94002

In the ENGINEERING REFERENCE MANUAL SERIES

Engineer-In-Training Reference Manual
    Engineering Fundamentals Quick Reference Cards
    Engineer-In-Training Sample Examinations
    Mini-Exams for the E-I-T Exam
    1001 Solved Engineering Fundamentals Problems
    E-I-T Review: A Study Guide
Civil Engineering Reference Manual
    Civil Engineering Quick Reference Cards
    Civil Engineering Sample Examination
    Civil Engineering Review Course on Cassettes
    Seismic Design of Building Structures
    Seismic Design Fast
    Timber Design for the Civil P.E. Examination
    Fundamentals of Reinforced Masonry Design
    246 Solved Structural Engineering Problems
Mechanical Engineering Reference Manual
    Mechanical Engineering Quick Reference Cards
    Mechanical Engineering Sample Examination
    101 Solved Mechanical Engineering Problems
    Mechanical Engineering Review Course on Cassettes
    Consolidated Gas Dynamics Tables
Electrical Engineering Reference Manual
    Electrical Engineering Quick Reference Cards
    Electrical Engineering Sample Examination
Chemical Engineering Reference Manual
    Chemical Engineering Quick Reference Cards
    Chemical Engineering Practice Exam Set
Land Surveyor Reference Manual
Petroleum Engineering Practice Problem Manual
Expanded Interest Tables
Engineering Law, Design Liability, and Professional Ethics
Engineering Unit Conversions

In the ENGINEERING CAREER ADVANCEMENT SERIES

How to Become a Professional Engineer
The Expert Witness Handbook—A Guide for Engineers
Getting Started as a Consulting Engineer
Intellectual Property Protection—A Guide for Engineers
E-I-T/P.E. Course Coordinator's Handbook
Becoming a Professional Engineer

TIMBER DESIGN for the CIVIL P.E. EXAM
Third Edition

Printed in the United States of America

ISBN: 0-912045-13-2

Professional Publications, Inc.
1250 Fifth Avenue, Belmont, CA 94002
(415) 593-9119

Current printing of this edition (last number): 6 5 4 3 2

Copyediting: Shelley Arenson
Typesetting: Sylvia Osias
Cover Design: Lynelle Dodge

Table of Contents

Guide To Figures

Guide To Tables

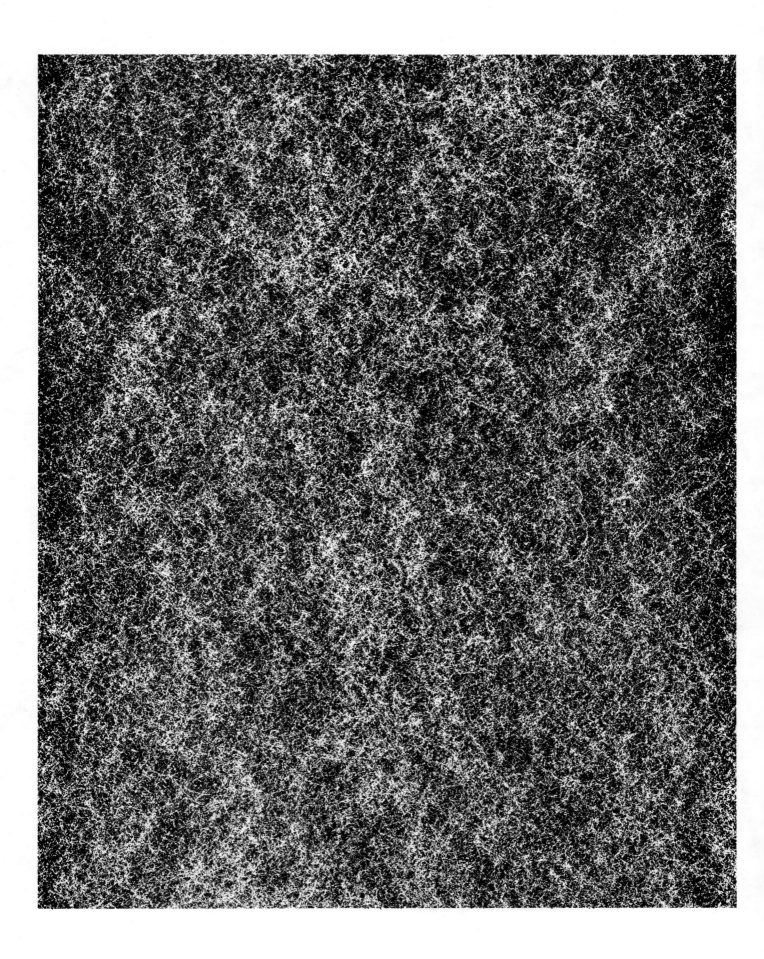

Acknowledgments

The timber industry has been very supportive of this and all other books dealing with wood structures. The National Forest Products Association, which promulgates a widely accepted timber design code, was particularly generous in sharing tables from their publication.

I would like to thank my parents for providing me with support, both financial and spiritual, throughout my academic career. Colorado State University's fine Timber Structures Program gave me the specific background required for this work. The Construction Management Program at Stanford was extremely generous with their computer and printer facilities. The corrections and revisions in this third edition were accomplished through the tolerance of Benson Woodworking and the careful review of James Magee. The many revisions in the second edition of this work (occasioned by author errors and changes in the timber code) were accomplished through the efforts of Major William W. Watkin III. Both the second and third editions include corrections made in response to the careful reading of past readers. Finally, profound thanks go to my wife Joel, for her unflagging encouragement and willingness to accommodate this work in our lives.

Robert L. Brungraber, Ph.D., P.E.

Introduction

This book is intended to help you prepare for timber structural questions on a professional engineering exam. While this book was written to be self-contained, it is strongly recommended that you also use the National Design Specification for Wood Construction (NDS), published by the National Forest Products Association.[1] The NDS is the basic timber code used in the United States, and recent professional engineering exam questions on timber structures have required that the examinee cite the edition of the NDS used in answering specific problems. The third edition of this book references the 1986 edition of the NDS.

For those engineers who design timber structures in practice, this book will be a useful reference due to its worked examples illustrating the principles found in the code. The book is necessarily problem oriented and, therefore, cannot be exhaustive in its treatment of wood science. If, for example, you are interested in sophisticated wood mechanics, there are several references listed in the bibliography.

The interesting thing about the need for this book is that questions on timber structures are reappearing on P.E. exams after a lengthy hiatus. Why the renewed emphasis on the material after so many years? The answer is that timber has moved beyond the realms of residential and temporary construction, structures that have neither required nor received much engineering attention.

Many structures being built with wood in the U.S. today would have been made of steel or concrete only a few years ago. The major advance has been in glue-laminating large members from smaller, standard size lumber. With its high strength-to-weight ratio, glue-laminated timber now dominates the long-span rigid dome market, for example.

The proven durability of preservative-treated timber has also opened up a large market in the replacement of bridges in the short to medium span range. Because of economic and schedule considerations, more low-rise commercial buildings are being framed with timber joists and rafters.

Timber's unique characteristics have made it the material chosen for immense and sophisticated structures, such as the 200 foot wide, 590 foot long Air Force trestle in New Mexico which holds a B-52 124 feet in the air for testing in a non-magnetic environment. Finally, increases in rehabilitating buildings have involved engineers in evaluating and strengthening older timber structures.

Besides its primary role as the world's most widely used fuel, timber is the most common building material—both in number of structures and total floor area. It is easy to believe that it was the first material used for above-ground shelters. The marvel is that timber design methods are as relatively simplistic as they are after all those years and structures.

Timber's characteristics and technology's timing have combined to hold back the development of timber analysis from the sophistication levels seen in steel and concrete. Timber is the only organic building material. Its natural source not only makes it renewable, but in many ways the most complex of building materials. Even the most powerful computer analyses can be overwhelmed by modeling the complete response of a timber structure. Timber has also been overlooked by engineers because as they were finding methods to analyze complex problems, timber was being replaced in large structures by steel and concrete—simpler materials with which to deal.

The timber codes are changing rapidly, however, as new products are introduced, larger and longer timber members are used, more timber research is performed, and more powerful analytical tools are developed. So, while the present codes may not address issues that arise frustratingly often, engineers might appreciate the freedom available in the timber codes, and supplement them with current research when required.

---

[1] National Forest Products Association, 1250 Connecticut Avenue N.W., Suite 200, Washington, D.C. 20036.

Notice To Examinees

Nomenclature

Nomenclature

A	cross-sectional area	inches^2
A_1	in fastener group analysis, area of main member(s), before drilling	inches^2
A_2	in fastener group analysis, area of side member(s), before drilling	inches^2
b	width of rectangular cross section	inches
c	distance from neutral axis to extreme bending fiber	inches
C_c	curvature factor; allowable bending stress in curved members	–
C_F	size factor; allowable bending stress in deep members	–
C_f	form factor; allowable bending stress in non-rectangular cross sections	–
C_k	dividing value between intermediate and long beams	–
C_s	slenderness factor for beams	–
CUF	condition of use factor	–
d	rectangular cross section depth	inches
d'	member depth remaining, after notching	inches
d_x	cross-sectional dimension resisting buckling about local x axis	–
d_y	cross-sectional dimension resisting buckling about local y axis	–
D	connector diameter	inches
e	eccentricity (of axial loads)	inches
E	Young's modulus of elasticity	psi
f_b	actual maximum bending stress at a cross section	psi

f_c	actual compression parallel to grain stress	psi
$f_{c\perp}$	actual compression perpendicular to grain stress	psi
f_g	actual end grain bearing stress	psi
f_r	actual radial stress in curved bending member	psi
f_t	actual tension parallel to grain stress	psi
f_v	actual "horizontal" (along the grain) shear stress	psi
F_b	allowable bending stress in extreme fiber	psi
F_b'	allowable bending stress in extreme fiber, adjusted for member slenderness	psi
F_c	allowable compression parallel to grain stress	psi
F_c'	allowable compression parallel to grain stress, adjusted for member slenderness	psi
$F_{c\perp}$	allowable compression perpendicular to grain stress	psi
F_g	allowable end grain bearing stress	psi
F_n	allowable load (or stress) at an angle to the grain (found with Hankinson's Formula)	psi
F_{rc}	allowable radial bending compression stress	psi
F_{rt}	allowable radial bending tension stress	psi
F_t	allowable tension parallel to grain stress	psi
F_v	allowable "horizontal" (along the grain) shear stress	psi
G	specific gravity	–
I	cross-sectional moment of inertia	inches^4

I_n	net cross-sectional moment of inertia	inches^4
J	convenient grouping of other factors, used in assessing combined stresses in members, considering slenderness	–
K	slenderness ratio separating intermediate from long columns, or modification factor for number of connectors in a row	–
K_e	effective column length factor (see Table 6.1)	–
ℓ	span length, or length of bolt in main member	inches
ℓ_b	bearing length in compression perpendicular to grain	inches
ℓ_e	effective length of member, considering slenderness	inches
ℓ_u	laterally unsupported length of beam	inches
ℓ_x	distance between restraints against column buckling about local x axis	–
ℓ_y	distance between restraints against column buckling about local y axis	–
L	member length	inches
LDF	Load Duration Factor	–
M	bending moment at cross section	in-lb
MC	moisture content	%
N	load on fastener(s) at angle to grain between 0° and 90°	–
P	load; or load on connector(s), parallel to grain	pounds
Q	first moment of the cross-sectional area beyond y about the neutral axis or load on connectors(s), perpendicular to grain	inches^3 or pounds
r	radius of curvature	feet or inches
s	cross-sectional modulus = $I/c = bd^2/6$ for rectangular section	inches^3
t	thickness	inches

V	shear force at cross section	pounds
WGT	weight of a sample	pounds
y	distance from neutral axis to point in cross section where shear stress is being evaluated (see Q)	inches
Y	deflection	inches

Symbols

θ	angle between the longitudinal wood axis (or grain) and the load or stress direction

Subscripts

1	in fastener group analysis, area of main member(s), before drilling
2	in fastener group analysis, area of side member(s), before drilling
b	bending stress (or length of bearing, when used with L)
c	curvature factor when used with C
$c_\parallel$	compressive stress parallel to the grain
$c_\perp$	compressive stress perpendicular to the grain
DRY	after oven-drying
e	effective, as in column length
f	form factor, when used with C
F	size factor, when used with C
g	end grain bearing stress
k	dividing value between long and intermediate beams, when used with C
n	specific angle with grain for evaluated property; or net, as in net moment of inertia
r	radial stress
rc	radial compression
rt	radial tension
t	tensile stress along the grain; or total, as in total moment of inertia
v	shear stress
WET	moisture content being evaluated

Superscripts

$'$	allowable stress after adjustments for slenderness

Part 1

Wood Anatomy and Physical Properties

Wood is an exceedingly complex organic material. Scientists have been studying its structure for centuries. The fields of wood anatomy and physics are immense and growing. In order to keep this book focused on structural applications, the wood anatomy presented will be superficial, even below the detail level of high school biology. Only those features and orientations of wood's internal structure that most significantly affect its behavior as a building material will be covered.

1 HARDWOODS AND SOFTWOODS

The terms *hardwood* and *softwood*, while commonly used and understood, are often misnomers. Hardwoods such as balsa and aspen are quite soft, while softwoods such as white pine and true fir are quite hard. The less common, but more precise, terms *deciduous* and *coniferous* are not universally applicable either. Deciduous (hardwood) trees are defined as those that lose their broad leaves annually, a rule violated every year in the tropics. Coniferous (softwood) trees, on the other hand, are not supposed to lose their leaves (needles) and should have seeds in cones. Again, there are species commonly recognized as softwoods that ignore this definition. But, the hardwood/softwood distinction is so widespread that time spent disputing it is largely wasted.

There are other differences between the two basic tree types. Internal structure in the softwoods is far simpler than in the hardwoods. There are only 650 softwood species, and they can be found in vast tracts, often containing only one species. There are more than 250,000 hardwood species, however, and they are widely scattered and interspersed.

The entire issue of softwood versus hardwood is largely an academic one, however, as far as the structural applications of this book are concerned. The majority of structural timber requirements are filled with softwoods. Hardwoods are mostly used for fuel, railroad ties, pallets, furniture and paneling, and many other non-structural products. Exceptions to this pattern are the older structures built amid the hardwood forests of the eastern United States.

2 WOOD ANATOMY

The most crucial aspect of wood anatomy, as it governs the behavior and design of timber members and connections, is that wood is basically a bundle of tubes bound together by a natural glue. The tubes are wood cells aligned along the major axes of the tree trunk and its branches. These cells are an eighth to a half inch long with walls composed primarily of cellulose. The glue binding the cells together is lignin, a very complex and tough compound.

As a tree grows, cells are laid up in concentric layers under the bark. The bark splits and expands, making room for new wood. Once a cell is in place, it does not move within the tree. Fences nailed to trees are encased by them, but not lifted. Except in the tropics, the new cells are not formed identically throughout the year. The difference in appearance of spring and summer wood causes wood's growth rings and grain.

3 LUMBER DEFECTS

As a tree grows, it responds to its environment in many ways. It inevitably develops characteristics that reduce the strength of lumber cut from it. The worst of these defects are: knots, cross grain, checks and splits, and reaction wood.

A. Knots

Knots are the most obvious lumber characteristic. A knot is a section of a branch that has been enveloped by the tree as it grew. If the branch was an early and low one that died and was encased along with its dead bark, the resulting knot is said to be *loose* or *encased*. A branch that was alive when the tree was cut produces *intergrown* or *tight* knots in the lumber, with uninterrupted contact between the wood cells and branch bark.

A knot's shape is a function of how the plane of the lumber face intersects the branch. A face normal to the axis of the branch results in a *round knot*. If the face is nearly parallel to the branch axis, the knot is called a *spike knot*. Any orientation between normal and parallel makes *oval knots*.

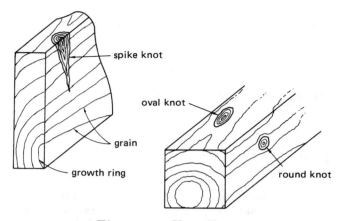

Figure 1.1 Knot Shapes

Knots reduce lumber's strength in several ways. A knot is an interruption in the fibers that would otherwise be aligned along the strong axis of the piece. The fibers that are left also deviate from that axis to pass around the knot. Finally, significant stress concentrations exist near the knot.

B. Cross Grain

Cross grain is a generic term describing wood fibers that are not aligned with the member's major axis. Severe cross grain occurs when trees that have grown spirally or with pronounced taper are cut for lumber. Some cross grain is the inevitable result of cutting prismatic, rectangular pieces from a tapered mass of concentric cylinders. Cross grain drastically reduces the tensile strength of lumber and can precipitate abrupt and early bending failures.

The most direct measure of cross grain is the *slope of grain*. Slope of grain is the angle, expressed as a ratio, between the wood fibers and the longitudinal axis of the lumber. A large slope (1 in 6) of grain is second only to knots in reducing the grade of a piece of lumber. Grain is a misleading term. The growth ring tracings on the lumber face can be parallel to the face, while the fibers are not. Often, a small pattern of checks will be the only indication of misaligned fibers.

C. Checks, Shakes, and Splits

Checks and splits are fractures in the wood that open as the lumber dries. Checks align with the longitudinal axis of the piece and are normal to the growth rings. Splits run through checks and are usually found at the ends of timber. The worst of the splits are often trimmed off after the lumber is dried as a final step in cutting lumber. Improper kiln-drying can accentuate splitting at the ends.

Shakes are thin voids within the tree that seem to occur naturally as the tree is growing. Shakes also align with the axis of the tree, but they lie in plane with the growth

rings. It is as if the tree had delaminated slightly at a transition between spring and summer wood.

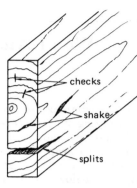

Figure 1.2 Checks, Shakes, and Splits

Timber's strength relies upon the connection between adjacent wood cells. Though checks, shakes, and splits may close, the cells never reconnect across the fracture. By physically separating pieces of lumber, checks, shakes, and splits are detrimental in many ways. Just what and how much effect these separations have depends on the location and severity of the defects, and the end use of the timber.

D. Reaction Wood

Reaction wood is created by the tree as a response to its own changing dead load. As branches get longer and heavier, or if the tree is tilted for some reason, the wood is subjected to bending stresses. The tree responds by growing thicker-walled, denser cells at these locations. Most softwoods grow *compression wood* on the underside of the branches. Most hardwoods, however, grow *tension wood* on branch topsides. The denser reaction wood shrinks more as it dries than does the surrounding normal wood, resulting in dramatic and abrupt warps in any lumber that contains reaction wood.

4   WOOD DENSITY

The density of wood varies a great deal within a single species, and even within a single tree. Increased density is the most reliable indicator of a species' higher strength. Density is principally a function of the amount of wood present, any extractives, and the amount of moisture present.

A. Amount of Wood

The specific gravity of the basic wood material, the cell wall, is a nearly constant 1.5, regardless of species. What does vary is the amount of that material present in the tree. Oak cells have relatively thick walls, while balsa cell walls are very thin.

Within a species, growth rate is the major variable in establishing density. The slower a softwood grows, the higher its percentage of the denser summer wood, and subsequently, its density. A tree's growth rate is affected by local environmental conditions more than anything else.

B. Extractives

Only cells within several inches of the bark are alive and transfer fluids within the tree. As the tree grows, this sapwood gradually transforms into heartwood. That transformation process involves the deposition on the cell walls of chemicals known as *extractives* or *infiltrates*. There is wide variety in types and amounts of extractives. Silicas in tropical woods, for example, dull saw blades rapidly. The most naturally rot-resistant timbers result from the presence of certain extractives, such as resins and waxes. The densest tropical woods, some of which sink in water, have large amounts of extractives.

C. Amount of Moisture

The amount of water present is the major influence on the density of a given piece of wood. Cellulose is a hygroscopic material, meaning it absorbs and gives up water readily. Since wood is primarily made of cellulose, it will change moisture content in response to changing conditions.

The most common measure of the amount of water present in wood is *moisture content* (MC).

$$\text{MC} = (100) \left(\frac{\text{WGT}_{wet} - \text{WGT}_{dry}}{\text{WGT}_{dry}} \right) \qquad 1.1$$

Moisture content varies widely with species and time. Fresh-cut cedar can have a moisture content as high as 250 percent.

Water in wood exists in two forms. The majority of the water is known as *free water* and simply fills the hollow cells while the tree is alive. This is the first water to go after the tree is cut, and only the weight of the wood changes as it does. There is about five times as much free water as there is *bound water*. The bound water is chemically bonded in the walls of the wood cells. As the bound water leaves, the wood shrinks and generally gets stronger.

There are certain moisture contents that are of interest:

- *Green*: When the tree is cut, its moisture content starts to drop as the free water is lost. The term *green* wood can mean the fresh-cut state. Green wood is also defined in allowable stress tables as having a moisture content level of 19 percent and above.

- *Fiber Saturation Point* (FSP): When the free water is mostly gone, but the bound water is still intact, the moisture content of the wood is defined as being at the *fiber saturation point*. The fiber saturation point is about 30 percent for all wood species. It is only below FSP that wood starts to shrink.

- *Equilibrium Moisture Content* (EMC): The wood continues to dry by losing bound water until it stabilizes at the *equilibrium moisture content*. The equilibrium moisture content of wood varies with species, and ambient temperature and humidity. In the United States, equilibrium moisture content can range from 5 percent to 25 percent, and 10 percent to 15 percent is the common range.

- *Oven-Dry*: In order to lower the moisture content below its equilibrium level, the remaining bound water must be driven off. Wood is heated in a ventilated oven at a temperature just above water's boiling point, and the weight is monitored. There is no absolutely dry wood, but once a baking specimen has reached a relatively stable weight, it is said to be *oven-dry*.

D. Shrinkage

The amount wood shrinks as it passes from its fiber saturation point to oven-dry varies with fiber orientation. The shrinkage along the fibers (longitudinally) is very small—0.1 to 0.2 percent. This means that a ten foot long timber will typically shorten less than an eighth of an inch.

Since it is the cell wall that shrinks with decreasing moisture content, it is not surprising that wood shrinks much more transverse to the cells than along them. There is a further difference in the shrinkage across the fibers, which depends on the orientation of the growth rings. Along the rings (the tangential direction), wood shrinks about eight percent from fiber saturation point to oven-dry. Across the rings (the radial direction), wood shrinks only three or four percent. An eight inch wide timber might be expected to shrink as much as a quarter inch or more as it passes from fiber saturation point to its equilibrium moisture content. This change in dimension can cause problems for unsophisticated designers, particularly in the area of connection detailing.

The difference in shrinkage between radial and tangential directions can also cause difficulties. The differential shrinkage means that the circumference shrinks more than the radius. The resultant hoop residual tensions in the wood make longitudinal splits in dry timber virtually inevitable. Since lumber is typically cut from green wood and then dried, the differential shrinkage also causes some distortion of the cross sections.

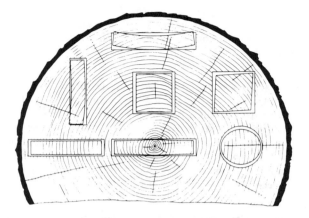

Figure 1.3 Characteristic Shrinkage, Distortion, and Checking

Since both volume and weight are functions of the amount of water present in wood, comparing species on the basis of density can be misleading and confusing. Specific gravity is the measure commonly used for comparing species. Specific gravity is the ratio of the wood's density to that of water. Wood density must be derived from weights and volumes evaluated at a specified moisture content. Unfortunately, several different benchmark conditions have been used over the years. Since the structural codes generally use the oven-dry condition for both weight and volume, that condition is assumed throughout this book.

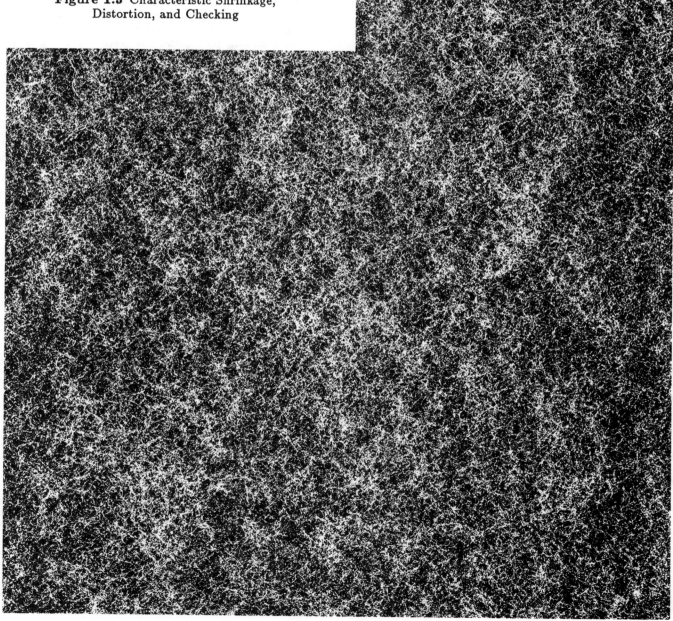

Part 2
Thermal Properties

Growing interest in energy efficiency has focused attention on thermal performance of building materials; wood is no exception. Most of the recent research is well beyond the scope of this book. A material's response to dynamic environmental conditions is a complex function of several material properties. Table 2.1 illustrates the low thermal conductivity of wood relative to other structural materials.

Table 2.1
Representative Thermal Conductivities

material	thermal conductivity, k BTU/hr-ft^2-in-°F
air	0.168
wood (softwood average)	0.80
glass	5.5
concrete	7.5
steel	312.0
aluminum	1,416.0

The dimensional changes wood undergoes because of variation in moisture content are much greater than those caused by temperature changes. Elevated temperatures drive off water and the wood shrinks, while its thermal response expands it. The accepted practice, in face of these conflicting effects, is to neglect thermal expansion and contraction under all normal circumstances.

One characteristic of timber's thermal properties which should interest structural engineers is larger members' resistance to fire. Even though wood supports combustion at lower temperatures than other structural materials, it still needs oxygen and elevated temperature to do so. Wood is such a good insulator that the temperature inside a large timber in an inferno is elevated only slightly. Consequently, timbers char and lose cross section and structural capacity very slowly. The longer and higher endurance of timbers in fire can mean reduced fire insurance rates for heavy timber structures.

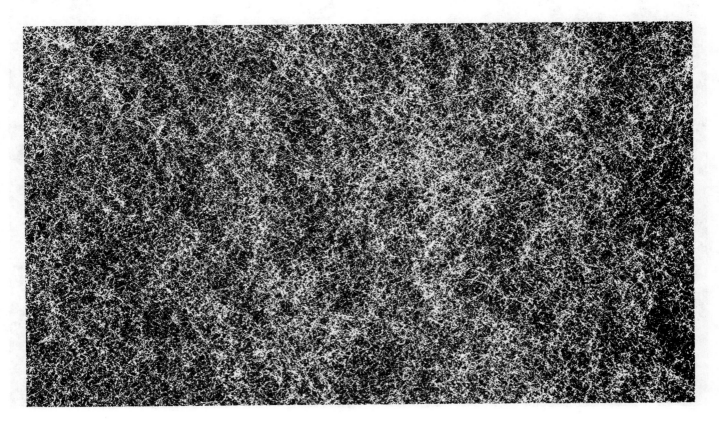

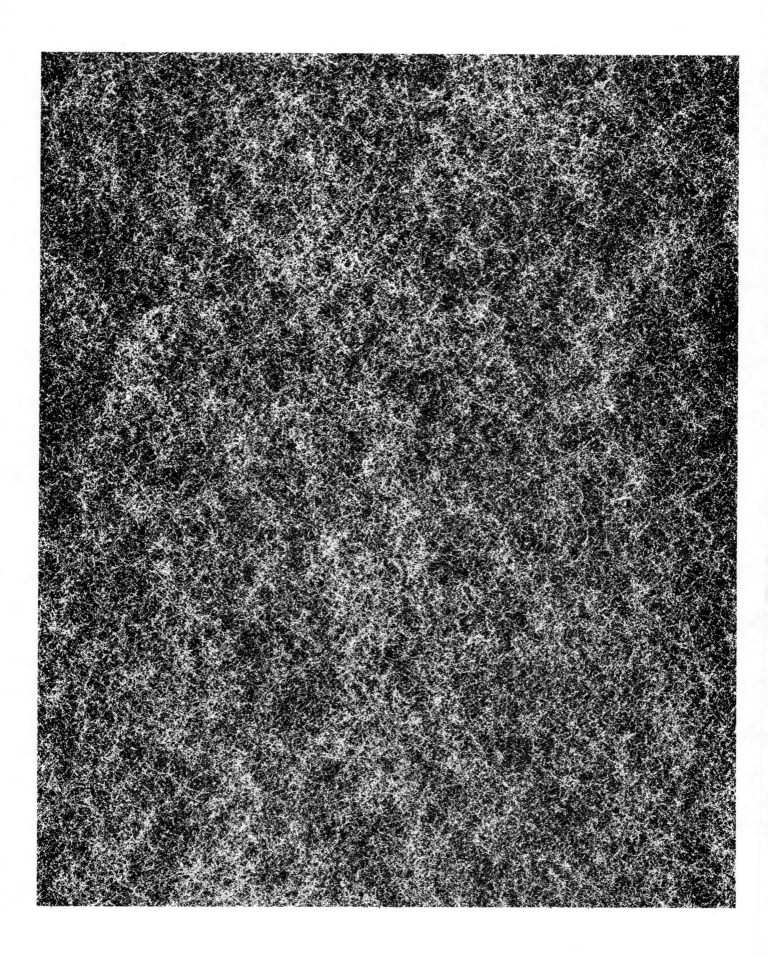

Part 3
Mechanical Properties of Wood

1 INTRODUCTION

As described earlier, wood consists of cells oriented in concentric cylinders in the tree. As a result of this and its growth irregularities, wood is an anisotropic material. Thus, wood's mechanical properties will be functions of position and orientation.

A common model of wood imposes three perpendicular axes of symmetry. Wood can then be treated as an orthotropic material, requiring consideration in three directions only. The three axes are related to the growth rings and are commonly designated as longitudinal, radial, and tangential.

The *longitudinal axis* is parallel to the wood fibers and is sometimes called the *strong axis*. The *radial axis* has its origin at the center of the tree and points outward. In a rectangular piece of lumber, the radial axis lies in the cross section and is perpendicular to the growth rings. The *tangential axis* follows the growth rings. In a tree, the tangential axis is circumferential; but in a piece of lumber, it is assumed to lie in a plane parallel to the growth rings.

By cutting trees in different ways, sawyers produce planks with the tangential and radial axes in a variety of positions. The two basic options, *plain-sawed* and *quarter-sawed*, are shown in Fig. 3.1.

Though the orthotropic model reduces anisotropic wood to a material with only three axes, designing still remains more complex with wood than with other common structural materials. For example, there are six separate Poisson's ratios involving the three different directions for load application and strain measurement. There are also three compressive stress directions.

In order to further simplify these orientation options to a manageable level, some assumptions and groupings are widely used. The radial and tangential directions are usually lumped into a *perpendicular-to-grain* category. Some properties, such as modulus of elasticity, are only needed for the longitudinal direction. Finally, certain properties, such as the various Poisson's ratios, are so unlikely to concern structural designers that they are usually neglected.

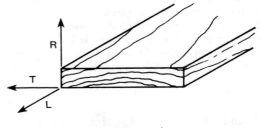

plain-sawed

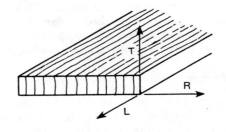

quarter-sawed

Figure 3.1 Orientation Axes

2 STRENGTH AND STIFFNESS: TEST AND DESIGN VALUES

Timber design has traditionally compared stresses caused by design loads with those judged to be allowable. Limit-state design procedures are being developed, but they have yet to appear in the U.S. codes. Timber strength depends on many different parameters. Strength varies with species, within a species, within trees from the same stand, and even within the same tree. Clearly, establishing safe design values for such a variable material is a paramount issue.

There are two basic methods used to establish allowable working stresses for timber design. The older method, historically used in the United States, is to test small clear specimens in the lab and correct for defects and service conditions found in actual use. The newer method, developed in Europe and gaining acceptance here, is to test the full-size timbers in nondestructive ways, correlate the measured quantity with a predicted capacity, and correct only for actual service conditions—not for defects.

A. Small Clear Specimen Method

This method relies completely on the validity of the test specimen sampling methods, which are correspondingly precise and complicated. A large enough number of tests lead to meaningful values. Even with apparently identical small clear specimens there is a spread in the test results. The corrections for actual timber defects and expected service are applied to a strength level below which only five percent of the tested specimens fail. This starting point for corrections is known as the *five percent exclusion limit*. There is a variety of correction factors applied to this five percent exclusion limit.

Defects

In its Standard D245, the American Society of Testing and Materials (ASTM) includes an exhaustive list of strength ratios to be applied to the five percent exclusion limit on the basis of various defects. Strength ratios vary from 4 to 99 percent, depending on the relative severity of the defect. Published design values include strength ratios that are specific to species, stress type, nature of use, moisture content, and lumber grade.

Safety Factor

Wood's variability is accounted for by using the five percent exclusion limit. The *safety factor* is intended to adjust properties for potential overload. The size of this safety factor depends on the predictability of behavior and the consequences of failure. There is no safety factor applied to compression across the grain nor to modulus of elasticity. A timber failure due to either of these properties would only be a matter of unacceptable deflection—generally not an actual collapse. Other safety factors range from about 0.8 for bending to 0.4 for shear, with shear failure considered more unpredictable than bending failure.

Special Grading

Certain species have significantly variable properties due to widely varying density within the species. The denser examples are stronger, and they can be graded accordingly. Since density variation within a species is largely a function of growth rate, the distinction is often done on the basis of growth ring, or grain, spacing. The closer the ring spacing, the denser the wood will be.

Special Conditions

This catchall factor covers a variety of issues. The depth of a bending member has an influence on its behavior, and is accounted for by normalizing the tabulated allowable stresses to a 12 inch deep beam and readjusting

from there for the actual depth. The modulus of elasticity is also decreased to account for the shear deflections in beams, which are then conveniently neglected.

Moisture Content

The test specifications call for specimens to be green when tested. Lumber in service may have varying moisture content, which the engineer must take into account. As wood dries below the fiber saturation point, it becomes stronger, but the larger members also split and are possibly weakened. Lumber is therefore divided into sizes larger than 4 inches wide and those that are narrower. The smaller lumber may be distinguished by as many as three moisture content ranges: above 19 percent (green), between 19 percent and 15 percent, and below 15 percent (kiln-dried, or K-D).

There are other factors, called *condition of use factors* (CUF), which are used to account for the special problem of designing connections in members that are expected to undergo changes in moisture content and dimension during their service life.

Load Duration

A further example of wood's complexity is its rheological, or time-dependent, stress-strain behavior. In general, a timber's capacity decreases as the load duration increases. Load durations range from sudden and brief (impact) loading to permanent, dead load.

The design life of timber structures is longer than the duration of typical tests; therefore, a factor is used to normalize the properties to a ten year duration. The engineer then corrects the allowable stresses to the expected load duration. Figure 3.2 illustrates the range of factors to be applied for load duration. The durations are cumulative over the life of the structure. The most commonly used load duration factors (LDF), listed in all the codes, are given in Table 3.1. These load duration factors apply to all connection design loads and allowable stress levels except modulus of elasticity and compression across the grain.

Table 3.1
Common Load Duration Factors

dead load (50 years)	0.90
snow load (2 months)	1.15
roof live load (7 days)	1.25
(7 days duration commonly used for concrete forming)	
wind or seismic load (1 day)	1.33
impact load	2.00

Reproduced from Wood Handbook: Wood as an Engineering Material, Agriculture Handbook No. 72, by Forest Products Laboratory, Forest Service, U.S. Department of Agriculture, 1974.

Load Combinations

The duration of any given combination of load types is that of the shortest duration load in the combination. That least value, therefore, establishes the load duration factor applied to the allowable stresses for a given combination. Some authors make an issue of only applying the load duration factor to the allowable stresses and not to the load, but the correct load duration factor must be applied to each of the possible design load combinations to determine which one is critical. The designer can apply the load duration factor either to load or to allowable stress, as long as it is not applied to both, or neither.

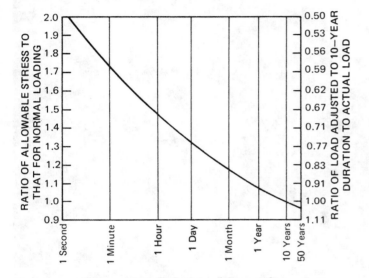

Figure 3.2 Relation of Strength to Duration of Load

Example 3.1

Determine the critical load combination on a roof rafter with the following loads: 20 psf dead load, 35 psf snow load, and 25 psf wind load.

To determine which load combination will control after modifying the allowable stresses for load duration, divide each combination by the load duration factor of

the shortest duration load included in the combination. The maximum of these effective design loads establishes the controlling load combination.

load combination	total load (psf)	adjusted load (psf)	design load (psf)
dead alone	20	$\frac{20}{0.9}$	22.2
dead + snow	55	$\frac{55}{1.15}$	47.8
dead + wind	45	$\frac{45}{1.33}$	33.8
dead + wind + $\frac{snow}{2}$	62.5	$\frac{62.5}{1.33}$	47.0
dead + snow + $\frac{wind}{2}$	67.5	$\frac{67.5}{1.33}$	50.75

The dead, snow, and half wind load combination controls. The design could now proceed with 50.75 psf and the tabulated values for allowable stresses, or with 67.5 psf and allowable stresses increased by 33% (this author's preferred method). Dividing the snow load in half when combining it with wind loads is a common building code recommendation. This may be unconservative, particularly where unusual roof shapes could concentrate drifting snow, and should only be done with care and consideration of the applicable code provisions.

B. Full-Size Testing

Another method for establishing allowable stresses requires testing full-size members and modifying the predicted capacities for design service conditions. The most common tests measure bending deflection or frequency when vibrated. These nondestructive tests provide stiffness data which are correlated with the strength of the member.

Lumber that has been *stress-graded* by one of these methods will include an allowable bending stress in the grade stamp. For example, a 1600f-1.4E machine-stress-rated (MSR) board would have an allowable bending stress of 1600 psi and a modulus of elasticity (E) of 1.4×10^6 psi. The principal uses of stress-graded lumber in the United States are on glue-laminated timbers and prefabricated trusses.

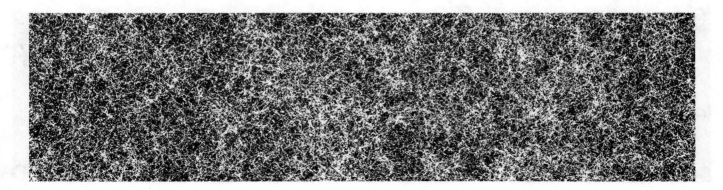

Part 4

Design Stresses in Lumber

1 INTRODUCTION

The vast majority of structural timber used in the United States is softwood. The major species are pine, fir, hemlock, spruce, cedar, and redwood. Most of these species have several varieties, such as red and ponderosa pine. When two or more similar species grow in the same area, they are often grouped together for manufacturing and marketing convenience. For example, hem-fir is a common pairing of hemlock and fir.

Trade associations developed around many of the species, and these associations promulgated their own grading standards. The proliferation of different standards left a legacy of confusion that is still being settled. Public Standard 20-70, administered by the American Lumber Standards Committee, has done much to standardize lumber grading across the nation. All the grading associations now use some form of a *select structural, no. 1, no. 2,* or *no. 3,* and *utility* rankings to grade their lumber. A no. 2 douglas fir 2×4 meets the same grading criteria as a no. 2 southern pine 2×4. The allowable stresses and stiffnesses may not be equal, but their characteristics will be equivalent.

There are many grading standards that do not usually concern engineers, such as ladder stock and pencil stock rules. This book uses the allowable stresses found in the Uniform Building Code. A few of the species found in that publication are reproduced in Appendix B of this book.

2 THE ALLOWABLE STRESS TABLES

The tables of allowable stresses are reasonably easy to use once the terms are understood. The footnotes at the ends of the tables are as important as the tables themselves, but they are often ignored by the uninformed.

A. Species/Variety

Determining the species of an old sawn timber can be extremely difficult, even for experts in the field. Specifying a precise species for new construction can cause unnecessary expense and delays. Unless there is a real need for a specific species, it is best to determine what is commonly available, or simply to be conservative in species assumption.

B. Moisture Content

Southern pine is a species that is further divided into categories depending on its moisture content when in use and while being manufactured. It is safe to assume that a timber protected from the elements will achieve and remain at a sub-fifteen percent moisture content, unless the timber is used in a cooling tower or other wet application.

C. Grade and Size

Lumber is graded at the mill and grouped into lots. Grades better than no. 2 (e.g., no. 1, select structural, etc.) are generally in the minority. A common practice is to put the higher grades together as "no. 1 and better." Unless available vertical clearance in the design is a serious problem, the engineer should check prices and availability before specifying lumber in the higher grades. It will often be less expensive to specify a larger member (or more of the same size) in a lower grade.

D. Sizes

Many seem to lament that a 2×4 isn't one anymore. In other words, there is a difference between nominal and actual sizes. Lumber shrinks during manufacture through drying and surfacing. A nominal 2×4 may start as nearly 2 inches by 4 inches, but it only has to be $1\frac{1}{2}$ inches by $3\frac{1}{2}$ inches to be sold as 2×4 and meet the appropriate standard.

Lumber's larger faces are known as sides, and the narrower faces are called edges. Lumber surfaced on one side and one edge is abbreviated as 1S1E, while the common lumber surfaced on all four sides is called S4S.

The section properties of Appendix E use the actual size of the member and neglect the standard corner rounding that is done to reduce splintering. A 4×2 is listed as well as a 2×4 to aid the engineer using the member in the flat orientation.

Older structures and some newer ones with heavy solid-sawn timbers may have full-size members in them. These members are generally rough sawn and unfinished. It is, of course, safe and conservative to assume that a given member size is a nominal one, and that the timber is not full-size unless specifically stated.

There are three basic size categories used in the allowable stress tables: dimension lumber, posts and timbers, and beams and stringers. Dimension lumber is further broken down by size and use. Two of the dimension lumber subgroups deal with the same sizes—maximum dimension 4 inches—but are designated by either numbered grades (no. 1, etc.) or use grades (stud, etc.). The grade names used depend on local supply and practice. The last dimension lumber subgroup contains those sizes with a depth larger than 4 inches.

Posts and timbers are graded with the expectation, but not the requirement, that the members will be used as compression members. The minimum dimension of the post and timber size category is 5 inches (nominally), with no more than 2 inches difference between the two dimensions. Beams and stringers, on the other hand, also have a minimum dimension of 5 inches, but there must be more than a 2 inch difference between the two dimensions. A 6×8, then, is categorized as a post and timber, while a 6×10 is a beam and stringer.

Glue-laminated members most commonly come in $5\frac{3}{8}$, $6\frac{3}{4}$, and $8\frac{3}{4}$ inch widths, laminated from 2×6's, 2×8's, and 2×10's respectively. After gluing, the members are planed to a finish width. The depth is a multiple of $1\frac{1}{2}$ or $\frac{3}{4}$ inch, depending on the numbers and thicknesses of the laminae. The laminae are usually oriented parallel to the principle bending axis, e.g., the X–X axis in Appendix B. Since the nominal size is equal to the actual size, section properties for glue-laminated members are readily calculated.

3   LISTED PROPERTIES

Design properties are listed in the National Design Specification tables. Once the correct row has been found in the allowable stress table for the appropriate species, it is a simple matter to read across to the required value in the appropriate column. The design properties contained in these tables, duplicated in Appendix B, are:

- *Extreme Fiber Stress in Bending* (F_b): This value is the allowable tension in a bending member cross section. F_b will be significantly higher than the allowable tension parallel to the grain (F_t) found in the adjacent column.

  There is a subcategory under F_b called *repetitive use members*, which has a higher F_b. The likelihood and consequences of any one of a large number of interconnected members failing are so reduced that a lower safety factor has been used to derive the allowable bending stress. There are three criteria that repetitive members must meet: there must be at least three members; they must not be more than 24 inches on center; and they must all be joined by a load-sharing mechanism such as plywood or decking.

- *Tension Parallel to the Grain* (F_t): This column contains the allowable tension in the longitudinal direction. Tension across the grain (perpendicular), either radial or tangential, is limited to one third the allowable horizontal shear (F_v). For certain species (notably, douglas fir), the allowable tension across the grain is further reduced to as low as 15 pounds per square inch.

- *Horizontal Shear* (F_v): Shear across the grain is seldom a concern. The allowable stresses listed in the column are for shears in the plane of the fibers, which tend to slide the wood cells by each other. Since shear forces and stresses tend to be higher in beams than in columns, this along-the-grain stress, oriented horizontally, is commonly defined as *horizontal shear stress*. Provision for increased allowable shear stresses can be found in the footnotes to Table 3.1. Allowable shear stresses are fairly low because of the susceptibility of an individual member to end splits that may open after grading.

- *Compression Perpendicular to the Grain* $(F_{c\perp})$: To simplify design, there is no distinction made between compression in the radial and tangential directions. No adjustment factor is applied to the average of the test values for this property since overstressing will generally cause only localized crushing.

- *Compression Parallel to the Grain* (F_c): This value is used to design columns and other compression members. The allowable stress is in the longitudinal direction. Long columns are designed for buckling, a phenomenon that is governed by stiffness (modulus of elasticity), not strength.

  When the compression parallel to the grain is applied to the end of a member, the design values of Appendix A, End Grain in Bearing F_g, apply. If the end grain bearing stress is larger than 75 percent of the allowable stress of Appendix A, a metal bearing plate is required to distribute the load across the member face.

- *Modulus of Elasticity* (E): The number in this column is the longitudinal modulus of elasticity. The value is based on an average of test results, not the five percent exclusion limit, so a calculated deflection will also be an average expected value. The tabulated modulus has been decreased by ten percent from actual averages in order to allow for shear deflections in beams.

4   GLUE-LAMINATED ALLOWABLE STRESS TABLES

The allowable stress tables for glue-laminated members (Appendix B) are similar to the equivalent lumber tables. The meanings of the various combination symbols are explained in the footnotes. The allowable stresses vary, depending on the bending axis orientation and whether the applied load is mainly a transverse bending load or an axial one.

Part 5

Connections

1 INTRODUCTION

In many ways, the connections are the most demanding aspect of timber structural design. Timber members can be very strong, and yet it can be impossible to develop that capacity with appropriate connection details. Designing a connection requires attention to connection capacity, net sections, maintaining certain minimum clearances, and avoiding critical detailing errors. Maintaining required edge and end distances in all the connected members may actually force the engineer to use a larger member than required by stresses in the member itself.

In roughly ascending order of holding capacity, the common mechanical fasteners used in the United States are: nails and spikes, lag screws, bolts, shear plates, and split rings. Shear plates and split rings are manufactured by TECO Products and are commonly referred to as *connectors*.[2] Adhesives are widely used to manufacture many timber structural elements, but adhesives have not found many applications in field-installed connections. With advances in technology and quality control, adhesives may be used more frequently.

2 FASTENER/GRAIN RELATIONSHIP AND LOAD APPLICATION DIRECTION

The fastener's orientation with respect to the wood fibers is a major consideration. Fasteners that terminate within the member, such as nails and lag screws, can be installed either along the wood fibers (into the *end grain*), or across the wood fibers (into the *side grain*). The member that contains the point of these fasteners is the *holding member*. The member through which the fastener passes is the *side member*. Figure 5.1 illustrates these definitions.

As shown in Fig. 5.2, the two basic load application directions are along the fastener axis (in tension or withdrawal), and normal to the fastener axis (in shear or lateral load).

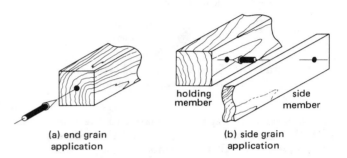

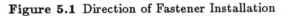

(a) end grain application   (b) side grain application

Figure 5.1 Direction of Fastener Installation

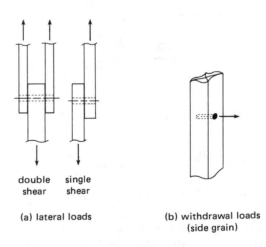

double shear   single shear

(a) lateral loads   (b) withdrawal loads (side grain)

Figure 5.2 Types of Load Application

Lateral loads must be further distinguished by their orientation with respect to the wood fibers, or longitudinal axis, of the wood members. Figure 5.3 shows a load, applied parallel to the longitudinal axis, that bears on the ends of the cells exposed in the hole through which the fastener passes. The load capacity of such *parallel-to-grain* connections is significantly larger than those loaded *perpendicular-to-grain*, (also shown in Fig. 5.3). Tension perpendicular to the grain, intentional or inadvertent, is a chief cause of connection failures.

2 TECO Products, P.O. Box 203, Colliers, WV 26035

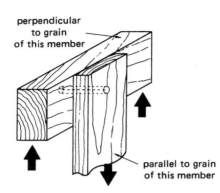

Figure 5.3 Direction of Load Application
Relative to Grain Direction

The difference in capacities related to the orientation with the wood fibers is so profound that the engineer must investigate all the members in a multi-member bolted connection. When the load is applied at an angle that is neither parallel nor perpendicular to the grain, the Hankinson formula (Eq. 5.1) is used to interpolate between the two limiting capacities.

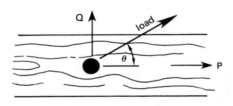

Figure 5.4 Hankinson's Formula Components

$$F_n = \frac{PQ}{P \sin^2 \theta + Q \cos^2 \theta} \qquad 5.1$$

A. Combinations of Load Types

A timber connection's response to lateral and withdrawal loadings is different enough that there is little interaction to consider when the two occur simultaneously. In a situation that combines load types, each applied load can be compared independently with its respective capacity.

B. Load Duration

The established practice is to assume that the capacity of all fasteners increases as loads are applied for shorter time periods. The load duration factors (LDF) of Table 3.1 and Fig. 3.2 apply to all connections (NDS 8.1.1.2).

C. Species Grouping

The capacity of any timber connection depends on the wood species involved. Through-bolt capacities are specific in Table 5.11 for a wide variety of species. For other fastener types, species are grouped together in capacity ranges. Withdrawal capacity is also a function of the specific gravity of the holding member. Table 5.1 is a list of species, their specific gravities, and the four common species groupings.

Glue-laminated members are classified, for connection design purposes, in footnote 14 of the glue-laminated allowable stress tables of Appendix B.

D. Conditions of Use

Changing moisture conditions can have a tremendous influence on a connection's strength and endurance. The condition of use factors (CUF) of Table 5.2 and the footnotes of the allowable stress tables include capacity decreases as large as 75 percent.

3 NAILS AND SPIKES

Nails and spikes are the simplest and most common of the mechanical fasteners. They are often power-driven in both shop and field installations. Table 5.3 lists the lengths and diameters of the most common sizes.

A. Connection Capacity—Multiple Nails and Spikes

Whether the nailed connection is loaded laterally or in withdrawal, the connection capacity is a simple multiple of the number of nails and their individual capacities. This is because a nail's capacity is limited by its stiffness, not its strength, and all the nails of a group are likely to be contributing equally to the overall connection stiffness. The only limit on this linear increase in strength is reached when driving another nail would split the member.

B. Lateral Loads

Figure 5.5 shows a typical load-deformation curve for a laterally loaded, nailed connection. Clearly, the deformations become unacceptably high long before actual failure occurs. A 0.015 inch deflection is an accepted proportional limit for the connections and is used as the failure criterion. The loads corresponding to this deformation are so low that the load direction makes no difference in the nail capacity. Therefore, there is no distinction drawn between loads parallel and perpendicular to the grain with nails, nor is there any application for the Hankinson formula.

Table 5.1
Species Groupings for Connection Design

Species	Bolt Group[a]	Timber Connector Load Group[b] (Shear Plates and Split Rings)	Grouping for Lag Bolts, Drift Bolts, Nails, Spikes, Wood Screws, Staples, and Metal Plate Connectors	
			Group	Specific Gravity(G)[c]
Ash, Commercial White	2	A	I	0.62
Aspen	12	D	IV	0.40
Aspen, Northern[e]	12	C	III	0.42
Beech	4	A	I	0.68
Birch, Sweet and Yellow	4	A	I	0.66
Cedar, Northern White	12	D	IV	0.31
Cedars, Western[d]	9	D	IV	0.35
Coast Species[e]	12	D	IV	0.39
Cottonwood, Black	12	D	IV	0.33
Cottonwood, Eastern	12	D	IV	0.41
Cypress, Southern	3	C	III	0.48
Douglas Fir-Larch[d]	3	B	II	0.51
Douglas Fir-Larch (dense)	1	A	II	—[f]
Douglas Fir, South	6	C	III	0.48
Eastern Woods	12	D	IV	0.38
Fir, Balsam	11	D	IV	0.38
Hem-Fir[d]	8	C	III	0.42
Hemlock				
Eastern-Tamarack[e]	8	C	III	0.45
Mountain	9	C	III	0.47
Western[d]	8	C	III	0.48
Hickory and Pecan	2	A	I	0.75
Maple, Black and Sugar	4	A	I	0.66
Northern Species[e]	12	D	IV	0.35
Oak, Red and White	5	A	I	0.67
Pine				
Eastern White[d]	11	D	IV	0.38
Idaho White	11	D	IV	0.40
Lodgepole	10	C	III	0.44
Northern	9	C	III	0.46
Ponderosa[e]	11	C	III	0.49
Ponderosa-Sugar	11	C	III	0.42
Red[e]	11	C	III	0.42
Southern	3	B	II	0.55
Southern (dense)	1	A	II	—[f]
Western White	11	D	IV	0.40
Poplar, Yellow	10	C	III	0.46
Redwood				
California	3	C	III	0.42
California (open grain)	8	D	IV	0.37
Spruce				
Eastern	10	C	III	0.43
Engelmann-Alpine Fir	12	D	IV	0.36
Sitka	10	C	III	0.43
Sitka, Coast[e]	10	D	IV	0.39
Spruce-Pine-Fir[e]	10	C	III	0.42
West Coast Woods (mixed species)	12	D	IV	0.35
White Woods (Western Woods)	12	D	IV	0.35

[a] See Tables 6.20–6.22 for species and density groupings applicable to bolt design.

[b] When stress graded.

[c] Based on weight and volume when oven-dry. These specific-gravity values are to be used for the determination of withdrawal design values for lag bolts, nails, spikes, and wood screws.

[d] Also applies when species name includes the designation "North."

[e] Applies when graded in accordance with National Lumber Grades Authority *Standard Grading Rules for Canadian Lumber* (2).

[f] The specific gravity of dense lumber is slightly higher than for medium-grain lumber. However, the design values for this group are based on the average specific gravity of the species, which is 0.51 for Douglas Fir-Larch and 0.55 for Southern Pine.

Table 5.2
Condition of Use Factors (CUF)
for Connections

| Type of fastener | Condition of wood[1] | | Factor |
	At time of fabrication	In service	
Timber connectors[2]	Dry	Dry	1.0
	Partially seasoned[3]	Dry	See Note 3
	Wet	Dry	0.8
	Dry or wet	Partially seasoned or wet	0.67
Bolts or lag screws	Dry	Dry	1.0
	Partially seasoned[3] or wet	Dry	See Table 8.1C
	Dry or wet	Exposed to weather	0.75
	Dry or wet	Wet	0.67
Drift bolts or pins - Laterally loaded	Dry or wet	Dry	1.0
	Dry or wet	Partially seasoned or wet, or subject to wetting and drying	0.70
Wire nails and spikes			
—Withdrawal loads	Dry	Dry	1.0
	Partially seasoned or wet	Will remain wet	1.0
	Partially seasoned or wet	Dry	0.25
	Dry	Subject to wetting and drying	0.25
—Lateral loads	Dry	Dry	1.0
	Partially seasoned or wet	Dry or wet	0.75
	Dry	Partially seasoned or wet	0.75
Threaded, hardened steel nails	Dry or wet	Dry or wet	1.0
Wood screws	Dry or wet	Dry	1.0
	Dry or wet	Exposed to weather	0.75
	Dry or wet	Wet	0.67
Metal plate connectors	Dry	Dry	1.0
	Partially seasoned or wet	Dry or wet	0.8

1. Condition of wood definitions applicable to fasteners are:

"Dry" wood has a moisture content of 19 percent or less.

"Wet" wood has a moisture content at or above the fiber saturation point (approximately 30 percent).

"Partially seasoned" wood, for the purposes of Table 8.1B, has a moisture content greater than 19 percent but less than the fiber saturation point (approximately 30 percent).

"Exposed to weather" implies that the wood may vary in moisture content from dry to partially seasoned, but is not expected to reach the fiber saturation point at times when the joint is under full design load.

"Subject to wetting and drying" implies that the wood may vary in moisture content from dry to partially seasoned or wet, or vice versa, with consequent effects on the tightness of the joint.

2. For timber connectors, moisture content limitations apply to a depth of 3/4 inch from the surface of the wood.

3. When timber connectors, bolts or laterally loaded lag screws are installed in wood that is partially seasoned at the time of fabrication but that will be dry before full design load is applied, proportional intermediate values may be used.

Reproduced from National Design Specification for Wood Construction, 1986 Edition, with permission from National Forest Products Association, Washington, D.C.

End Grain

Nails in the end grain of the holding member have only two-thirds the lateral load capacity of the same nail penetrating the same distance into the side grain of the same species (NDS 8.8.6).

Penetration

A nail must penetrate the holding member at least a minimum amount for the nail to develop its full lateral load capacity. The minimum required full-strength

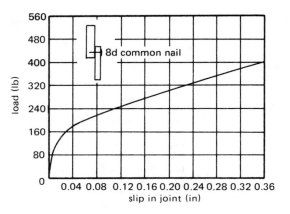

Figure 5.5 Load-Deformation Curve for Typical Laterally Loaded Nail

penetration is a function of the nail diameter and the density of the holding member species. For the species of group I in Table 5.1, the full-strength penetration in the holding member is ten nail diameters. Similarly, the minimum penetration is eleven diameters for group II species, thirteen diameters for group III species, and fourteen diameters for group IV species. These values are included in Table 5.4, for convenience.

The minimum allowable penetration is one-third the full-strength penetration. For any nail penetration less than full strength, the capacity can be determined by a simple interpolation between zero capacity at no penetration and full strength at the specified penetration (NDS 8.8.5.1).

Metal Side Plates

If nails attach an adequately stiff and strong metal sideplate to the timber holding member, the allowable loads can be increased 25 percent (NDS 8.8.5.4).

Different Species

If two different species are nailed together, the lesser design value controls regardless of whether it is the holding or side member (NDS 8.8.5.6).

Toe-Nailed Connections

Some nailed connections must have the nails installed as *toe-nails* because of clearance restrictions or construction sequence. The lateral capacity of these connections is five-sixths that of the corresponding lateral load nail-species combination. The withdrawal capacity of toe-nailed connections is two-thirds of the corresponding straight nailed connection (NDS 8.8.7.1).

Table 5.3
Common Nail and Spike Dimensions

Sizes of bright, common wire nails

Size	Gage	Length	Diameter
		In.	*In.*
6d	11½	2	0.113
8d	10¼	2½	.131
10d	9	3	.148
12d	9	3¼	.148
16d	8	3½	.162
20d	6	4	192
30d	5	4½	.207
40d	4	5	.225
50d	3	5½	.244
60d	2	6	.262

Sizes of smooth box nails

Size	Gage	Length	Diameter
		In.	*In.*
3d	14½	1¼	0.076
4d	14	1½	.080
5d	14	1¾	.080
6d	12½	2	.098
7d	12½	2¼	.098
8d	11½	2½	113
10d	10½	3	.128
16d	10	3½	.135
20d	9	4	.148

Sizes of helically and annularly threaded nails

Size	Length	Diameter
	In.	*In.*
6d	2	0.120
8d	2½	.120
10d	3	.135
12d	3¼	.135
16d	3½	.148
20d	4	.177
30d	4½	.177
40d	5	177
50d	5½	.177
60d	6	.177
70d	7	.207
80d	8	.207
90d	9	.207

Sizes of common wire spikes

Size	Length	Diameter	Size	Length	Diameter
	In.	*In.*		*In.*	*In.*
10d	3	0.192	40d	5	0.263
12d	3¼	.192	50d	5½	.283
16d	3½	.207	60d	6	.283
20d	4	.225	5/16 inch	7	.312
30d	4½	.244	⅜ inch	8½	.375

Reproduced from Wood Handbook: Wood as an Engineering Material, Agriculture Handbook No. 72, by Forest Products Laboratory, Forest Service, U.S. Department of Agriculture, 1974.

C. Allowable Lateral Loads

The design values for laterally loaded nails and spikes are found in Table 5.4. These are normal load duration

values, specific for species group and nail size, and based on full-strength penetration.

Table 5.4
Design Values—Nails and Spikes in Lateral Loads

SIZE OF NAIL	STANDARD LENGTH (Inches)	WIRE GAUGE	PENETRATION REQUIRED (Inches)	LOADS (Pounds)[1][2][3]	
				Douglas Fir Larch or Southern Pine	Other Species
BOX NAILS					
6d	2	12½	1⅛	51	See U.B.C. Standard No. 25-17
8d	2½	11½	1¼	63	
10d	3	10½	1½	76	
12d	3¼	10½	1½	76	
16d	3½	10	1½	82	
20d	4	9	1⅝	94	
30d	4½	9	1⅝	94	
40d	5	8	1¾	108	
COMMON NAILS					
6d	2	11½	1¼	63	See U.B.C. Standard No. 25-17
8d	2½	10¼	1½	78	
10d	3	9	1⅝	94	
12d	3¼	9	1⅝	94	
16d	3½	8	1¾	108	
20d	4	6	2⅛	139	
30d	4½	5	2¼	155	
40d	5	4	2½	176	
50d	5½	3	2¾	199	
60d	6	2	2⅞	223	

[1]The safe lateral strength values may be increased 25 percent where metal side plates are used.
[2]For wood diaphragm calculations these values may be increased 30 percent. (See U.B.C. Standard No. 25-17.)
[3]Tabulated values are on a normal load-duration basis and apply to joints made of seasoned lumber used in dry locations. See U.B.C. Standard No. 25-17 for other service conditions.

Reproduced from the 1988 edition of the Uniform Building Code, © 1988, with the permission of the publishers, the International Conference of Building Officials.

D. Withdrawal Loads

The design withdrawal capacity of nails and spikes is so low and so susceptible to weakening with changed moisture content that consideration should be given either to other fastener types or to reconfiguring the connection to load the nail(s) laterally. There is no dependable capacity if the nail is in the end grain of the holding member (NDS 8.8.3 and 8.8.4).

If a nailed connection must be loaded in withdrawal, the capacity is a multiple of the total number of inches of nail penetration into the holding member and the allowable withdrawal load per inch of that nail type in the holding member's species. The allowable withdrawal load per inch of penetration, found in Table 5.5, is a function of the holding member's specific gravity (see Table 5.1) and of the nail type and size.

The withdrawal capacity is subject to the standard load duration factors and the condition of use factors of Table 5.2. There is no increase in withdrawal capacity with metal side plates.

Example 5.1

What is the allowable combined snow and dead load on the exterior, overhead trellis slat shown? All timber is treated with preservative.

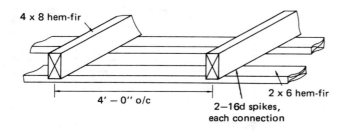

4 x 8 hem-fir

4' – 0'' o/c

2 x 6 hem-fir

2–16d spikes, each connection

The solution procedure is to establish the total penetration of the nails and multiply by the allowable withdrawal load per inch of penetration to calculate the connection capacity. Then, convert this capacity to a snow load on the slats.

Table 5.3 shows the spike is $3\frac{1}{2}''$ long. Subtracting the 2×6 hem-fir thickness, the actual nail penetration is $3.5'' - 1.5'' = 2''$.

From Table 5.1, hem-fir is in group III, and has a specific gravity of $G = 0.42$. Table 5.5 shows that common 16d spikes in wood with $G = 0.42$ have a withdrawal design value of 33 lb/in of penetration.

The condition of use factor from Table 5.2 is CUF = 0.25. From Table 3.1, the load duration factor for snow loading is LDF = 1.15.

The capacity per connection is

$$\left(2\,\frac{\text{nails}}{\text{connection}}\right)\left(2\,\frac{\text{in}}{\text{nail}}\right)\left(33\,\frac{\text{lb}}{\text{in}}\right)(1.15)(0.25)$$
$$= 40.0\ \text{lb/connection}$$

The allowable combined snow and dead load is

$$\frac{40.0\,\dfrac{\text{lb}}{\text{connection}}}{(4\ \text{ft})\left(\dfrac{5.5}{12}\ \text{ft}\right)} = 20.7\ \text{psf}$$

Note: The pressure treatment has no effect on capacity.

Example 5.2

Investigate the connection capacity at point A at the top of the backboard. Assume a 230 lb player occasionally and briefly hangs on the rim.

Table 5.5
Allowable Withdrawal Loads—Nails and Spikes

Normal load duration

Design values in withdrawal in pounds per inch of penetration into side grain of member holding point.

d = pennyweight of nail or spike. G = specific gravity of the wood, based on weight and volume when oven-dry.

Specific gravity G	Penny wt. Diam.	Size of box nail								Size of common spike							
		6d 0.099	8d 0.113	10d 0.128	12d 0.128	16d 0.135	20d 0.148	30d 0.148	40d 0.162	10d 0.192	12d 0.192	16d 0.207	20d 0.225	30d 0.244	40d 0.263	50d 0.283	60d 0.283	5/16'' 0.312	3/8'' 0.375
0.75		67	76	86	86	91	99	99	109	129	129	139	151	164	177	190	190	210	252
0.68		52	59	67	67	71	78	78	85	101	101	109	118	128	138	149	149	164	197
0.67		50	57	65	65	68	75	75	82	97	97	105	114	124	133	144	144	158	190
0.66		48	55	63	63	66	72	72	79	94	94	101	110	119	128	138	138	152	183
0.62		41	47	53	53	56	62	62	68	80	80	86	94	102	110	118	118	130	157
0.55		31	35	40	40	42	46	46	50	59	59	64	70	76	81	88	88	97	116
0.54		29	33	38	38	40	44	44	48	57	57	61	67	72	78	84	84	92	111
0.51		25	29	33	33	35	38	38	42	49	49	53	58	63	67	73	73	80	96
0.49		23	26	30	30	31	34	34	38	45	45	48	52	57	61	66	66	72	87
0.48		22	25	28	28	30	33	33	36	42	42	46	50	54	58	62	62	69	83
0.47		21	24	27	27	28	31	31	34	40	40	43	47	51	55	59	59	65	78
0.46		20	22	25	25	27	29	29	32	38	38	41	45	48	52	56	56	62	74
0.45		19	21	24	24	25	28	28	30	36	36	39	42	46	49	53	53	58	70
0.44		18	20	23	23	24	26	26	29	34	34	37	40	43	47	50	50	55	66
0.43		17	19	21	21	23	25	25	27	32	32	35	38	41	44	47	47	52	63
0.42		16	18	20	20	21	23	23	26	30	30	33	35	38	41	45	45	49	59
0.41		15	17	19	19	20	22	22	24	29	29	31	33	36	39	42	42	46	56
0.40		14	16	18	18	19	21	21	23	27	27	29	31	34	37	40	40	44	52
0.39		13	15	17	17	18	19	19	21	25	25	27	29	32	34	37	37	41	49
0.38		12	14	16	16	17	18	18	20	24	24	25	28	30	32	35	35	38	46
0.37		11	13	15	15	16	17	17	19	22	22	24	26	28	30	33	33	36	43
0.36		11	12	14	14	14	16	16	17	21	21	22	24	26	28	30	30	33	40
0.35		10	11	13	13	14	15	15	16	19	19	21	23	24	26	28	28	31	38
0.33		9	10	11	11	12	13	13	14	17	17	18	19	21	23	24	24	27	32
0.31		7	8	9	9	10	11	11	12	14	14	15	17	18	19	21	21	23	28

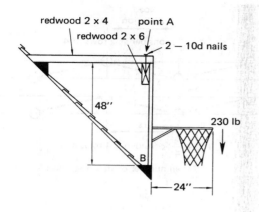

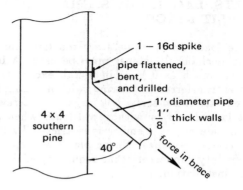

The solution procedure is to determine the load applied on the connection, check the actual penetration, and compare the capacity to the applied load.

Summing moments about Point B, the design load for connection at A is

$$(230 \text{ lb}) \left(\frac{2 \text{ ft}}{4 \text{ ft}} \right) = 115 \text{ lb}$$

From Table 5.2, CUF = 0.75. From Table 3.1, LDF = 2.0 (impact load). From Table 5.1, redwood is in group III. Group III species have a full-strength penetration of thirteen diameters, or 1.92″ with 10d nails (Table 5.4).

A 10d nail is 3″ long (Table 5.3). The actual penetration of the nails into the 2×6 is 3″ − 1.5″ = 1.5″. This actual penetration is greater than the absolute minimum required, one-third of the full strength, or 1.92″/3 = 0.64″. A simple interpolation factor of 1.5″/1.92″ will adjust the nail capacity for the actual penetration.

Table 5.4 gives the capacity of one 10d nail in a group III species as 77 lb/nail.

The connection capacity is

$$(2 \text{ nails}) \left(77 \frac{\text{lb}}{\text{nail}} \right) (2.0)(0.75) \left(\frac{1.5 \text{ in}}{1.92 \text{ in}} \right) = 180 \text{ lb}$$

The 180 lb capacity exceeds the 115 lb design load; therefore the design is satisfactory.

Example 5.3

What is the design capacity of the X-brace in the framing of a garage wall resisting wind load?

First, check the withdrawal capacity of the nail as it limits the withdrawal component of the load. Then, check the lateral capacity of the nail as it limits the lateral component of the load. The lower value will control the connection capacity.

Table 5.2 gives the CUF = 1.0. Wind load means a LDF = 1.33 (Table 3.1). The flattened pipe acts as a metal side plate and increases only the lateral nail capacity by 25%. Southern pine is a group II species with a specific gravity, $G = 0.55$ (Table 5.1).

A 16d spike is 3.5″ long (Table 5.3). After subtracting two pipe wall thicknesses, the penetration is 3.5″ − (2)(0.125″) = 3.25″. Table 5.5 gives a withdrawal capacity of 64 lb/in. The sine of 40° is used to determine the withdrawal component of the applied load.

The connection capacity, as limited by the withdrawal capacity, is

$$\frac{\left(64 \frac{\text{lb}}{\text{in}} \right) (3.25 \text{ in})(1.0)(1.33)}{\sin 40°} = 430 \text{ lb}$$

Group II species have a full lateral strength penetration of 11 diameters, or 2.28″ with 16d spikes (Table 5.4). The actual 3.25″ penetration exceeds the required 2.28″. There is no increase in the lateral capacity over the full-strength value for the extra penetration. Table 5.4 gives a capacity of 155 lb for a 16d spike. The cosine of 40° is used to convert the lateral component to an applied load.

The connection capacity, as limited by the lateral capacity is

$$\frac{(155 \text{ lb}) (1.0)(1.33)(1.25)}{\cos 40°} = 336 \text{ lb}$$

Therefore, lateral capacity limits design to 336 lb.

There is no interaction considered between the lateral and withdrawal loads.

4 BOLTS, LAG SCREWS, SHEAR PLATES, AND SPLIT RINGS

When the loads and members are too large for nails, a heavier mechanical fastener must be used. A bolt in timber acts much as it does in metal, except that all the load is transferred in bearing, with no clamping or friction effects. A lag screw is a large wood screw used to resist lateral and/or withdrawal loads when access to the far side of the member is restricted by its size or the erection sequence. Shear plates and split rings are heavy-duty connectors that require special cutting heads for installation.

A. Capacity Reduction with Multiple Fasteners

Unlike nailed connections, the shear capacity of a connection using the heavier mechanical fasteners is not a simple multiple of the number of fasteners and their individual capacities. Because their capacities are controlled by strength, not stiffness, and multiple fasteners do not share applied loads equally, capacities are reduced on the basis of connection layout, side member material, and relative size.

To determine the multiple fastener reduction factor, K, the number of fasteners in any row must first be determined. A row is defined as two or more fasteners lying in a line parallel to the direction of the applied load. Adjacent rows of staggered fasteners are considered to act as a single row if the distance between the rows is less than one-fourth the least distance along the load axis between fasteners in the adjacent rows (NDS 8.3.2.4b).

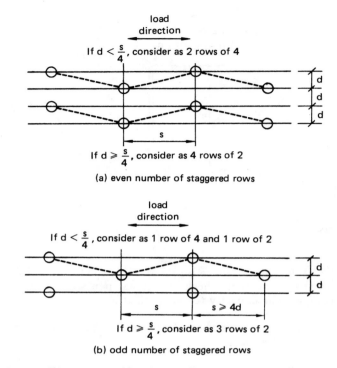

Figure 5.6 Number of Fasteners in a Row

Once the number of fasteners per row is known, the modification factor is found in Table 5.6A or Table 5.6B, depending on whether the side member is timber or metal. In either table, the relative and absolute gross (not net) sizes of the side and main members determine the modification factor applied to the sum of the individual capacities of the fasteners.

Table 5.6A
Modification Factor for Number of Fasteners in Row, K for Wood Side Plates

A_1/A_2	A_1 (in²)†	Number of fasteners in a row										
		2	3	4	5	6	7	8	9	10	11	12
	<12	1.00	0.92	0.84	0.76	0.68	0.61	0.55	0.49	0.43	0.38	0.34
	12 – <19	1.00	0.95	0.88	0.82	0.75	0.68	0.62	0.57	0.52	0.48	0.43
	19 – <28	1.00	0.97	0.93	0.88	0.82	0.77	0.71	0.67	0.63	0.59	0.55
0.5	28 – <40	1.00	0.98	0.96	0.92	0.87	0.83	0.79	0.75	0.71	0.69	0.66
•	40 – <64	1.00	1.00	0.97	0.94	0.90	0.86	0.83	0.79	0.76	0.74	0.72
‡	>64	1.00	1.00	0.98	0.95	0.91	0.88	0.85	0.82	0.80	0.78	0.76
	<12	1.00	0.97	0.92	0.85	0.78	0.71	0.65	0.59	0.54	0.49	0.44
	12 – <19	1.00	0.98	0.94	0.89	0.84	0.78	0.72	0.66	0.61	0.56	0.51
	19 – <28	1.00	1.00	0.97	0.93	0.89	0.85	0.80	0.76	0.72	0.68	0.64
1.0	28 – <40	1.00	1.00	0.99	0.96	0.92	0.89	0.86	0.83	0.80	0.78	0.75
•	40 – <64	1.00	1.00	1.00	0.97	0.94	0.91	0.88	0.85	0.84	0.82	0.80
‡	>64	1.00	1.00	1.00	0.99	0.96	0.93	0.91	0.88	0.87	0.86	0.85

A_1 = cross-sectional area of main member(s) before boring or grooving.
A_2 = sum of the cross-sectional areas of side members before boring or grooving.
*When A_1/A_2 exceeds 1.0, use A_2/A_1.
†When A_1/A_2 exceeds 1.0, use A_2 instead of A_1.
‡For A_1/A_2 between 0 and 1.0, interpolate or extrapolate from the tabulated values.

The multiple fastener factor, K, usually has little effect on connections with fewer than four fasteners in a row, but in longer rows the effect can be profound. This factor can make adding a fastener to a row actually decrease that row's overall capacity. Careful attention should be paid to connection layout in very heavy splices.

B. Condition of Use Factors

The condition of use factors for bolts, lags, shear plates, and split rings are similar to those used in nailed connections, with one very notable exception. As timber seasons in place, it shrinks across the grain. If a metal side plate restrains it from doing so, it is likely to split at the fasteners (see Fig. 5.7). This drastically reduces the fastener capacity, justifying the 60 percent reduction in design capacity. The situation is corrected by using separate splice plates with each row of fasteners across the

grain. This is only one example of how tension perpendicular to the grain can influence the behavior of a connection that might appear to have no applied loads in a direction perpendicular to the grain.

C. Net Section

At connections, member stress levels have to be based on a cross-sectional area with the bolt or lag holes removed. Assume bolt holes have a one-sixteenth inch larger diameter than the bolt (NDS 8.5.4.2). Subtract the diameter times the penetration for lag screws. The author further reduces the cross-sectional area at critical areas by one-eighth, after subtracting holes, to allow for unfortunate knot locations. This is not required by the code. Bolts or lag screws in adjacent staggered rows are considered to be at the same section if they fall within a piece of the member that is four diameters long.

Table 5.6B
Modification Factor for Number of Fasteners in Row, K for Metal Side Plates

A_1/A_2	A_1 (in^2)	Number of fasteners in a row										
		2	3	4	5	6	7	8	9	10	11	12
2–12	5 – <8	1.00	0.78	0.64	0.54	0.46	0.40	0.35	0.30	0.25	0.20	0.15
	8 – <16	1.00	0.85	0.73	0.63	0.54	0.48	0.42	0.38	0.34	0.30	0.26
	16 – <24	1.00	0.91	0.83	0.74	0.66	0.59	0.53	0.48	0.43	0.38	0.33
	24 – <39	1.00	0.94	0.87	0.80	0.73	0.67	0.61	0.56	0.51	0.46	0.42
	39 – <64	1.00	0.96	0.92	0.87	0.81	0.75	0.70	0.66	0.62	0.58	0.55
	64 – <119	1.00	0.98	0.95	0.91	0.87	0.82	0.78	0.75	0.72	0.69	0.66
	119 – <199	1.00	0.99	0.97	0.95	0.92	0.89	0.86	0.84	0.81	0.79	0.78
12–18	17 – <24	1.00	0.94	0.88	0.81	0.74	0.67	0.61	0.55	0.49	0.43	0.37
	24 – <39	1.00	0.96	0.91	0.86	0.80	0.74	0.68	0.62	0.56	0.50	0.44
	39 – <64	1.00	0.98	0.94	0.90	0.85	0.80	0.75	0.70	0.67	0.62	0.58
	64 – <119	1.00	0.99	0.96	0.93	0.90	0.86	0.82	0.79	0.75	0.72	0.69
	119 – <199	1.00	1.00	0.98	0.96	0.94	0.92	0.89	0.86	0.83	0.80	0.78
	>199	1.00	1.00	1.00	0.98	0.97	0.95	0.93	0.91	0.90	0.88	0.87
18–24	40 – <64	1.00	1.00	0.96	0.93	0.89	0.84	0.79	0.74	0.69	0.64	0.59
	64 – <119	1.00	1.00	0.97	0.94	0.92	0.89	0.86	0.83	0.80	0.76	0.73
	119 – <199	1.00	1.00	0.99	0.98	0.96	0.94	0.92	0.90	0.88	0.86	0.85
	>199	1.00	1.00	1.00	1.00	0.98	0.96	0.95	0.93	0.92	0.92	0.91
24–30	40 – <64	1.00	0.98	0.94	0.90	0.85	0.80	0.74	0.69	0.65	0.61	0.58
	64 – <119	1.00	0.99	0.97	0.93	0.90	0.86	0.82	0.79	0.76	0.73	0.71
	119 – <199	1.00	1.00	0.98	0.96	0.94	0.92	0.89	0.87	0.85	0.83	0.81
	>199	1.00	1.00	0.99	0.98	0.97	0.95	0.93	0.92	0.90	0.89	0.89
30–35	40 – <64	1.00	0.96	0.92	0.86	0.80	0.74	0.68	0.64	0.60	0.57	0.55
	64 – <119	1.00	0.98	0.95	0.90	0.86	0.81	0.76	0.72	0.68	0.65	0.62
	119 – <199	1.00	0.99	0.97	0.95	0.92	0.88	0.85	0.82	0.80	0.78	0.77
	>199	1.00	1.00	0.98	0.97	0.95	0.93	0.90	0.89	0.87	0.86	0.85
35–42	40 – <64	1.00	0.95	0.89	0.82	0.75	0.69	0.63	0.58	0.53	0.49	0.46
	64 – <119	1.00	0.97	0.93	0.88	0.82	0.77	0.71	0.67	0.63	0.59	0.56
	119 – <199	1.00	0.98	0.96	0.93	0.89	0.85	0.81	0.78	0.76	0.73	0.71
	>199	1.00	0.99	0.98	0.96	0.93	0.90	0.87	0.84	0.82	0.80	0.78

A_1 = Cross-sectional area of main member before boring or grooving.
A_2 = Sum of cross-sectional areas of metal side plates before drilling.

Reproduced from National Design Specification for Wood Construction, 1986 Edition, with permission from National Forest Products Association, Washington, D.C.

PROFESSIONAL PUBLICATIONS, INC. ● Belmont, CA

Table 5.7
Special Condition of Use Factors for
Connections Seasoning in Place

Factors apply when wood is at or above the fiber saturation
point (wet) at time of fabrication but dries to a moisture
content of 19 percent or less (dry) before full design load is
applied. For wood partially seasoned when fabricated,
adjusted intermediate values may be used.

Arrangement of bolts or lag screws	Type of splice plate	Modification factor
—One fastener only, or —Two or more fasteners placed in a single line parallel to grain, or —Fasteners placed in two or more lines parallel to grain with separate splice plates for each line	Wood or metal	1.0
—All other arrangements	Wood or metal	0.4

*Reproduced from National Design Specification for Wood Construction,
1986 Edition, with permission from National Forest Products Association,
Washington, D.C.*

D. Angle of Load to Grain

Lag screw and bolt design capacities are tabulated for
use in parallel and perpendicular to the grain directions.
For other load directions, use the Hankinson formula to
interpolate.

5   LAG SCREWS

A lag screw will only develop its full lateral and withdrawal capacities if installed correctly. The proper installation tool is a wrench, not a hammer. A pilot hole
must be drilled and sized according to established standards (NDS 8.6.4). Lag bolt capacities are subject to
the condition of use factors found in Table 5.2.

A. Withdrawal Loads

The withdrawal capacity of a lag screw is a function of
its diameter, the holding member's specific gravity, and
the effective threaded length in the holding member.
The dimension T-E, found in Appendix C, is the length
of effective thread. This effective length, multiplied by
the allowable load per inch found in Table 5.8, is the
allowable withdrawal load for a lag screw.

It is possible for the lag screw-to-timber capacity to
exceed the tensile strength of the lag screw. If the effective threaded length is less than seven diameters in
group I species, eight diameters in group II, ten diameters in group III, and eleven diameters in group IV, the
lag screw should not break before it is pulled out (NDS
8.6.6.1).

If a lag screw must unavoidably be loaded in withdrawal
while installed in end grain, the capacity should be reduced by 25 percent (NDS 8.6.6.3).

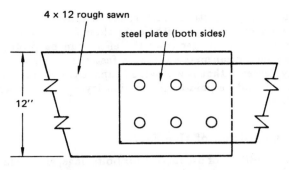

(a) plate installed while wood is wet

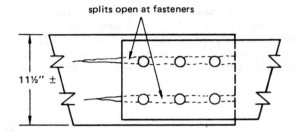

(b) after seasoning and shrinkage

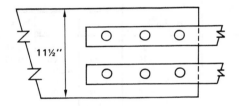

(c) with separate side plates

Figure 5.7 Seasoning in Place

B. Lateral Loads in Lag Screws

Tables 5.9 and 5.10 give the allowable lateral loads, parallel and perpendicular to the grain, for all lag screw
diameters and lengths in the four species groups found
in Table 5.1. The only difference in the two tables is
the side member material. If the load is at an angle to
the grain between the two listed values, the Hankinson
formula should be used.

End Grain Installation

The listed values are for side grain installation. If the
lag screw is in the end grain, reduce the side grain lateral load capacity by a third (NDS 8.6.7.6).

Combined Loadings

Just as with nails, no interaction between combined lateral and withdrawal loads needs to be considered. Each
load component is compared with its own respective
design value.

Table 5.8
Allowable Withdrawal Loads—Lag Screws

Normal load duration, dry service conditions

Design values for load in withdrawal in pounds per inch of penetration of threaded part into side grain of member holding point.

D = the shank diameter in inches.
G = specific gravity of the wood based on weight and volume when oven-dry.

Specific gravity G	Lag screw diameter D											
	1/4	5/16	3/8	7/16	1/2	9/16	5/8	3/4	7/8	1	1-1/8	1-1/4
	0.250	0.3125	0.375	0.4375	0.500	0.5625	0.625	0.750	0.875	1.000	1.125	1.250
0.75	413	489	560	629	695	759	822	942	1058	1169	1277	1382
0.68	357	422	484	543	600	656	709	813	913	1009	1103	1193
0.67	349	413	473	531	587	641	694	796	893	987	1078	1167
0.66	341	403	463	519	574	627	678	778	873	965	1054	1141
0.62	311	367	421	473	523	571	618	708	795	879	960	1039
0.55	260	307	352	395	437	477	516	592	664	734	802	868
0.54	253	299	342	384	425	464	502	576	646	714	780	844
0.51	232	274	314	353	390	426	461	528	593	656	716	775
0.49	218	258	296	332	367	401	434	498	559	617	674	730
0.48	212	250	287	322	356	389	421	482	542	599	654	708
0.47	205	242	278	312	345	377	408	467	525	580	634	686
0.46	199	235	269	302	334	365	395	453	508	562	613	664
0.45	192	227	260	292	323	353	382	438	492	543	594	642
0.44	186	220	252	283	312	341	369	423	475	525	574	621
0.43	179	212	243	273	302	330	357	409	459	508	554	600
0.42	173	205	235	264	291	318	344	395	443	490	535	579
0.41	167	198	226	254	281	307	332	381	428	473	516	559
0.40	161	190	218	245	271	296	320	367	412	455	497	538
0.39	155	183	210	236	261	285	308	353	397	438	479	518
0.38	149	176	202	227	251	274	296	340	381	422	461	498
0.37	143	169	194	218	241	263	285	326	367	405	443	479
0.36	137	163	186	209	231	253	273	313	352	389	425	460
0.35	132	156	179	200	222	242	262	300	337	373	407	441
0.33	121	143	164	184	203	222	240	275	309	341	373	403
0.31	110	130	149	167	185	202	218	250	281	311	339	367

The threaded part shall not include the length of the tapered tip of standard lag screws

Reproduced from National Design Specification for Wood Construction, 1986 Edition, with permission from National Forest Products Association, Washington, D.C.

Lag Screw Spacing

The design values of Tables 5.9 and 5.10 assume the lag screws are spaced according to the spacing requirements for bolts.

Example 5.4

Select the 2 lag screws for attaching the light to the field house roof. Determine the lateral and withdrawal components of the applied load. Select a trial lag screw and compare its capacities with those required. It would be wasteful to use a lag screw that is at its design capacity in one component, while significantly underloaded in the other.

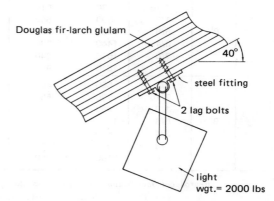

Douglas fir-larch glulam
40°
steel fitting
2 lag bolts
light wgt.= 2000 lbs

Table 5.9
Allowable Lateral Loads in Lag Screws—Wood Side Pieces

Thickness of side member (inches)	Length of lag screw (inches)	Diameter of lag screw shank (inches)	Species Group							
			GROUP I		GROUP II		GROUP III		GROUP IV	
			Total lateral load per lag screw in single shear (pounds)		Total lateral load per lag screw in single shear (pounds)		Total lateral load per lag screw in single shear (pounds)		Total lateral load per lag screw in single shear (pounds)	
			Parallel to grain	Perpendicular to grain	Parallel to grain	Perpendicular to grain	Parallel to grain	Perpendicular to grain	Parallel to grain	Perpendicular to grain
1½"	4"	1/4	200	200	170	170	130	130	100	100
		5/16	290	240	220	180	150	130	120	110
		3/8	330	250	250	190	180	140	140	110
		7/16	370	260	280	190	200	140	160	110
		1/2	390	250	290	190	210	140	170	110
		5/8	470	280	360	210	260	160	200	120
	5"	1/4	240	230	200	200	180	180	160	160
		5/16	340	290	290	250	240	200	190	160
		3/8	440	340	380	290	270	210	220	170
		7/16	550	380	420	290	300	210	240	170
		1/2	580	380	440	280	310	200	250	160
		5/8	710	420	530	320	380	230	310	180
	6"	1/4	270	260	230	220	210	200	180	180
		5/16	380	320	330	280	290	250	260	220
		3/8	490	370	420	320	370	280	300	230
		7/16	600	420	520	360	410	280	330	230
		1/2	700	460	600	390	430	280	340	220
		5/8	850	510	710	430	510	310	410	250
	7"	1/4	280	270	240	230	210	210	190	180
		5/16	400	340	350	300	310	270	280	230
		3/8	530	400	460	350	410	310	360	270
		7/16	650	450	560	390	500	350	420	300
		1/2	760	490	660	430	550	360	440	290
		5/8	910	540	780	470	640	380	510	310
2½"	6"	3/8	450	340	380	290	270	210	220	170
		7/16	590	410	440	310	320	220	250	180
		1/2	620	410	470	310	340	220	270	180
		5/8	730	440	550	330	390	240	320	190
		3/4	830	460	630	350	450	250	360	200
		7/8	950	490	720	370	510	270	410	210
		1	1060	530	800	400	570	290	460	230
	7"	3/8	500	380	430	330	380	290	300	230
		7/16	670	470	580	410	430	300	350	240
		1/2	830	540	650	420	460	300	370	240
		5/8	1000	600	750	450	540	320	430	260
		3/4	1120	620	850	470	610	330	490	270
		7/8	1280	660	970	500	690	360	550	290
		1	1440	720	1090	540	780	390	620	310
	8"	3/8	560	420	480	370	430	330	380	290
		7/16	730	510	630	440	560	390	450	320
		1/2	890	580	770	500	600	390	480	310
		5/8	1230	740	970	580	700	420	560	340
		3/4	1440	790	1090	600	780	430	630	340
		7/8	1610	840	1220	630	870	450	700	360
		1	1810	910	1370	690	980	490	790	390
	9"	3/8	600	460	520	400	470	350	410	310
		7/16	790	550	680	480	610	430	540	380
		1/2	960	630	830	540	740	480	600	390
		5/8	1310	790	1130	680	860	520	690	420
		3/4	1680	920	1350	740	960	530	770	430
		7/8	1940	1010	1470	760	1050	550	840	440
		1	2190	2000	1660	830	1190	590	950	480

Reproduced from National Design Specification for Wood Construction, 1986 Edition, with permission from National Forest Products Association, Washington, D.C.

Table 5.10
Allowable Lateral Loads in Lag Screws—Metal Side Pieces

Length of lag screw (inches)	Diameter of lag screw shank (inches)	GROUP I Total lateral load per lag screw in single shear (pounds)		GROUP II Total lateral load per lag screw in single shear (pounds)		GROUP III Total lateral load per lag screw in single shear (pounds)		GROUP IV Total lateral load per lag screw in single shear (pounds)	
		Parallel to grain	Perpendicular to grain	Parallel to grain	Perpendicular to grain	Parallel to grain	Perpendicular to grain	Parallel to grain	Perpendicular to grain
3″	1/4	240	190	210	160	160	120	130	100
	5/16	350	240	270	180	190	130	150	100
	3/8	420	250	320	190	230	140	180	110
	7/16	480	270	360	200	260	140	210	120
	1/2	540	280	400	210	290	150	230	120
	5/8	650	310	490	230	350	170	280	130
4″	1/4*	270	210	240	180	210	160	190	150
	5/16	410	280	350	240	290	200	230	160
	3/8	570	350	480	290	340	210	280	170
	7/16	730	410	550	310	390	220	310	180
	1/2	810	420	610	320	440	230	350	180
	5/8	980	470	740	360	530	250	430	200
5″	5/16	440	300	380	260	340	230	300	200
	3/8	620	380	530	320	470	290	380	230
	7/16	810	460	700	390	530	300	430	240
	1/2	1040	540	840	440	600	310	480	250
	5/8	1330	640	1010	480	720	350	580	280
	3/4	1550	680	1170	520	840	370	670	300
6″	5/16*	450	300	390	260	340	230	300	210
	3/8	630	390	550	330	490	300	430	260
	7/16	850	480	730	410	660	370	540	300
	1/2	1100	570	950	490	760	400	610	320
	5/8	1640	790	1290	620	920	440	740	350
	3/4	1990	870	1500	660	1070	470	860	380
7″	3/8*	640	390	560	340	500	300	440	270
	7/16	870	490	750	420	670	380	590	330
	1/2	1120	580	970	500	870	450	740	380
	5/8	1710	820	1480	710	1130	540	900	430
	3/4	2380	1050	1840	810	1310	580	1050	460
8″	7/16*	880	490	760	420	680	380	600	330
	1/2	1140	590	980	510	880	460	780	400
	5/8	1750	840	1510	720	1320	630	1060	510
	3/4	2470	1090	2130	940	1560	690	1250	550
	7/8	3260	1360	2480	1030	1770	740	1420	590
9″	1/2*	1150	600	990	510	890	460	780	410
	5/8	1770	850	1530	730	1370	660	1210	580
	3/4	2510	1100	2160	950	1790	790	1440	630
	7/8	3360	1400	2880	1200	2060	860	1650	690
10″	5/8*	1790	860	1550	740	1380	660	1220	590
	3/4	2550	1120	2200	970	1970	870	1630	720
	7/8	3430	1420	2960	1230	2340	970	1880	780
	1	4410	1770	3680	1470	2640	1050	2110	850
11″	3/4*	2570	1130	2220	980	1990	880	1750	770
	7/8	3470	1440	3000	1250	2620	1090	2100	870
	1	4490	1800	3880	1550	2960	1180	2370	950
12″	7/8	3490	1450	3020	1260	2700	1120	2320	960
	1	4520	1810	3900	1560	3260	1310	2620	1050
	1-1/8	5670	2270	4890	1960	3630	1450	2910	1170
13″	7/8*	3510	1460	3030	1260	2710	1130	2390	1000
	1	4550	1820	3930	1570	3520	1410	2870	1150
	1-1/8	5710	2280	4930	1970	3980	1590	3200	1280
14″	1	4570	1830	3950	1580	3530	1410	3110	1250
	1-1/8	5750	2300	4960	1980	4330	1730	3470	1390
	1-1/4	7030	2810	6070	2430	4750	1900	3810	1520
15″	1	4590	1830	3960	1580	3540	1420	3130	1250
	1-1/8	5770	2310	4990	1990	4460	1780	3750	1500
	1-1/4	7070	2830	6110	2440	5130	2050	4120	1650
16″	1*	4590	1830	3960	1580	3540	1420	3130	1250
	1-1/8*	5790	2320	5000	2000	4480	1790	3950	1580
	1-1/4*	7120	2850	6150	2460	5500	2200	4430	1770

*Greater lengths do not provide higher loads.

Reproduced from National Design Specification for Wood Construction, 1986 Edition, with permission from National Forest Products Association, Washington, D.C.

Table 5.1 has Douglas fir-larch in group II, with $G = 0.51$. The CUF = 1.0, from Table 5.2. Table 3.1 gives a LDF = 0.9 for this dead load.

The required lateral capacity per lag screw is

$$\frac{(2000 \text{ lb}) (\sin 40°)}{(0.9)(2 \text{ lag screws})} = 714 \text{ lb/lag screw}$$

The required withdrawal capacity per lag screw is

$$\frac{(2000 \text{ lb}) (\cos 40°)}{(0.9)(2 \text{ lag screws})} = 851 \text{ lb/lag screw}$$

Try a $6'' \times \frac{7}{16}''$ lag screw. The lateral capacity = 730 lb, parallel-to-grain (Table 5.10). The withdrawal capacity = (T-E)(allowable load). The effective penetration, T-E = $3\frac{7}{32}''$ (Appendix C). The allowable withdrawal loading = 353 lb/in (Table 5.8). The withdrawal capacity is therefore equal to (3.219 in)(353 lb/in) = 1136 pounds.

The $6'' \times \frac{7}{16}''$ lag screw satisfies both the applied withdrawal and lateral loads. Similar calculations show a $5'' \times \frac{1}{2}''$ lag to have 840 lb lateral capacity and 1048 lb in withdrawal. A $4'' \times \frac{5}{8}''$ has 740 lb lateral capacity and 980 lb withdrawal. While all three sizes work, the $5'' \times \frac{1}{2}''$ most evenly exceeds the two applied load components and is the author's choice.

Example 5.5

The lag screw shown is intended to hold the wharf against wind load. What is its capacity?

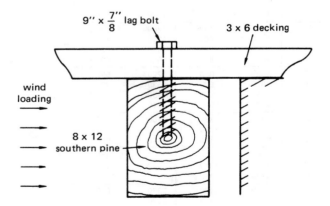

Determine the lag screw capacity and modify for condition of use and load duration.

Southern pine is a group II species (Table 5.1). The wind load duration factor is 1.33 (Table 3.1). Assuming the wharf is subjected to a wet-dry cycle, Table 5.2 gives a CUF = 0.75. The lag screw capacity is 760 lb, found in Table 5.9.

lag screw capacity = (760 lb) (1.33) (0.75) = 760 lb

6 BOLTS

The shear capacity of a bolt depends on the wood species holding the bolt, the length and diameter of the bolt, the load directions, and the number of members and their configuration. Table 5.11 is a straightforward list of design values based on an assumed layout for a typical connection. The listed values are for dry conditions and normal load duration. Enter an appropriate bolt length for the actual configuration into the table and modify the table value for the design condition of use and load duration factors.

A. Reading Load Tables

An assumption inherent in Table 5.11 is that with two side members, each is half as thick as the main member sandwiched between them. This *double-shear* assumption is not true for connections with two members, nor for ones with more than three members. Other connection configurations are accommodated by using a modified or substitute main member thickness in Table 5.11, while still using the actual bolt size and member species (NDS 8.5.7 and 8.5.8).

Use the following criteria to find the length of bolt, ℓ, in main member to enter into Table 5.11.

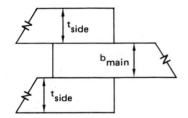

Figure 5.8 Connection Member Thicknesses

In the case where all members are aligned with one another in double shear (three members),

- $t_{\text{side members}} = \dfrac{b_{\text{main member}}}{2}$

  use the tabulated value $\ell = b_{\text{main member}}$

- $t_{\text{side members}} > \dfrac{b_{\text{main member}}}{2}$

  use the tabulated value $\ell = b_{\text{main member}}$

- $t_{\text{side members}} < \dfrac{b_{\text{main member}}}{2}$

  use the tabulated value $\ell = (2)(t_{\text{thinner side member}})$

In the case where all members are aligned with one another in single shear (only two members), and load is at the same angle to the grain in both pieces,

- for side members of equal thickness, use (0.5)(tabulated value), with $\ell = t_{\text{member}}$

Table 5.11
Lateral Loads in Bolts—Design Values

p = Safe loads parallel to grain in pounds
q = Safe loads perpendicular to grain in pounds

Length of Bolt in Main Wood Member[3] (in inches)		DIAMETER OF BOLT (IN INCHES)								
		3/8	1/2	5/8	3/4	7/8	1	1-1/8	1-1/4	1-1/2
1½	Single p	325	470	590	710	830	945			
	Shear q	185	215	245	270	300	325			
	Double p	650	940	1180	1420	1660	1890			
	Shear q	370	430	490	540	600	650			
2½	Single p		630	910	1155	1370	1575			
	Shear q		360	405	450	495	540			
	Double p	710	1260	1820	2310	2740	3150			
	Shear q	620	720	810	900	990	1080			
3½	Single p			990	1400	1790	2135	2455	2740	3305
	Shear q			565	630	695	760	825	895	1020
	Double p	710	1270	1980	2800	3580	4270	4910	5480	6610
	Shear q	640	980	1130	1260	1390	1520	1650	1780	2040
5½	Single p				1950	2535	3190		3820	4975
	Shear q				1090	1190	1300		1395	1605
	Double p		1270	1990	2860	3900	5070	6380	7640	9950
	Shear q		930	1410	1880	2180	2380	2600	2790	3210
7½	Single p								3975	5680
	Shear q								1900	2185
	Double p			1990	2860	3890	5080	6440	7950	11,360
	Shear q			1260	1820	2430	3030	3500	3800	4370
9½	Single p									5730
	Shear q									2765
	Double p				2860	3900	5080	6440	7950	11,460
	Shear q				1640	2270	2960	3710	4450	5530
11½	Single p									
	Shear q									
	Double p				3900	5080	6440	7950		11,450
	Shear q				2050	2770	3540	4360		6150
13½	Single p									
	Shear q									
	Double p						5100	6440	7960	11,450
	Shear q						2530	3310	4160	6040

[1]Tabulated values are on a normal load-duration basis and apply to joints made of seasoned lumber used in dry locations. See U.B.C. Standard No. 25-17 for other service conditions.

[2]Double shear values are for joints consisting of three wood members in which the side members are one half the thickness of the main member. Single shear values are for joints consisting of two wood members having a minimum thickness not less than that specified.

[3]The length specified is the length of the bolt in the main member of double shear joints or the length of the bolt in the thinner member of single shear joints.

[4]See U.B.C. Standard No. 25-17 for wood-to-metal bolted joints.

Reproduced from the 1988 Edition of the Uniform Building Code, copyright © 1988, with the permission of the publishers, the International Conference of Building Officials.

- for side members of unequal thickness, use the lesser of:

  · (0.5)(tabulated value), with

    $\ell = t_{\text{thicker member}}$

  · (0.5)(tabulated value), with

    $\ell = (2)(t_{\text{thinner member}})$

In the case where the load is at a different angle to the grain in each of two members, use the lesser of the following two values:

- tabulated value for main member

- tabulated value, with $\ell = (2)(t_{\text{side member}})$ and loaded in the appropriate direction. Use the Hankinson formula.

Note: Connection details are extremely important in timber because of the effect they can have on load direction. See Figs. 5.9 through 5.12 for illustrations.

Members of Different Materials

When the members used at the same connection are different species of timber, use the lesser of the following two values:

- tabulated value for all members of side member species

- tabulated value for all members of main member species

When metal members are in the connection as side members(s) (straps or plates) and load is perpendicular to the grain, there is no increase in the tabulated values. If the load is parallel to the grain, increase the tabulated value for main members by:

- 75 percent for bolts $\frac{1}{2}$ inch or less in diameter

- 25 percent for bolts $1\frac{1}{2}$ inches in diameter

- proportional percentage for intermediate diameter bolts (i.e., between $\frac{1}{2}$ inch and $1\frac{1}{2}$ inches)

When the main member is metal and load is perpendicular to the grain, there is no increase in the tabulated value (with $\ell = (2)(t_{\text{side member}})$. When the load is parallel to the grain, increase the tabulated value for a piece with $\ell = (2)(t_{\text{side members}})$ by:

- 75 percent for bolts $\frac{1}{2}$ inch or less in diameter

- 25 percent for bolts $1\frac{1}{2}$ inches in diameter

- proportional percentage for intermediate diameter bolts

Note: The 75 percent increase in allowable loads with steel side members is a three-fold increase over the former 25 percent value. This is a somewhat volatile issue, and should be checked carefully against the current codes.

Connection with Four or More Members

In cases where all members are of equal thickness, evaluate single-shear capacity of two of the members, and multiply by the total number of shear planes. In cases where members are of unequal thicknesses (this situation is complex and arises rarely (NDS 8.5.8.6)):

- resolve into all possible adjacent three-member joints

- evaluate capacity of each with above methods

- divide each capacity in half and assign to shear planes

- the lesser of any two capacities applies for each plane

- connection capacity is a multiple of the number of shear planes and the least capacity of those evaluated

B. Load Distribution as Influenced by Connection Details

Connection details can alter the direction in which loads are applied to members in connections. In the following example, a simple truss is used to demonstrate the crucial effect that connection details have on the angle of load application with the grain.

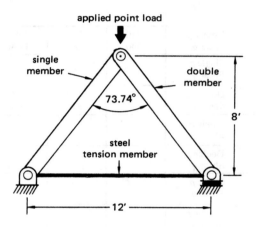

Figure 5.9 Entire Truss, as Loaded

At the truss peak connection, the 800 pound load can be imposed on the fastener, the single member, or the doubled members, depending upon how the connection is detailed. In all cases, the timber members are simple compression members; the difference is in the angles of load application at the fasteners. In this and all multi-member connections, dividing up the connection into pieces and investigating each piece as a free body is the best way to analyze the load distribution.

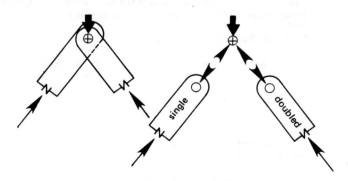

Figure 5.10 Load Applied through Bolt

If the load is applied to the bolt as shown in Fig. 5.10, both pieces act as simple truss members, and the fastener load is parallel to the grain in all members.

In Fig. 5.11, the doubled members are two-force bodies or simple truss members. Therefore, the fastener load is parallel to the grain in the doubled members. In the single member, however, the load applied by the doubled members through the fasteners is at an angle of 73.74° to the grain.

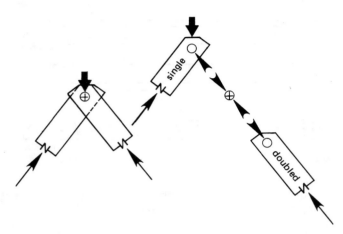

Figure 5.11 Load Applied through Single Member

The load application shown in Fig. 5.12 gives an opposite response to those of Fig. 5.11. The single member has the fastener load parallel to the grain. The fastener load in the doubled members is at an angle of 73.74° to the grain.

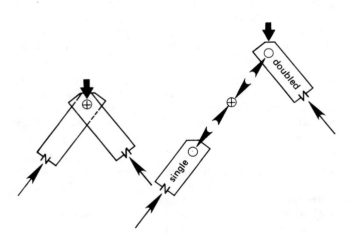

Figure 5.12 Load Applied through Doubled Members

7 SPACING REQUIREMENTS FOR BOLTS AND LAG SCREWS

The design values for both lag screws and bolts are valid only if certain spacing requirements are met. Some of the design spacings can be reduced (but not below other, absolute, minimums) with a reduced design capacity calculated by linear interpolation to zero capacity at zero spacing. A row is defined as two or more fasteners in a line parallel to the load direction. All spacings are given as center-to-center distances, and distances are measured from a surface of the member to the center of the bolt.

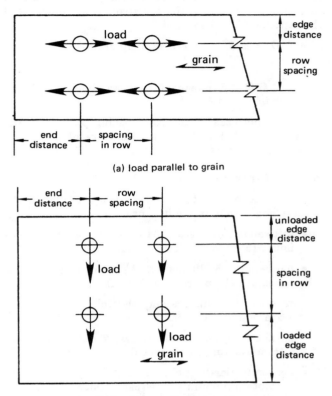

(a) load parallel to grain

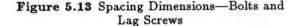

(b) load perpendicular to grain

Figure 5.13 Spacing Dimensions—Bolts and Lag Screws

The following outlines the required spacings for bolts and lag screws. The spacings will vary with load direction. Some spacings may be reduced to an absolute minimum value with a linear decrease in capacity. See Fig. 5.6 for an explanation of staggered rows of bolts. The bolt length used in this outline, ℓ, should be the effective bolt length that governs in finding the allowable load. The bolt diameter, D, is in inches, too (NDS 8.5.11–17).

Fasteners in a Row

The minimum full-strength spacings required for spacing of fasteners in a row when the load is parallel to the grain are:

- four diameters for full-strength

- three diameters absolute minimum (75 percent bolt design value)

When the load is perpendicular to the grain, the spacing is limited by spacing requirements of attached members (wood or metal), loaded parallel to the grain.

Fastener Rows

The required spacing of fastener rows loaded parallel to the grain is $1\frac{1}{2}$ diameters, across the grain. For a load perpendicular to the grain, the spacing is a function of the fastener ℓ/D ratio.

- $\ell/D = 2$; $2\frac{1}{2}$ diameters, along grain
- $\ell/D \geq 6$; 5 diameters, along grain
- $2 < \ell/D < 6$; linear interpolation between $2\frac{1}{2}$ and 5 diameters

Note: In any case, if the row spacing parallel to the member exceeds 5 inches, separate splice plates are required for each row.

End Distance

The required end distances for a load parallel to the grain, when members are in tension are:

- softwood: 7 diameters, $3\frac{1}{2}$ diameters absolute minimum (50 percent design value)
- hardwood: 5 diameters, $2\frac{1}{2}$ diameters absolute minimum (50 percent design value)

For members in compression, the following end distances are required for loads:

- parallel-to-grain: 4 diameters; 2 diameters absolute minimum (50 percent design value)
- perpendicular-to-grain: 4 diameters; 2 diameters absolute minimum (50 percent design value)

Edge Distance

The required edge distance for a load parallel to the grain is a function of the fastener ℓ/D ratio.

- $\ell/D \leq 6$; $1\frac{1}{2}$ diameters
- $\ell/D > 6$; use the greater of the following values:
  · $1\frac{1}{2}$ diameters
  · $\frac{1}{2}$ the distance between fastener rows

For a load perpendicular to grain, the required edge distance is four diameters for a loaded edge, and $1\frac{1}{2}$ diameters for an unloaded edge.

Note: Loads should not be hung from beams on fasteners below the neutral axis.

When loads are at angles other than parallel and perpendicular to the grain, the engineer should ensure uniform load distribution by aligning the center of the connection resistance with the centroids of the connected members. The spacing constraints should be met as well as is feasible in the members, recognizing that these situations can be complex and conflicting.

Example 5.6

The drawing below shows five feasible bolt patterns using six $\frac{5}{8}''$ bolts to splice a 4×6 member with two 2×6 splice plates. The members will be in tension. Deter-

mine the capacity and the minimum splice plate lengths for each pattern. All members are southern pine no. 1, surfaced and used at 15% moisture content. Design will be for normal load duration.

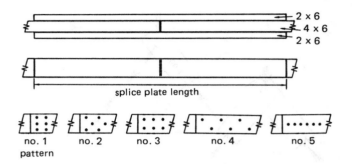

In designing tension splices, the engineer is trying to maximize the load capacity while keeping the splice length within reasonable limits. This optimization process often involves balancing connector and member capacities. There are several variables to consider: the distance between bolts in a row, the row spacing, the row staggering, and the end and edge distances. These dimensions influence the numbers of connector rows and connectors within those rows that the connection is considered as having in the connector capacity analysis. The layout also governs the number of connectors considered to be within a given net cross section in the member capacity analysis. The purpose of this example is to demonstrate the interaction of these design variables in optimizing the design.

Check the capacity of the bolts, correcting for multiple connectors. Make sure the net section left after drilling does not limit load capacity. Use required spacing and end distances to determine the minimum length splice members.

The allowable tension stress in the members and basic allowable load in the bolts do not change with the bolt pattern. To find the basic bolt capacity, use Table 5.11 with the correct member thickness. This is double shear with aligned members, but the member thickness must be compared to determine which controls.

$$t_{\text{side member}} = 1.5 \text{ in} < (0.5)(b_{\text{main}})$$
$$= (0.5)(3.5 \text{ in})$$
$$= 1.75 \text{ in}$$

Therefore, use $\ell = (2)(t_{\text{thinner side member}}) = 3$ in.

With southern pine, $\frac{5}{8}''$ bolt, and load parallel to grain, Table 5.11 gives $P = 1960$ lb/bolt.

The stress tables of Appendix B give an allowable tension stress of 1050 psi. Note that with the no. 1 grade and 6″ width, Footnote 3 does not decrease the allowable stress.

Table 5.2 gives the CUF = 1.0 for this protected exposure condition. The LDF is 1.0 (Table 3.1).

The area of the main member is 19.25 in^2 and that of each side plate is 8.25 in^2, before drilling any holes. The holes are assumed to be $\frac{1}{16}$″ oversized, or $\frac{11}{16}$″ diameter. The minimum spacings are given as multiples of the bolt diameter. For the $\frac{5}{8}$″ bolts, the minimum spacings are:

end distance (tension)	7 diameters	4.375 in
edge distance	$1\frac{1}{2}$ diameters	$\frac{15}{16}$ in
row spacing	$1\frac{1}{2}$ diameters	$\frac{15}{16}$ in
spacing in row	4 diameters	2.5 in

The edge spacing varies with the ℓ/D ratio. In this case, $\ell/D = 3 \text{ in}/\left(\frac{5}{8} \text{ in}\right) = 4.8 < 6$, so the $1\frac{1}{2}$ diameters controls.

With these common numbers, start evaluating the different pattern capacities.

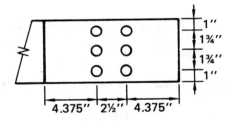

There is adequate space across the member for the three rows of two bolts. The minimum splice plate length is

$$(2)[(2.5 \text{ in}) + (2)(4.375 \text{ in})] = 22.5 \text{ in}$$

Check the bolt capacity first. This pattern is considered as three rows of two bolts each. Table 5.6A shows a K of 1.0 for two bolts, no matter what the member sizes are. Therefore, the bolt capacity is

$$(6 \text{ bolts}) \left(1960 \frac{\text{lb}}{\text{bolt}}\right)(1.0) = 11,760 \text{ lb}$$

Now check the net section capacity. A one-eighth reduction in area is made to account for the possibility of knots also falling in the critical cross section. The splice plates will control because they are thinner than the main member. The area of three holes will be removed.

$$\text{net area} = (2)\left[(8.25 \text{ in}^2) - (3)(1.5 \text{ in})\left(\frac{11}{16} \text{ in}\right)\right]\left(\frac{7}{8}\right)$$
$$= 9.02 \text{ in}^2$$

The net section capacity, therefore, is

$$(9.02 \text{ in}^2)(1050 \text{ psi}) = 9475 \text{ lb}$$

For bolt pattern no. 1, the splice plates control the capacity at 9475 pounds.

Because the bolts will not be loaded to capacity when the splice plates are in pattern no.1, the bolt spacing may be reduced somewhat. The bolts will be at $9475/11,760 = 0.81$, or 81% of their design capacity. The bolt spacing could be reduced to 2″ ($0.81 \times 2.5″$) (three diameters is the absolute minimum allowed), resulting in an absolute minimum splice plate length of 21.5″.

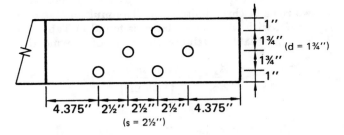

Since the member controls the capacity in pattern no. 1, it seems reasonable to stagger the pattern to increase the net section. The in-row spacing must be at least eight bolt diameters, while keeping $d > S/4$. If $d < S/4$ this pattern would be considered as one row of four bolts and one row of two bolts.

The minimum splice plate length is

$$2[(3)(2.5 \text{ in}) + (2)(4.375 \text{ in})] = 32.5 \text{ in}$$

Check the bolt capacity first. This pattern is still considered as three rows of two bolts each ($d > S/4$). Therefore, the bolt capacity is

$$(6 \text{ bolts}) \left(1960 \frac{\text{lb}}{\text{bolt}}\right)(1.0) = 11,760 \text{ lb}$$

Now check the net section capacity. With this staggered spacing there is a maximum of only two bolts in any four diameter (2.5 in) length of the members. Therefore, only two holes will be subtracted from the area.

$$\text{net area} = (2)\left[(8.25 \text{ in}^2) - (2)(1.5 \text{ in})\left(\frac{11}{16} \text{ in}\right)\right]\left(\frac{7}{8}\right)$$
$$= 10.83 \text{ in}^2$$

The net section capacity, therefore, is

$$(10.83 \text{ in}^2)(1050 \text{ psi}) = 11,370 \text{ lb}$$

For bolt pattern no. 2, the splice plates control the capacity at 11,370 pounds. The bolt and member capacities are very nearly balanced, making this a reasonable design choice.

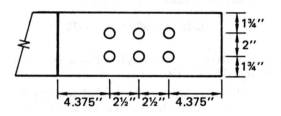

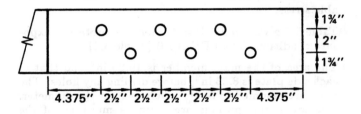

The minimum splice plate length is

$$(2)[(2)(2.5 \text{ in}) + (2)(4.375 \text{ in})] = 27.5 \text{ in}$$

Check the bolt capacity first. This pattern is considered as two rows of three bolts each. The multiple fastener factor, K, with wood side plates, is found in Table 5.6. To use that table, evaluate the ratio of the member areas.

$$\frac{A_1}{A_2} = \frac{19.25 \text{ in}^2}{(2)(8.25 \text{ in}^2)}$$
$$= 1.17$$

Since this is greater than 1.0, use the reciprocal,

$$\frac{1}{1.17} = 0.86$$

When using this reciprocal, also use

$$A_2 = (2)(8.25 \text{ in}^2)$$
$$= 16.5 \text{ in}^2$$

This value falls in the 12–19 in² range.

Interpolating between 0.95 for a 0.5 ratio, and 0.97 for a 1.0 ratio, K is 0.97 in this case.

Therefore, the bolt capacity is

$$(6 \text{ bolts}) \left(1960 \frac{\text{lb}}{\text{bolt}}\right)(0.97) = 11,410 \text{ lb}$$

Now check the net section capacity. Only two holes will be subtracted from the area.

$$\text{net area} = (2)\left[(8.25 \text{ in}^2) - (2)(1.5 \text{ in})\left(\frac{11}{16} \text{ in}\right)\right]\left(\frac{7}{8}\right)$$
$$= 10.83 \text{ in}^2$$

The net section capacity, therefore, is

$$(10.83 \text{ in}^2)(1050 \text{ psi}) = 11,370 \text{ lb}$$

For bolt pattern no. 3, the splice plates control the capacity at 11,370 pounds. This is another well-balanced connection design, with an even shorter length than the previous layout.

The minimum splice plate length is

$$(2)[(5)(2.5 \text{ in}) + (2)(4.375 \text{ in})] = 42.5 \text{ in}$$

Check the bolt capacity first. This pattern is considered as two rows of three bolts each. Again because $d > S/4$, the multiple connector factor is the same as for bolt pattern no. 3. Therefore, the bolt capacity is

$$(6 \text{ bolts}) \left(1960 \frac{\text{lb}}{\text{bolt}}\right)(0.97) = 11,410 \text{ lb}$$

Check the net section capacity. Because only one hole occurs in any four diameter (2.5″) length of the members, only the area of one hole need be subtracted.

$$\text{net area} = (2)\left[(8.25 \text{ in}^2) - (1)(1.5 \text{ in})\left(\frac{11}{16} \text{ in}\right)\right]\left(\frac{7}{8}\right)$$
$$= 12.63 \text{ in}^2$$

The net section capacity, therefore, is

$$(12.63 \text{ in}^2)(1050 \text{ psi}) = 13,260 \text{ lb}$$

For bolt pattern no. 4, the bolts control the capacity at 11,410 pounds. This capacity is slightly larger than that of pattern no. 3, but probably not enough to justify the extra 15 inches of splice plate length.

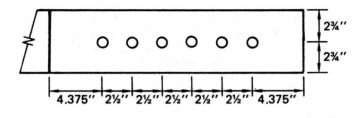

The minimum splice plate length is still

$$(2)[(5)(2.5 \text{ in}) + (2)(4.375 \text{ in})] = 42.5 \text{ in}$$

Check the bolt capacity first. This pattern is considered as one row of six bolts. The multiple connector factor is found with the same relative areas used in bolt pattern no. 3, except for six bolts. Now the interpolation for $A_2/A_1 = 0.86$ is between $K = 0.75$ and 0.84. That interpolation gives a $K = 0.81$. Therefore, the bolt capacity is

$$(6 \text{ bolts})\left(1960\,\frac{\text{lb}}{\text{bolt}}\right)(0.81) = 9,530 \text{ lb}$$

Check the net section capacity. The area of only one hole need be subtracted.

$$\text{net area} = (2)\left[(8.25 \text{ in}^2) - (1)(1.5 \text{ in})\left(\frac{11}{16} \text{ in}\right)\right]\left(\frac{7}{8}\right)$$
$$= 12.63 \text{ in}^2$$

The net section capacity, therefore, is

$$(12.63 \text{ in}^2)(1050 \text{ psi}) = 13,260 \text{ lb}$$

For bolt pattern no. 5, the bolts control the capacity at 9530 pounds. This is almost as low as the capacity of bolt pattern no. 1. Note that bolt patterns no. 4 and no. 5 differ only in the amount of staggering. The minimum amount of row stagger that would qualify the six bolts as two separate rows is the along-the-grain spacing divided by four, or $\frac{5''}{8}$.

Considering splice plate length and balanced capacity, either bolt pattern no. 3 or no. 4 would be a good design.

Example 5.7

What is the capacity of this connection against snow load? The spruce-pine-fir seasons in place, and it is expected to stay dry.

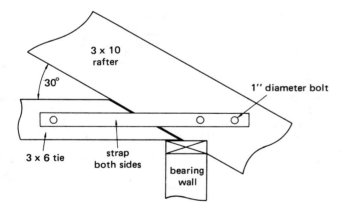

Check the tie bolt capacity and the capacity of the bolts in the rafter. Use the Hankinson formula to determine the rafter bolts' capacity.

Table 3.1 gives a LDF of 1.15 with snow loads. According to Table 5.2, the CUF for this connection is 1.0. There will be an increase in the bolt capacity, parallel to the grain only, because of the metal side plates. Table 5.6B shows that the multiple fastener factor, K, for any connection with only two fasteners in a row is 1.0.

First, evaluate the capacity in the tie beam. Table 5.11, with spruce-pine-fir, 1" bolts, and $\ell = 2.5''$, gives $P = 2260$ lb/bolt. The bolt capacity is

$$(1 \text{ bolt}) \left(2260\frac{\text{lb}}{\text{bolt}}\right)(1.15)(1.0)(1.50)(1.0) = 3900 \text{ lb}$$

The 1.50 metal plate increase is an interpolation between 75% increase for $\frac{1}{2}''$ diameter and 25% increase for $1\frac{1}{2}''$ diameter bolts (NDS 8.5.6.3).

When evaluating the bolt capacity in the rafter, the CUF of Table 5.7 must be included because the connection seasons in place. The strap does cross the grain, so the CUF of Table 5.7 is 0.4. Table 5.11 gives a capacity perpendicular to the grain, Q, of 700 lb. Before using the Hankinson formula, find the adjusted bolt capacities in both directions.

$$P = (2260 \text{ lb})(1.15)(1.50)(0.4) = 1559 \text{ lb/bolt}$$
$$Q = (700 \text{ lb})(1.15)(0.4) = 322 \text{ lb/bolt}$$

Note that only the component parallel to the grain is increased 50% for the metal side plates. Using the Hankinson formula,

$$F_{30°} = \frac{(322 \text{ lb})(1559 \text{ lb})}{(1559 \text{ lb})(\sin^2 30°) + (322 \text{ lb})(\cos^2 30°)}$$
$$= 795 \text{ lb/bolt}$$

The rafter connection capacity is

$$(2 \text{ bolts}) \left(795\,\frac{\text{lb}}{\text{bolt}}\right) = 1590 \text{ lb}$$

The two bolts in the rafter limit the connection capacity to 1590 lb, significantly less than the capacity of the single bolt in the tie beam.

The connection was weakened most by having the timbers season in place with the steel strap bolted across the grain. Since the strap is not exactly across the grain, but at an angle to it, some less severe CUF might be justified. One possible approach would be to use the Hankinson formula to interpolate between the 1.0 and 0.4 factors (CUF = 0.73). The rafter connection capacity would then be

$$(2 \text{ bolts}) \left(1450\frac{\text{lb}}{\text{bolt}}\right) = 2900 \text{ lb}$$

8 SHEAR PLATES AND SPLIT RINGS (CONNECTORS)

Shear plates and split rings are highly effective mechanical fasteners which can have capacities five to six times greater than those of bolts or lag screws. Shear loads are transmitted between members through the metal connectors which fit into carefully cut grooves, or daps.

The bolt or lag screw that lies on the connector axis serves only to hold the joint together. Both connector types are manufactured by TECO Products, whose design charts and tables form the basis of this section.

Split rings come in $2\frac{1}{2}$ inch and 4 inch diameters, and provide wood-to-wood connection. Lag screws are used to hold a split ring connection together when the holding member is very large or has an inaccessible far side. Shear plates have $2\frac{5}{8}$ inch or 4 inch diameters. Shear plates are used singly to attach a metal side member, or in pairs back-to-back to connect two wood members. In either case, lag screws can be used with shear plates for the same reasons they are used with split rings. Figure 5.14 illustrates the sizes and types of timber connectors.

split ring

pressed steel shear plate

malleable iron shear plate

Figure 5.14 Types of Split Rings and Shear Plates

Used with permission from Design Manual for TECO Timber Connector Construction, published by TECO Products, Colliers, West Virginia.

9 CONSIDERATIONS IN CONNECTOR DESIGN

Most of the factors applied to other fasteners also apply to connectors. The load duration factors are the same. The condition of use factors specific to connectors are found in Table 5.2. The modifier for number of connectors in a row is found in Tables 5.6A and 5.6B. The TECO capacity tables are specific to angle of load and grain, and incorporate the Hankinson formula interpolation. There is an absolute maximum load for the shear plates established by the bolt bearing on the plate. This maximum capacity is found in the lower right-hand corner of the shear plate capacity tables.

There are several special design considerations specific to shear plates and split rings.

- *Lag Screws in Connectors*: If lag screws are used instead of bolts, the factors in Table 5.12 apply.

- *Net Sections*: Net sections are determined by subtracting the projected area of the cut daps and bolt holes. This calculation is aided by the projected connector areas tabulated in Appendix D.

A bolt hole should have a diameter no larger than $\frac{1}{16}$ inch more than the bolt diameter. Half-inch bolts and lag screws are used in $2\frac{1}{2}$ inch split rings, while $\frac{3}{4}$ inch bolts and lag screws are used in the other connectors, except the $\frac{7}{8}$ inch diameter bolts used in 4 inch diameter shear plates.

Because a knot near a connector would further reduce the net section, the allowable stresses in tension and compression are reduced by one-eighth. This reduction is applied only to solid-sawn lumber, not to glue-laminated members.

Connectors in adjacent staggered rows are treated as being in the same cross section if the parallel-to-grain spacing between them is less than one connector diameter (NDS 8.2.1.5).

Table 5.12
Capacity Modification Using Lag Screws in Connectors

Modification Factors C_{lb} for Timber Connectors Used with Lag Bolts[a]

Timber Connector Size and Type	Side Plates	Penetration	Fastener Species Load Group[c]				Modification Factor[b] C_{lb}
			I	II	III	IV	
$2\frac{1}{2}$-in. split ring, 4-in. split ring, or 4-in. shear plate	Wood or	Standard	7	8	10	11	1.00
	Metal	Minimum	3	$3\frac{1}{2}$	4	$4\frac{1}{2}$	0.75
$2\frac{5}{8}$-in. shear plate	Wood	Standard	4	5	7	8	1.00
		Minimum	3	$3\frac{1}{2}$	4	$4\frac{1}{2}$	0.75
	Metal	Standard and Minimum	3	$3\frac{1}{2}$	4	$4\frac{1}{2}$	1.00

[a]Factors apply to design values tabulated for connector units used with bolts.
[b]Use straight line interpolation for intermediate penetrations.

Used with permission from Timber Construction Manual, Third Edition, by American Institute of Timber Construction, published by John Wiley & Sons, Inc., 1985.

Example 5.8

What is the net section of the timber prepared as shown for a connector?

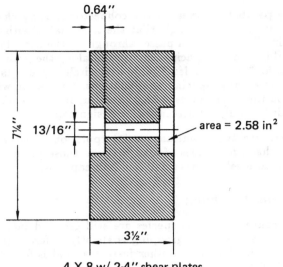

4 X 8 w/ 2-4" shear plates
3/4" bolt; 13/16" hole

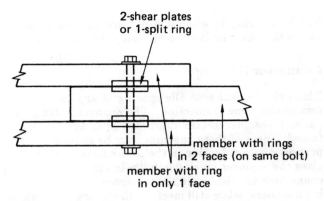
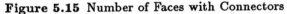

Figure 5.15 Number of Faces with Connectors

End Distance

The end distance charts are very similar to the edge distance charts. The tension line is used for a load with any component toward the near end of the member. For members in compression, there is a family of lines for various load-grain angles.

There are two limitations on end distance in members that are not cut square. The two can be converted to equivalent dimensions and compared with each other to determine which one controls.

Appendix E gives the 25.375 in² gross area for the 4×8. Appendix D lists the projected area of a 4" shear plate as 2.58 in². After subtracting two shear plates, the rest of the bolt hole between the plates must be subtracted. Appendix D also gives the depth of the connectors, 0.64" for a 4" shear plate. The $\frac{3}{4}$" bolt has a $\frac{13}{16}$" bolt hole.

The length of the hole between the plates is

$$3.5 \text{ in} - (2)(0.64 \text{ in}) = 2.22 \text{ in}$$

The net area then is

$$25.375 \text{ in}^2 - (2)(2.58 \text{ in}^2) - \left(\frac{13}{16}\text{ in}\right)(2.22 \text{ in})$$

$$= 18.51 \text{ in}^2$$

Minimum Lumber Sizes

TECO recommends minimum lumber widths and thicknesses in order to avoid members being unduly weakened by the cut daps and grooves. The minimum sizes depend on the connector type, diameter, and whether a member has connectors in one or two faces on any one bolt. These minimum sizes are found in the appropriate connector tables of Figs. 5.18 through 5.27.

Edge Distance

The edge distance charts give the minimum required loaded edge distances on the horizontal axis. The percentage of full load is the vertical axis. For loads parallel to the grain, and for any unloaded edge, the minimum edge distance is the value on the right-hand border of the chart. For any other load-grain angle, the diagonal lines represent the acceptable minimum edge distances as a function of percentage of full load.

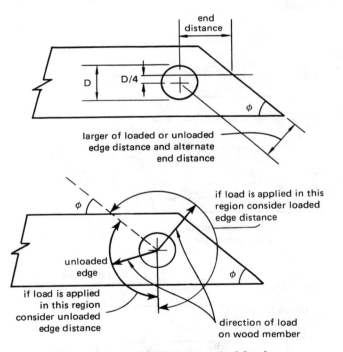

Figure 5.16 End Distance in Members without Square Ends

To determine which of the limitations controls, find the larger of these two values:

loaded or unloaded edge distance (see Fig. 5.16 for choice)

(tabulated end distance) $(\sin \phi) + \left(\frac{D}{4}\right)(\cos \phi)$ 5.2

The longer length, when laid out normal to the angled cut, is the outer limit of acceptable connector positions.

Connector Spacing

These charts deal with the spacing of any two connectors in the same connection. The connector design capacities assume certain minimum spacings are maintained. Some of these spacings may be reduced, with a proportionate reduction in the connector capacity. This gives the engineer much flexibility in making the overall connection fit within the limited space of two intersecting members, while still meeting all spacing restrictions.

The spacing charts in Figs. 5.18 through 5.27 allow for simultaneous adjustment of spacings both along and across the grain. The distances are measured from center to center of the connectors. These charts incorporate load angles and reductions for underloading. The vertical axis is the across-the-grain spacing of any two connectors, while the horizontal axis has a range of along-the-grain spacings. The lines radiating from the origin represent the angle that the line connecting the centers of two connectors makes with the grain, if they are spaced according to the grid position. This should not be confused with the angle that the load makes with the grain.

The parabolic curves on the connector spacing charts are specific to the angle that the load makes with the grain. Each parabola passes through all the acceptable combinations of spacings across and along the grain for that load-grain angle. The quarter circle represents all the acceptable spacing combinations, no matter what angle the load makes with the grain, for a connector loaded to only 50 percent of its design capacity.

There are two simultaneous interpolations used with this chart; for angles of load between those given, and for load levels between full and half capacity.

Species Grouping

For convenience, the species are still grouped into capacity ranges. The grouping is slightly different from the one used with the other fasteners, and is found in Table 5.1.

Connectors in End Grain

Connectors are installed in the end grain of timber very rarely. For a rather complex treatment of this difficult subject, refer to the National Design Specification, section 8.4.15.

Example 5.9

What is the snow load capacity of the splice? Check connector and net section capacities, and spacings. The splice is on the lower chord of a truss that was fabricated wet and is always dry in service.

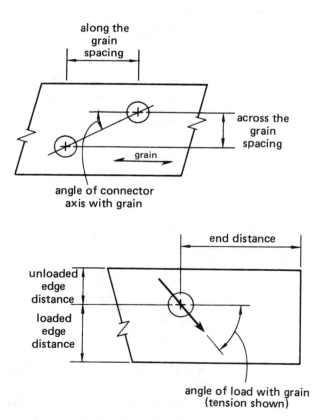

Figure 5.17 Connector Spacing and Angle
to the Grain

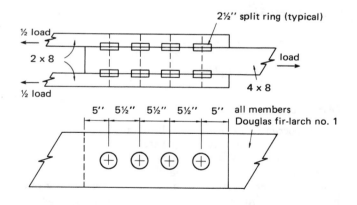

Check the connector capacity using the multiple connector correction. Then, check the net section capacity after subtracting the connector projected area. Use appropriate design values for the timber and any necessary footnoted considerations. Finally, check that the spacing is at least the minimum required for the members, connectors, and load levels involved.

The snow load has a LDF of 1.15 (Table 3.1). Table 5.2 gives a CUF of 0.8. According to Table 5.1, Douglas fir-larch is a group B species.

The split ring capacities must be looked up for both the main members and the splice plates. Figure 5.18 has both capacities. In the 4×8, using the 2″ THICK-2 FACES curve, the capacity at 0° to the grain is 2740 lb. Even though the member is actually 3.5″ thick, the curve for 2″ thick members is used as the highest available. In the 2×8 splice plates, using the $1\frac{1}{2}$″ THICK-1 FACE curve, the capacity along the grain is 2740 lb.

The multiple connector factor, K, of Table 5.6A is evaluated next. The ratio A_1/A_2, with information from Appendix E, is

$$\frac{25.375 \text{ in}^2}{(2)(10.875 \text{ in}^2)} = 1.167$$

This ratio is greater than 1.0. Therefore, use $A_2/A_1 = 1/1.167 = 0.857$, and use A_2 instead of A_1 to get K. The K for $A_2/A_1 = 0.5$ is 0.93; and for $A_2/A_1 = 1.0$, K is 0.97. Interpolating for the actual A_2/A_1, $K = 0.96$.

connector capacity =
$$(8 \text{ connectors})\left(2740\,\frac{\text{lb}}{\text{connector}}\right)(0.96)(1.15)(0.8)$$
$$= 19,360 \text{ lb}$$

The net section capacities are determined in both the main member and the splice plates. The 4×8 net area is

$$25.375 \text{ in}^2 - (2)(1.10 \text{ in}^2) - \left(\frac{9}{16} \text{ in}\right)$$
$$\times \, [3.5 \text{ in} - (2)(0.375 \text{ in})]$$
$$= 21.63 \text{ in}^2$$

Appendix D yields the 1.10 in² area for the connectors and the 0.375″ depth of the connector. The $\frac{1}{2}$″ bolt has a $\frac{9}{16}$″ hole that must be subtracted between the connectors.

The 2×8's net area is

$$(2)(10.875 \text{ in}^2) - (2)(1.10 \text{ in}^2) - \left(\frac{9}{16} \text{ in}\right)$$
$$\times \, [(2)(1.5 \text{ in}) - (2)(0.375 \text{ in})]$$
$$= 18.28 \text{ in}^2$$

The net area is less than the main members. With equal allowable stresses, the stress in the splice plates will control.

The allowable tension is

$$F_t = (1000 \text{ psi})(0.8)\left(\frac{7}{8}\right) = 700 \text{ psi}$$

The 0.8 factor comes from footnote 3, Appendix B. The $\frac{1}{8}$ reduction is recommended for critical sections, in order to account for possible knots.

The member capacity, as limited by the two 2×8's, is

$$(18.28 \text{ in}^2)(700 \text{ psi})(1.15) = 14,715 \text{ lb}$$

The splice capacity is, therefore, limited by net section stresses in the splice plates to 14,715 lb.

The spacing requirements are checked against the requirements in Fig. 5.19. The minimum member width with $2\frac{1}{2}$″ in split rings is 3.5″, less than the actual 7.25″. The minimum member thickness, with $2\frac{1}{2}$″ split rings, is 1″ in with connectors in one face and 1.5″ with connectors in one face and 1.5″ with connectors in two faces. These are both less than provided, so the members are adequate.

When the splice plates are at capacity, the connectors are only loaded to 14,715/19,360 = 0.76, or 76%. The end distance chart in Fig. 5.19 shows that the minimum required is 4″, again less than provided.

The minimum spacing (parallel to grain) is found in the spacing chart of Fig. 5.19. With the 76% load, interpolate between the 50% value of 3.5″ and the 6.75″ required for full strength:

$$3.5 \text{ in} + \frac{76\% - 50\%}{100\% - 50\%}(6.75 \text{ in} - 3.5 \text{ in})$$
$$= 5.19 \text{ in} < 5.5 \text{ in provided (O.K.)}$$

All the spacing provided is adequate for loads applied to connectors.

Example 5.10

Check the capacity of the members and the four $2\frac{1}{2}$″ split rings under the design snow load. Lay out the dimensions for the connectors. The connection was fabricated when dry and is sheltered from the elements.

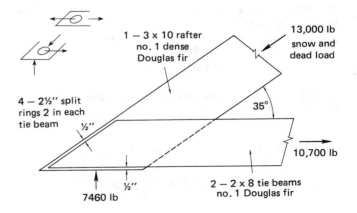

Check the net section and connector capacities in the rafter and tie beams. Laying out the connector dimensions is a complicated process with many available options. One way to systematically lay out the connection is first to consider each member separately and then to look at the entire connection. For each member, lay out the acceptable region for connectors. This region will be defined by the end and edge distances for the given connector, angle of load, and percentage of load capacity used. Then, determine the acceptable connector region for the entire connection by overlaying the acceptable regions for each member. Once this region is found, various layouts for the required number of connectors can be investigated for acceptability with the connector spacing chart. Note that because the vertical support is applied to the rafter (not to the ties), the connectors are loaded parallel to the grain in the ties and at 35° to the grain in the rafter.

First, find the net section of the 3×10 rafter.

$$(23.125 \text{ in}^2) - (2)(1.10 \text{ in}^2) - \left(\frac{9}{16} \text{ in}\right)$$
$$\times \left[(2.5 \text{ in} - (2)(0.375 \text{ in})\right]$$
$$= 19.94 \text{ in}^2$$

Appendix D has the 1.10 in² connector area and the 0.375″ connector depth. The capacity is

$$(19.94 \text{ in}^2)(1.15)\left(\frac{7}{8}\right)(1250 \text{ psi}) = 25,100 \text{ lb}$$

The 1.15 load duration factor comes from Table 3.1. The $\frac{7}{8}$ is an allowance for knots in the net section.

The connector capacity in the rafters, with four $2\frac{1}{2}''$ split rings, a group A species, 35° to grain, and the 2″ THICK-2 FACES curve, is 2830 lb/connector (see Fig. 5.18). The rafter split rings capacity is

$$\left(2830 \frac{\text{lb}}{\text{connector}}\right)(4 \text{ connectors})(1.15) = 13,000 \text{ lb}$$

The connectors are adequate in the rafter, and at 82% of their capacity.

$$\frac{10,650}{13,018} = 0.82$$

Now the tie beams' capacity is checked. The net section of the two 2×8's is

$$(2)\left[10.875 \text{ in}^2 - 1.10 \text{ in}^2 - \left(\frac{9}{16} \text{ in}\right)\right.$$
$$\left.\times (1.5 \text{ in} - 0.375 \text{ in})\right] = 18.28 \text{ in}^2$$

The connector dimensions are found in Appendix D. The tie beam capacity is

$$(18.28 \text{ in}^2)(1.15)\left(\frac{7}{8}\right)(1000 \text{ psi})(0.8) = 14.700 \text{ lb}$$

The connector capacity in the tie beams is found in Fig. 5.18 for $2\frac{1}{2}''$ split rings, load at 0° to grain, a group B species, and the $1\frac{1}{2}''$ THICK-1 FACE curve, to be 2740 lb/connector. The capacity of the four connectors is

$$\left(2740 \frac{\text{lb}}{\text{connectors}}\right)(4 \text{ connectors})(1.15) = 12,600 \text{ lb}$$

This is also greater than the applied 10,700 lb load.

The connection has adequate capacity, as long as the connectors fit into the available space without violating minimum spacing requirements. These spacing requirements should be checked next.

First, lay out the acceptable area for connectors in the rafter, as limited by edge and end distances. This member is in compression and at 82% capacity.

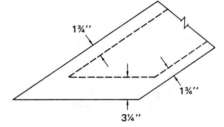

Next, the tie beams can have connectors in this region, considering that these connectors are at 10,700 lb/12,600 lb, or 85% of their capacity and in tension.

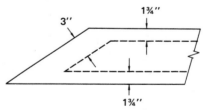

Overlapping these regions while maintaining the half-inch clearances means the connectors can be located anywhere in the common region. The more confining of any two parallel limits is the one that controls.

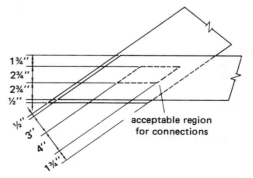

acceptable region
for connections

Within the acceptable region, many options remain for spacing the connectors. The widest allowable spacing should be checked first, to make sure there is room for the required connectors to fit and still meet the spacing requirements between individual connectors. If there is extra room, the engineer should compromise between the widest spacing permitted by the edge and end distances, and the closest spacing allowed for the given connectors. The spacings must be checked parallel and perpendicular to the grain in each of the connected members.

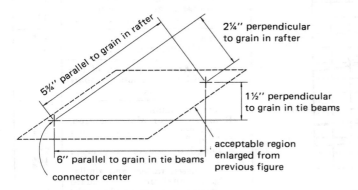

This set of connector spacings fulfills all the spacing and clearance requirements in each connected member. It also contains at least one set of reasonably simple layout dimensions.

Example 5.11

Check the $2\frac{5}{8}''$ shear plates for capacity and determine the spacing requirements for their layout. Determine the minimum required lag bolt size. The connection will be kept dry in service.

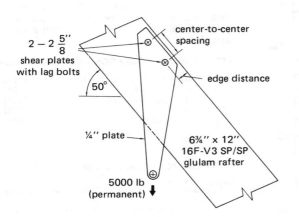

The connector capacity is found in Fig. 5.22. The lag screw used to hold the connector in place must be considered. The angle of load to grain has to be determined. The spacing considerations will include edge distances and center-to-center spacings.

Footnote 14 to Appendix B puts the connectors in a group A (or II) species. The connector capacity is found in Fig. 5.22 with the load at 40° to the grain and the $2\frac{1}{2}''$ THICK-2 FACES curve, to be 2820 lb/connector. The 2 FACES curve is used even with a connector in only one face because it is safe to assume a one-face connector is as strong as if there were another connector in the far face.

This means the connection capacity is

$$(2 \text{ connectors})\left(2820 \; \frac{\text{lb}}{\text{connector}}\right)(0.9)(1.0)(1.0)$$
$$= 5075 \text{ lb}$$

The 1.0 is the lag bolt modification factor, found in Table 5.12. The other 1.0 is the CUF of Table 5.2, and the 0.9 is the LDF from Table 3.1.

The connection is adequately strong. Now, establish the required spacings.

The connectors are loaded at 5000 lb/5075 lb, or 98.5% of their capacity. Figure 5.23 contains the necessary charts. The edge distance is an unloaded one, and must be at least $1\frac{3}{4}''$. The center-to-center spacing must be at least $4\frac{1}{2}''$. This parallel-to-grain spacing was interpolated for a 40° load angle and 98.5% of capacity, with the perpendicular-to-grain spacing equal to zero.

The lag screw, in a group II species, is determined from Table 5.12 to require a $3\frac{1}{2}$ diameter penetration. With a $\frac{3}{4}''$ lag screw, this means a $(3.5)(0.75'') + 0.25'' = 2.875''$ minimum length. The 0.25″ is included to account for the metal plate. Therefore, use a $\frac{3}{4}'' \times 3''$ lag screw.

Note the difference in meaning for lag bolt penetration. In lateral loading, the length of lag screw in the timber is the penetration. In withdrawal loads, the penetration is the length of the threaded portion of lag screw in the member.

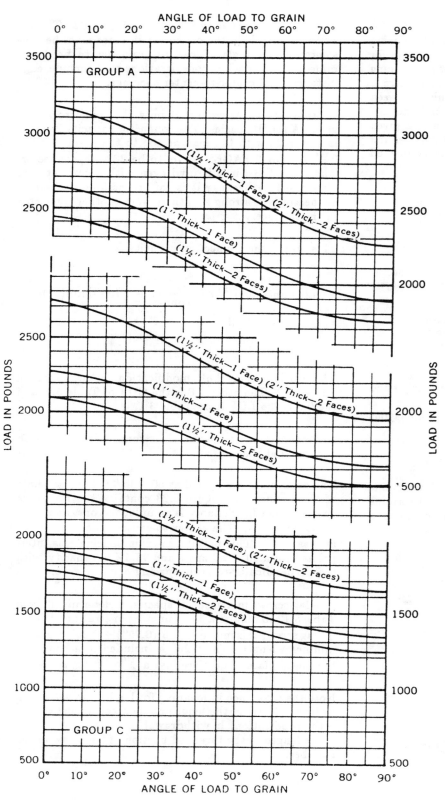

2½″ SPLIT RING DATA

Split Ring—Dimensions	
Inside Diameter at center when closed......................	2½″
Inside diameter at center when installed.....................	2.54″
Thickness of ring at center.......	0.163″
Thickness of ring at edge........	0.123″
Depth...........................	¾″
Lumber, Minimum dimensions allowed	
Width.........................	3½″
Thickness, rings in one face.....	1″
Thickness, rings opposite in both faces.....................	1½″
Bolt, diameter	½″
Bolt hole, diameter............	9/16″
Projected Area for portion of one ring within a member, square inches.....................	1.10
Washers, minimum	
Round, Cast or Malleable Iron, diameter.................	2⅛″
Square Plate	
Length of Side..............	2″
Thickness...................	⅛″
(For trussed rafters and similar light construction standard wrought washers may be used.)	

SPLIT RING SPECIFICATIONS

Split rings shall be TECO split rings as manufactured by TECO, Washington, D.C. Split rings shall be manufactured from hot rolled S. A. E.—1010 carbon steel. Each ring shall form a closed true circle with the principal axis of the cross section of the ring metal parallel to the geometric axis of the ring. The ring shall fit snugly in the prepared groove. The metal section of each ring shall be beveled from the central portion toward the edges to a thickness less than that at mid-section. It shall be cut through in one place in its circumference to form a tongue and slot.

PERCENTAGES FOR DURATION OF MAXIMUM LOAD

Two Months Loading, as for snow.......	115%
Seven Days Loading...................	125%
Wind or Earthquake Loading...........	133⅓%
Impact Loading......................	200%
Permanent Loading...................	90%

DECREASES FOR MOISTURE CONTENT CONDITIONS

Condition when Fabricated....	Seasoned	Unseasoned	Unseasoned
Condition when Used........	Seasoned	Seasoned	Unseasoned or Wet
Split Rings......	0%	20%	33%

Figure 5.18 Design and Load Data for TECO Connectors
2½″ TECO Split Rings

Used with permission from Design Manual for TECO Timber Connector Construction, published by TECO Products, Colliers, West Virginia.

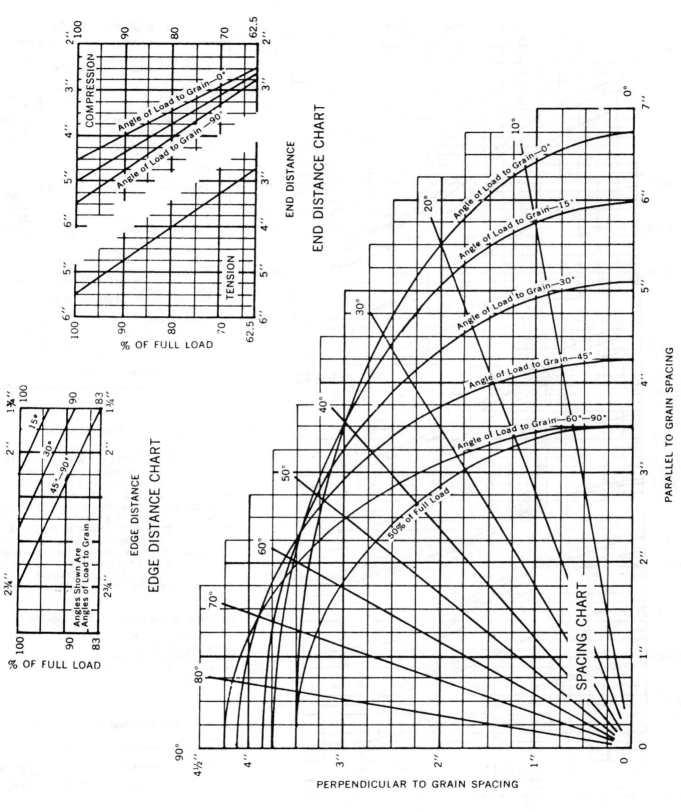

Figure 5.19 Design and Load Data for TECO Connectors
$2\frac{1}{2}''$ TECO Split Rings

Used with permission from Design Manual for TECO Timber Connector Construction, published by TECO Products, Colliers, West Virginia.

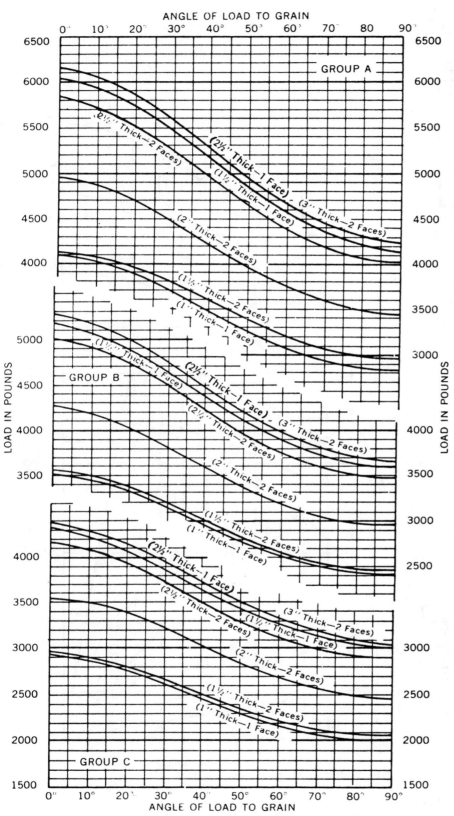

4" SPLIT RING DATA

Split Ring—Dimensions	
Inside Diameter at center when closed........................	4"
Inside diameter at center when installed.....................	4.06"
Thickness of ring at center.......	0.193"
Thickness of ring at edge........	0.133"
Depth....................	1"
Lumber, Minimum dimensions allowed	
Width....................	5½"
Thickness, rings in one face......	1"
Thickness, rings opposite in both faces........................	1½"
Bolt, diameter....................	¾"
Bolt hole, diameter............	13/16"
Projected Area for portion of one ring within a member, square inches........................	2.24
Washers, minimum	
Round, Cast or Malleable Iron, diameter....................	3"
Square Plate	
Length of Side..............	3"
Thickness....................	3/16"
(For trussed rafters and similar light construction standard wrought washers may be used.)	

SPLIT RING SPECIFICATIONS

Split rings shall be TECO split rings as manufactured by TECO, Washington, D.C. Split rings shall be manufactured from hot rolled S. A. E.—1010 carbon steel. Each ring shall form a closed true circle with the principal axis of the cross section of the ring metal parallel to the geometric axis of the ring. The ring shall fit snugly in the prepared groove. The metal section of each ring shall be beveled from the central portion toward the edges to a thickness less than that at mid-section. It shall be cut through in one place in its circumference to form a tongue and slot.

PERCENTAGES FOR DURATION OF MAXIMUM LOAD

Two Months Loading, as for snow.......	115%
Seven Days Loading....................	125%
Wind or Earthquake Loading...........	133⅓%
Impact Loading........................	200%
Permanent Loading....................	90%

DECREASES FOR MOISTURE CONTENT CONDITIONS

Condition when Fabricated....	Seasoned	Unseasoned	Unseasoned
Condition when Used........	Seasoned	Seasoned	Unseasoned or Wet
Split Rings......	0%	20%	33%

Figure 5.20 Design and Load Data for TECO Connectors
4″ TECO Split Rings

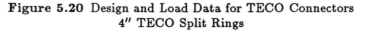

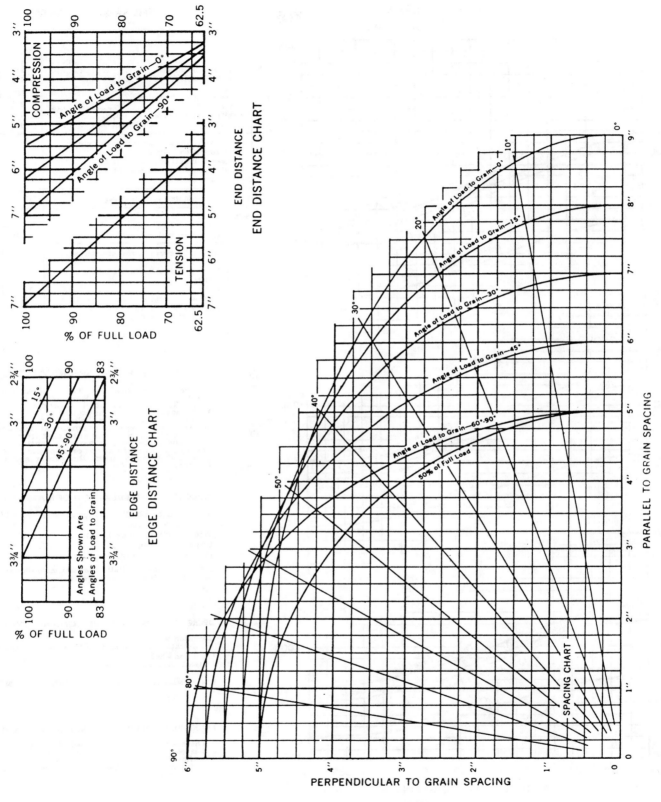

Figure 5.21 Design and Load Data for TECO Connectors
4″ TECO Split Rings

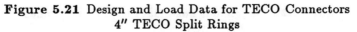
PROFESSIONAL PUBLICATIONS, INC. • Belmont, CA

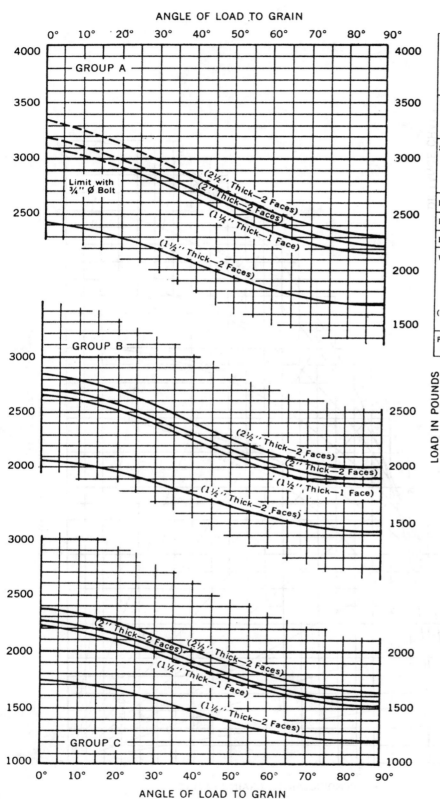

ANGLE OF LOAD TO GRAIN

2⅝" SHEAR PLATE DATA

Shear Plates, Dimensions	Pressed Steel	
Material	Reg.	Lt. Ga.
Diameter of plate	2.62"	2.62"
Diameter of bolt hole	.81"	.81"
Depth of plate	.42"	.35"
Lumber, minimum dimensions		
Face, width	3½"	3½"
Thickness, plates in one face only	1½"	1½"
Thickness, plates opposite in both faces	1½"	1½"
Steel Shapes or Straps (Thickness required when used with shear plates) Thickness of steel side plates shall be determined in accordance with A.I.S.C. recommendations.		
Hole, diameter in steel straps or shapes	13/16"	13/16"
Bolt, diameter	3/4"	3/4"
Bolt Hole, diameter in timber	13/16"	13/16"
Washers, standard, timber to timber connections only Round, cast or malleable iron, diameter . . . . . . Square Plate	3"	3"
Length of side	3"	3"
Thickness	1/4"	1/4"
(For trussed rafters and other light structures standard wrought washers may be used.)		
Projected Area, for one shear plate, square inches	1.18	1.00

SHEAR PLATE SPECIFICATIONS

Shear Plates shall be TECO shear plates as manufactured by TECO, Washington, D.C. Pressed Steel Type—Pressed steel shear-plates shall be manufactured from hot-rolled S. A. E.—1010 carbon steel. Each plate shall be a true circle with a flange around the edge extending at right angles to the face of the plate and extending from one face only, the plate portion having a central bolt hole and two small perforations on opposite sides of the hole and midway from the center and circumference.

PERCENTAGES FOR DURATION OF MAXIMUM LOAD

Two Months Loading, as for snow *115%
Seven Days Loading *125%
Wind or Earthquake Loading *133⅓%
Impact Loading *200%
Permanent Loading 90%

* Do not exceed limitations for maximum allowable loads for shear plates given elsewhere on this page.

DECREASES FOR MOISTURE CONTENT CONDITIONS

Condition when Fabricated	Seasoned	Unseasoned	Unseasoned
Condition when Used	Seasoned	Seasoned	Unseasoned or Wet
Shear Plates	0%	20%	33%

MAXIMUM PERMISSIBLE LOADS ON SHEAR PLATES

The allowable loads for all loadings except wind shall not exceed 2900 lbs for 2⅝" shear plates with ¾" bolts. The allowable wind load shall not exceed 3870 s. If bolt threads bear on the shear plate, reduce the preceding values by one-ninth.

ANGLE OF LOAD TO GRAIN

Figure 5.22 Design and Load Data for TECO Connectors
2⅝" TECO Shear Plates

Used with permission from Design Manual for TECO Timber Connector Construction, published by TECO Products, Colliers, West Virginia.

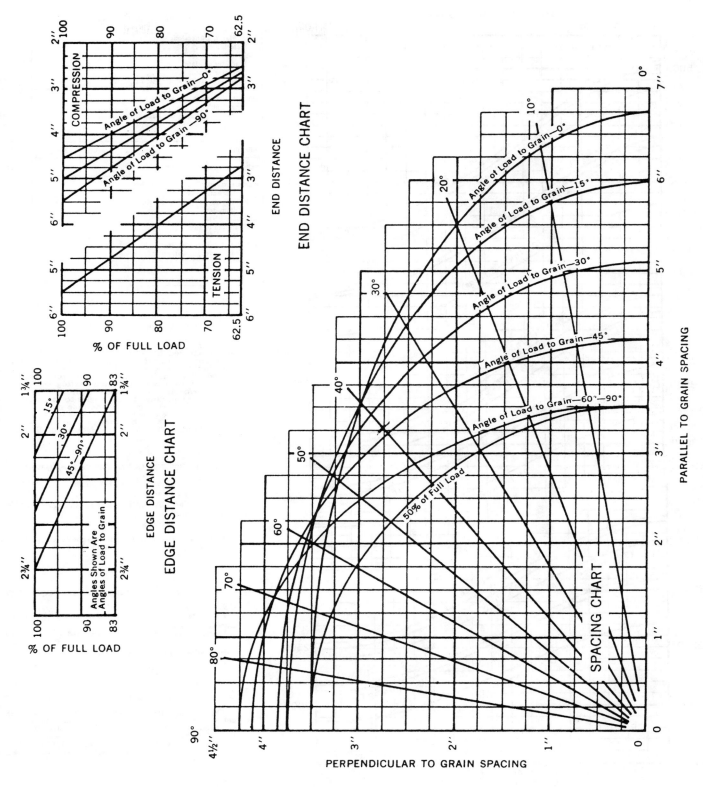

Figure 5.23 Design and Load Data for TECO Connectors
$2\frac{5}{8}''$ TECO Shear Plates

*Used with permission from Design Manual for TECO Timber Connector Construction, published by
TECO Products, Colliers, West Virginia.*

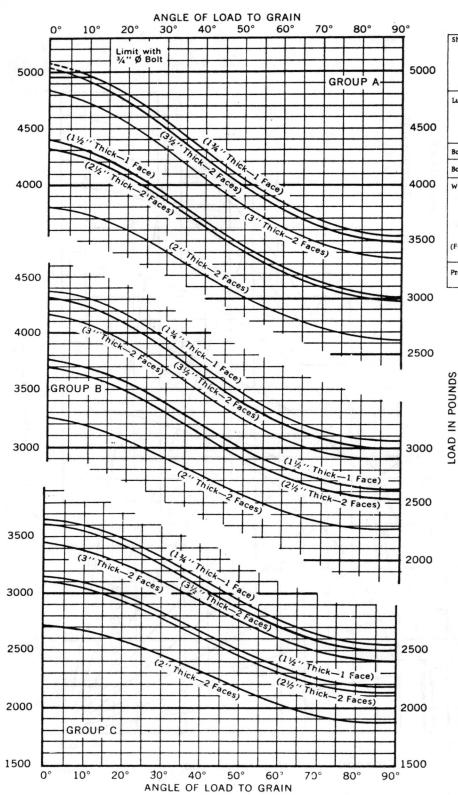

4" SHEAR PLATE DATA

Shear Plates, Dimensions Material	Malleable Iron	Malleable Iron
Diameter of plate	4.03"	4.03"
Diameter of bolt hole	.81"	.94"
Depth of plate	.64"	.64"
Lumber, minimum dimensions		
Face, width	5-1/2"	5-1/2"
Thickness, plates in one Face only	1½"	1½"
Bolt, diameter	3/4"	7/8"
Bolt Hole, diameter in timber	13/16"	15/16"
Washers, standard, timber to timber connections only		
Round, cast or malleable iron, diameter	3"	3-1/2"
Square Plate		
Length of side	3"	3"
Thickness	1/4"	1/4"
(For trussed rafters and other light structures standard wrought washers may be used.)		
Projected Area, for one shear plate, square inches	2.58	2.58

SHEAR PLATE SPECIFICATIONS

Shear plates shall be TECO shear plates as manufactured by TECO, Washington, D.C. Malleable Iron Types—Malleable iron shear plates shall be manufactured according to current A.S.T.M. Standard Specifications A 47, Grade 32510, for malleable iron castings. Each casting shall consist of a perforated round plate with a flange around the edge extending at right angles to the face of the plate and projecting from one face only, the plate portion having a central bolt hole reamed to size with an integral hub concentric to the bolt hole, and extending from the same face as the flange.

PERCENTAGES FOR DURATION OF MAXIMUM LOAD

Two Months Loading, as for snow	*115%
Seven Days Loading	*125%
Wind or Earthquake Loading	*133⅓%
Impact Loading	*200%
Permanent Loading	90%

* Do not exceed limitations for maximum allowable loads for shear plates given elsewhere on this page.

DECREASES FOR MOISTURE CONTENT CONDITIONS

Condition when Fabricated	Seasoned	Unseasoned	Unseasoned
Condition when Used	Seasoned	Seasoned	Unseasoned or Wet
Shear Plates	0%	20%	33%

MAXIMUM PERMISSIBLE LOADS ON SHEAR PLATES

The allowable loads for all loadings except wind shall not exceed 4970 lbs for 4" shear plates with ¾" bolts and 6760 lbs for 4" shear plates with ⅞" bolts. The allowable wind loads shall not exceed 6630 lbs when used with a ¾" bolt and 9020 lbs when used with a ⅞" bolt. If bolt threads bear on the shear plate, reduce the preceding values by one-ninth.

Figure 5.24 Design and Load Data for TECO Connectors
4" TECO Shear Plates (Wood-to-Wood)

Used with permission from Design Manual for TECO Timber Connector Construction, published by
TECO Products, Colliers, West Virginia.

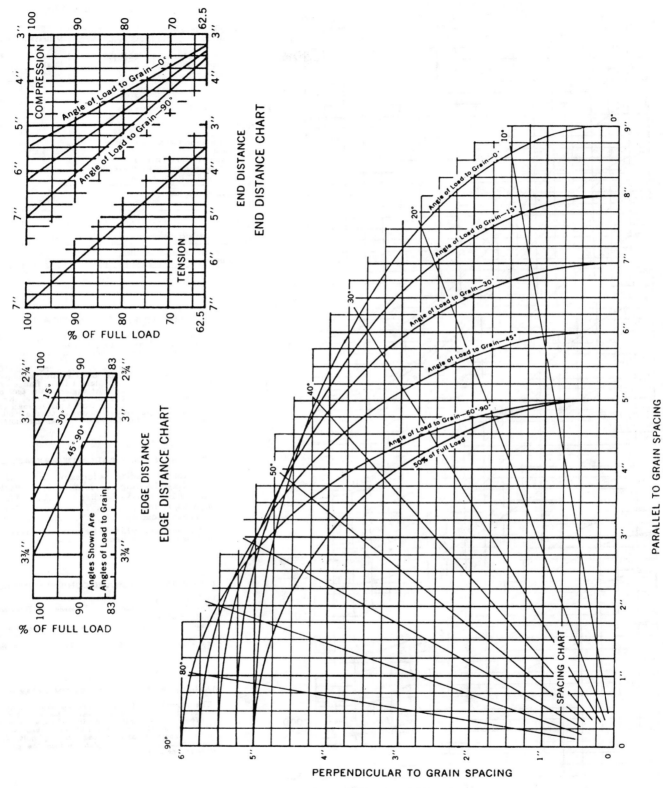

Figure 5.25 Design and Load Data for TECO Connectors
4″ TECO Shear Plates (Wood-to-Wood)

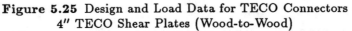

Used with permission from Design Manual for TECO Timber Connector Construction, published by
TECO Products, Colliers, West Virginia.

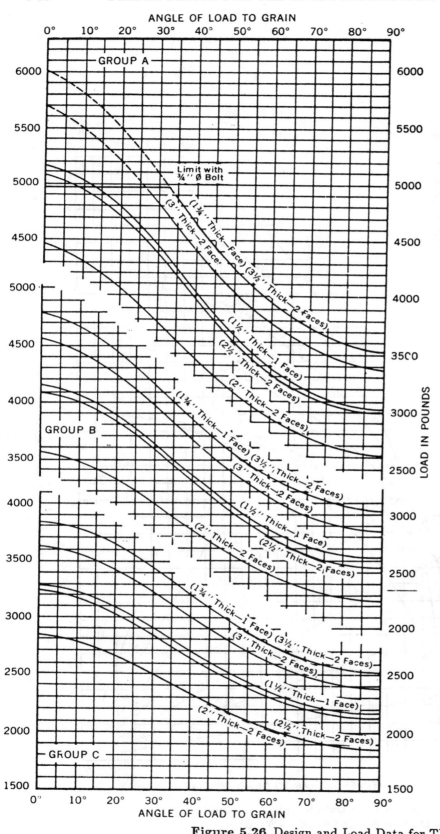

4" SHEAR PLATE DATA

Shear Plates, Dimensions	Malleable Iron	Malleable Iron
Material		
Diameter of plate	4.03"	4.03"
Diameter of bolt hole	.81"	.94"
Depth of plate	.64"	.64"
Lumber, minimum dimensions		
Face, width	5-1/2"	5-1/2"
Thickness, plates in one face only	1½"	1½"
Steel Shapes or Straps (Thickness required when used with shear plates) Thickness of steel side plates shall be determined in accordance with A.I.S.C. recommendations.		
Hole, diameter in steel straps or shapes	13/16"	15/16"
Bolt, diameter	3/4"	7/8"
Bolt Hole, diameter in timber	13/16"	15/16"
Projected Area, for one shear plate, square inches	2.58	2.58

SHEAR PLATE SPECIFICATIONS

Shear plates shall be TECO shear plates as manufactured by TECO, Washington, D.C. Malleable Iron Types—Malleable iron shear plates shall be manufactured according to current A. S. T. M. Standard Specifications A 47, Grade 32510, for malleable iron castings. Each casting shall consist of a perforated round plate with a flange around the edge extending at right angles to the face of the plate and projecting from one face only. The plate portion having a central bolt hole reamed to size with an integral hub concentric to the bolt hole and extending from the same face as the flange.

PERCENTAGES FOR DURATION OF MAXIMUM LOAD

Two Months Loading, as for snow. *115%
Seven Days Loading. *125%
Wind or Earthquake Loading. *133⅓%
Impact Loading. *200%
Permanent Loading. 90%

* Do not exceed limitations for maximum allowable loads for shear plates given below

DECREASES FOR MOISTURE CONTENT CONDITIONS

Condition when Fabricated. . . .	Seasoned	Unseasoned	Unseasoned
Condition when Used.	Seasoned	Seasoned	Unseasoned or Wet
Shear Plates.	0%	20%	33%

MAXIMUM PERMISSIBLE LOADS ON SHEAR PLATES

The allowable loads for all loadings except wind shall not exceed 4970 lbs for 4" shear plates with ¾" bolts and 6760 lbs for 4" shear plates with ⅞" bolts. The allowable wind loads shall not exceed 6630 lbs when used with a ¾" bolt and 9020 lbs when used with a ⅞" bolt. If bolt threads bear on the shear plate, reduce the preceding values by one-ninth.

Figure 5.26 Design and Load Data for TECO Connectors
4" TECO Shear Plates (Wood-to-Steel)

Used with permission from Design Manual for TECO Timber Connector Construction, published by TECO Products, Colliers, West Virginia.

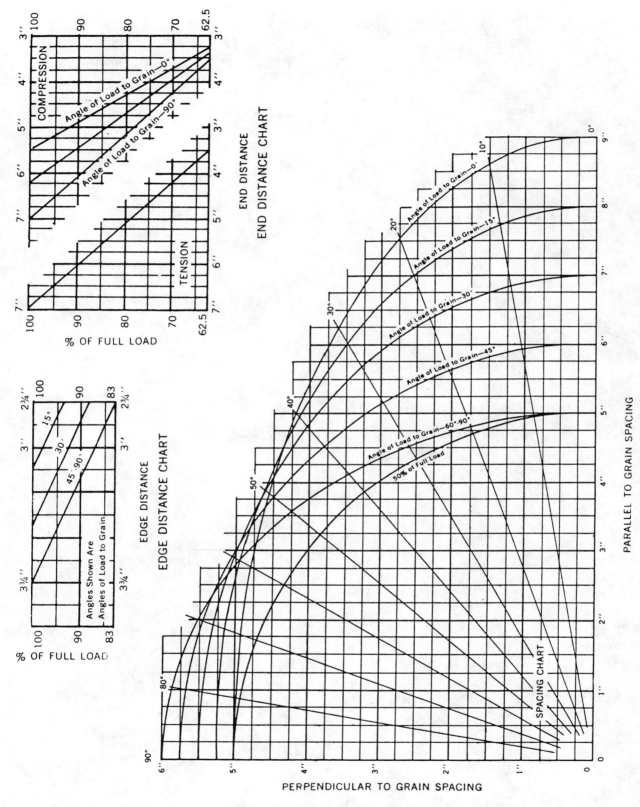

Figure 5.27 Design and Load Data for TECO Connectors
4″ TECO Shear Plates (Wood-to-Steel)

*Used with permission from Design Manual for TECO Timber Connector Construction, published by
TECO Products, Colliers, West Virginia.*

Part 6
Review of Essential Mechanics of Materials Concepts

1 INTRODUCTION

The material presented in this section is not intended as a complete treatment of mechanics of materials. Rather, it stresses the specifics and modifications of classical mechanics of materials concepts, as they apply to timber structural elements. The section is organized by loads in the axial and transverse directions, and their combinations.

2 AXIAL LOADING

Axial loads are applied along the longitudinal axis of the member. In wood, this means the loads are oriented with the fibers, or in the strong direction. Axial loads can be either tension or compression. If the load were aligned perfectly with the centroid of the cross section, the stresses caused by axial loads would be uniform on a cross section, at some distance from the ends.

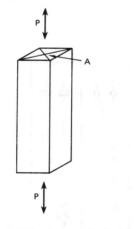

Figure 6.1 Member with Axial Load

A. Buckling

When an axially loaded member, commonly called a column, is in compression, a phenomenon known as *buckling* can drastically reduce the load capacity of the member. Buckling can be a reversible bow that develops in the column, or it can be a sudden and complete collapse initiated by lateral movement.

The basics of column buckling analysis were set down by Leonhard Euler in 1744. The Euler equation solves for the stress level at which a given column becomes unstable. At stress levels higher than this critical stress, any lateral displacement causes collapse or buckling.

$$\text{Euler's critical stress } f_{\text{cr}} = \frac{\pi^2 E}{\left(\dfrac{L}{k}\right)^2} \qquad 6.1$$

With the rectangular cross sections, $b \times d$ $(b > d)$, common in wood columns, the Euler equation becomes

$$f_{\text{cr}} = \frac{\pi^2 E}{(12)\left(\dfrac{L}{d}\right)^2} \qquad 6.2$$

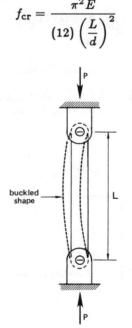

Figure 6.2 Column Subject to Buckling

The quantity L/d is a column's slenderness ratio. With wood columns, a factor of 2.74 is included to account for material variability, safety, and a correction of the tabled E values. This results in the following expression for allowable stresses in timber columns:

$$F_c' = \frac{0.3\,E}{\left(\dfrac{L}{d}\right)^2} \qquad 6.3$$

Limitations in material strengths place upper bounds on the applicability of the Euler equation, and wood is no exception. Figure 6.3 is a graph showing column failure stresses as a function of their slenderness ratios.

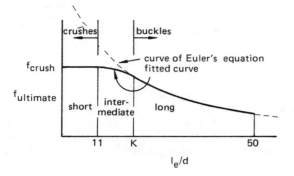

Figure 6.3 Column Failure Stresses

The National Design Specification divides the range of slenderness ratios into three regions:

- $\frac{L}{d} \le 11$: short column

- $11 < \frac{L}{d} < K;\ K = 0.671\sqrt{\frac{E}{F_c}}$:

  intermediate column

- $K \le \frac{L}{d} < 50$: long column

The Euler equation and the rest of the design equations are based on pinned-pinned end conditions. The design formula can be used with other end conditions by modifying the column length to an *effective length*, L_e, where $L_e = K_e L$. The most common end conditions and their effective lengths are included in Table 6.1.

B. Axial Deflections

The longitudinal deformation for both tension and compression members is

$$\text{change in length} = \frac{PL}{AE} \qquad 6.4$$

The tabulated E value in Appendix B is an average value that has been reduced in order to adjust bending deflections to include shear. The unadjusted average E is about nine percent larger than the table value.

3   TRANSVERSE LOADING

Transverse loads are applied perpendicular to the member's longitudinal axis. Transverse loading causes two different stresses in the member or beam. These distinct stresses are longitudinal bending stresses and shear stresses.

Table 6.1
Effective Column Lengths

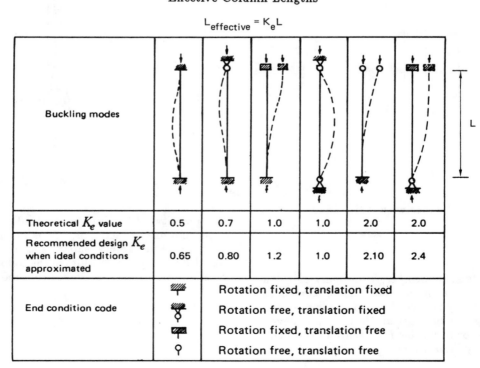

Buckling modes						
Theoretical K_e value	0.5	0.7	1.0	1.0	2.0	2.0
Recommended design K_e when ideal conditions approximated	0.65	0.80	1.2	1.0	2.10	2.4
End condition code		Rotation fixed, translation fixed				
		Rotation free, translation fixed				
		Rotation fixed, translation free				
		Rotation free, translation free				

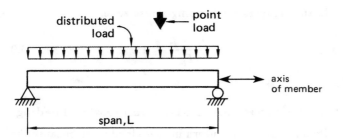

Figure 6.4 Transversely Loaded Member

A. Bending Stresses

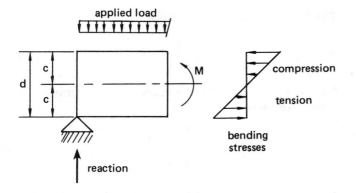

Figure 6.5 Longitudinal Bending Stresses

The classical equation for the maximum bending stress at a cross section is

$$f_b = \frac{Mc}{I} = \frac{M}{S} \qquad 6.5$$

Wood significantly violates several of the assumptions upon which this equation is based. To preserve the use of this common equation, the tabulated allowable bending stress values must be modified for certain specifics, such as beam depth, shape, and span-to-depth ratio.

B. Shear Stresses

The standard expression for shear stresses anywhere in a cross section is

$$f_v = \frac{VQ}{Ib} \qquad 6.6$$

In the rectangular cross sections common to wood members, the maximum shear stress is at the neutral axis where $Q = bd^2/8$. Since $I = bd^3/12$, the maximum shear stress in a rectangular cross section reduces to

$$f_v = \frac{3V}{2bd} = \frac{1.5V}{A} \qquad 6.7$$

There are shear stresses in two directions—along and across the grain. The shear strength across the grain is so much higher as to be of almost no concern. Since most transversely loaded members are horizontal beams, the shear stress component along the grain is horizontal. This is the only reason the tables give allowable horizontal shear stresses, although the shear component of concern in columns is vertical.

C. Deflections in Transversely Loaded Members

There are many numerical methods and copious tables available to determine bending deflections. In most materials, deflections due to the bending stresses are so much greater than those due to the shear stresses that the shear component is routinely neglected. This is not true in timber, which has a relatively low shear modulus of elasticity.

There are two ways to deal with the shear deflections. The standard method is to ignore them and to use a reduced modulus of elasticity in calculating the bending deflections, which are therefore increased in compensation. This reduced E is the value found in the design tables.

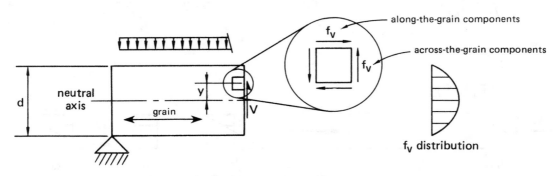

Figure 6.6 Shear Stresses due to Transverse Load

PROFESSIONAL PUBLICATIONS, INC. • Belmont, CA

The other method is to evaluate the two components separately and superpose them. In the shear deflection calculations, using a shear modulus equal to one-sixteenth of the modulus of elasticity is reasonable. In calculating the bending deflection component, the true modulus should be used to avoid providing for shear deflections twice. The true modulus of elasticity can be taken as nine percent higher than the tabulated value.

D. Lateral Stability of Bending Members

The compression zone of any bending member acts as a column, and issimilarly subject to buckling. When designing beams, the engineer must ensure that the member will either be stiff enough to resist lateral buckling itself, or be adequately restrained against sidesway. The other option is to reduce the allowable compression stresses in the member to a level safely below those that could cause buckling. That reduced bending stress, F_b', is discussed in the beam design section of this book.

4   COMBINED LOADING

When a member is subjected to both axial and transverse loads, the longitudinal bending stresses and axial stresses are superimposed. Since timber beams do not really behave as the bending stress equation assumes, the combined longitudinal stresses are treated in an interaction equation, rather than being simply added and then compared with some allowable value. The interaction equation includes buckling considerations.

A. Transverse and Axial Tension Loading

There are two interaction equations used with combined transverse and axial tension loading—one for the tensile bending-stress zone, where the two stresses add; and the other for the compressive bending-stress zone, where the net axial stress is considered in light of potential buckling.

In the tensile bending-stress zone,

$$\frac{f_t}{F_t} + \frac{f_b}{F_b} \leq 1.0 \qquad 6.8$$

In the compressive bending-stress zone,

$$\frac{f_b - f_t}{F_b'} \leq 1.0 \qquad 6.9$$

B. Transverse and Axial Compression Loading

Buckling is a real concern in these load cases because the transverse load displaces the member laterally, which is a particular concern in axial members. Just as with simple columns, members subjected to this combined loading are divided into categories by their slenderness ratio.

The basic interaction equation is

$$\frac{f_c}{F_c'} + \frac{f_b}{F_b' - J f_c} \leq 1.0 \qquad 6.10$$

The J factor includes the buckling consideration in these load cases.

$$0 \leq J = \frac{\dfrac{L_e}{d} - 11}{K - 11} \leq 1.0 \qquad 6.11$$

Note how the upper and lower limits on J work. With $L_e/d < 11$ (short columns), $J = 0$. With $L_e/d \geq K$ (long columns), $J = 1.0$. The intermediate columns gradually include buckling concerns as J grows from zero to one.

C. Eccentric Loading

An eccentric load is parallel to the longitudinal axis of the loaded member, but displaced from the centroid of the cross section. That displacement, or eccentricity, causes a bending moment whose stresses must be combined with the axial stresses. The most general formula contending with eccentric axial loads, end moments, and transverse loads is

$$\frac{f_c}{F_c'} + \frac{f_b + f_c \left(6 + 1.5J\right)\left(\dfrac{e}{d}\right)}{F_b' - J f_c} \leq 1.0 \qquad 6.12$$

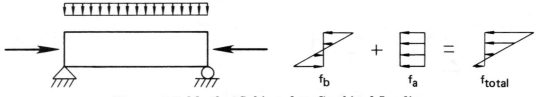

Figure 6.7 Member Subjected to Combined Loading

Appendix H of the National Design Specification contains many simplified design equations for various specific load cases.

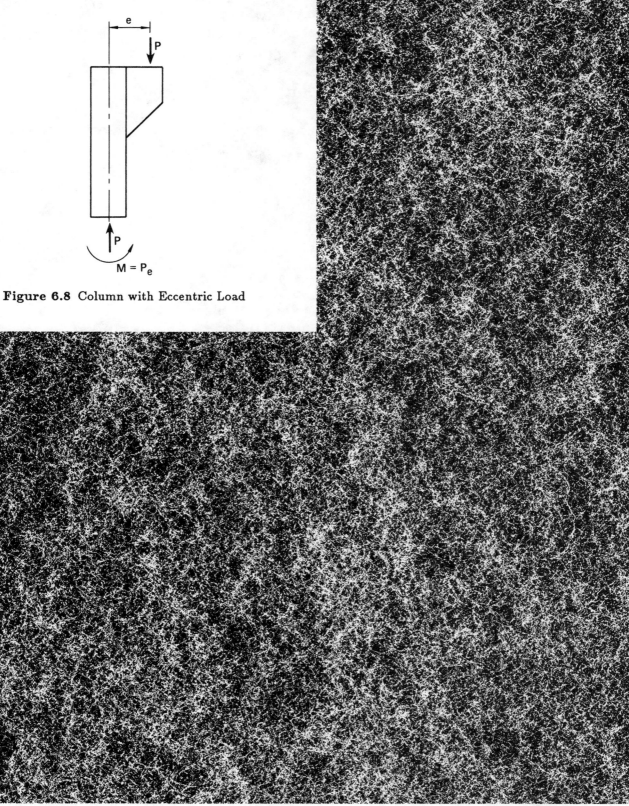

Figure 6.8 Column with Eccentric Load

Part 7

Design of Timber Structural Members—Axial Members

While load factor resistance design methods are already in use with timber structures, most are still designed by maintaining expected design stresses below allowable levels. Members subjected principally to axial loads include truss members, posts and columns, and diaphragm chords. Tension members are designed by comparing axial stresses at critical cross sections with allowable stresses. In compression members, stability considerations make their design more complex.

1   TENSION MEMBERS

The design process for tension members is a straightforward comparison of stresses at critical sections with the allowable stresses. The allowable stress is modified according to the design conditions. The design equation is

$$f_t = \frac{P}{A} \le F_t^{'}$$
$$= (F_t)(\text{CUF})(\text{LDF})$$

7.1

Both load duration and condition of use factors apply to $F_t^{'}$. Footnotes to the allowable stress tables contain condition of use reductions as high as 40 percent in the larger sizes. Net cross-sectional areas are often further reduced by one-eighth to account for the possibility of an otherwise acceptable knot falling right at the critical section. Design examples for tension members can be found in several of the connection design examples (see Part 5).

2   COMPRESSION MEMBERS

There are three common types of timber columns: solid, spaced, and built-up. Solid columns are the simplest and most common, and illustrate the basic design procedures for all columns. Spaced columns use timber more efficiently, but involve more labor. Spaced columns are mostly used in trusses where they can help to satisfy layout considerations. Built-up columns are solid assemblies of smaller members. A capacity reduction is necessary with built-up columns because of the imperfect connection between the distinct pieces.

The basic design equation for compression members looks as simple as the tension member equation:

$$f_c = \frac{P}{A} \le F_c^{'}$$

7.2

The cross-sectional area used to calculate the expected stress is either net or gross, because there are two distinct concerns in compression members: crushing at connections, and buckling in the main body of the member. The type of cross-sectional area used depends on where the column is braced relative to connections.

A. Connection at a Braced Point

If the connection is at a point that is restrained against buckling, both cross-sectional areas are used. Gross area is used to calculate the stress that is compared to the allowable buckling stress, $F_c^{'}$. Net area is used to calculate the stress at the connection for comparison with F_c, the allowable crushing stress.

B. Connection at an Unbraced Point

If the connection is at a point that is most subject to buckling, the net area is conservatively used to calculate the actual stress level. This actual stress level should be compared with the lower allowable buckling stress, $F_c^{'}$ (NDS 3.6.3).

C. $F_c^{'}$, Allowable Compression Stress, Considering Stability

The major factor determining allowable buckling stress is a member's slenderness ratio, L_e/d. Both the denominator (the minimum column dimension) and the numerator (the effective column length) will vary with a column's configuration.

Determining L_e, Effective Column Length

The Euler buckling-stress equation is based on an assumed pinned-pinned column. While this is probably the most common end condition in timber columns, it is possible to analyze other end conditions with the same equation by establishing an effective length for the column. To find a column's effective length, multiply its real length by a K_e appropriate factor from Table 6.1 (NDS Appendix N).

There may be more than one effective length to consider in a column. (See the following section for more information.) A truly fixed end condition is very difficult to achieve in timber, and it is generally not conservative to assume that one exists.

Determining d, Minimum Column Cross-Sectional Dimensions

The cross-sectional dimension, d, the denominator of a column's slenderness ratio, will vary with bracing layout.

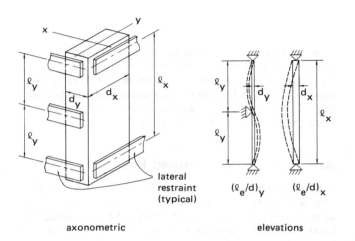

Figure 7.1 Determining the Slenderness Ratio for a Column

It is important to match the distance between bracing points with the cross-sectional dimension associated with buckling in the same plane as the braces. In a single column, several slenderness ratios might be calculated. The dimension d is always the actual dimension, not a nominal one. A column does not care if it is called a 4×6; it behaves as only a $3\frac{1}{2} \times 5\frac{1}{2}$ might.

D. Column Slenderness Categories

The slenderness ratio is used to categorize a column as short, intermediate, or long. These column types all behave differently, and each has different allowable stress. The first step is to determine a column's category.

Short Columns

If $(L_e/d) \leq 11$, the column is short. It should crush before it buckles. Therefore, there is no reduction in the allowable compression stress parallel to the grain. Equation 7.3 applies.

$$F_c' = (F_c)(\text{LDF})(\text{CUF}) \qquad 7.3$$

Intermediate Columns

If $11 < (L_e/d) < K$, the column is an intermediate column, which might fail in crushing, buckling, or both. K, the upper limit of this length category (where buckling clearly prevails) is a function only of material properties.

$$K = 0.671\sqrt{\frac{E}{F_c}} \qquad 7.4$$

The load duration factors of Table 3.1 are applied to F_c (NDS 3.6.6.3) in evaluating K, but they are not applied to E (NDS 3.6.6.4). Any applicable condition of use factors are applied to both E and F_c (NDS 3.6.6.1). (Note that the CUFs for E and F_c found in the allowable stress table footnotes are not necessarily equal, even for a single piece of wood in one condition of use.) The tabulated values for E are average values, meaning that there is a 50 percent chance of a column having a lower modulus of elasticity than the table value. For particularly critical columns, the conservative approach will reduce the tabulated E values by 40 percent in calculating capacities (NDS Appendix F). The reduced modulus is one that 95 percent of the qualified timbers should exceed.

The allowable stress in an intermediate column is

$$F_c' = F_c\left[1 - \left(\frac{1}{3}\right)\left(\frac{\frac{L_e}{d}}{K}\right)^4\right] \qquad 7.5$$

The load duration factor is also applied to F_c in this equation. Note that this means the load duration factor applies to both K and F_c of Eq. 7.5.

Long Columns

If $K \leq (L_e/d) \leq 50$, the column is a long column and is clearly subject to buckling. The Euler equation, with some extra safety factors and simplification (NDS Appendix G), is used to determine the allowable stress.

$$F_c' = \frac{0.30E}{\left(\frac{L_e}{d}\right)^2} \qquad 7.6$$

Note that since the load duration factor does not apply to E, the duration of a load has no effect on the allowable stress for a long column. For especially critical columns, 60 percent of the tabulated E value should be used.

The upper allowable limit on the slenderness ratio for a solid column is 50. Columns with slenderness ratios above 50 are too slender and must be braced or upsized.

Example 7.1

Design a 12 ft long, no. 1 Douglas fir-larch column to carry a combined snow and dead load of 14 kips. The column will be pinned-pinned at its ends and braced in one direction at its centerline. Assume the column is dry when installed, and is protected from the elements. Neglect possible load eccentricities.

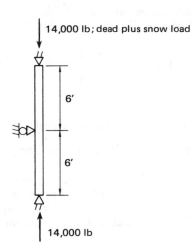

Since the allowable stress in a column is a function of its slenderness ratio, column design is necessarily a trial-and-error process.

In order to pick a reasonable first trial size, estimate an allowable stress. Assuming dimension lumber sizes, Appendix B gives an F_c of 1250 psi and an E of 1,800,000 psi. The LDF of Table 3.1 is 1.15 for snow loads. If these load duration and buckling considerations were to offset each other, the required cross-sectional area would be equal to 14,000 lb/1250 psi = 11.2 in^2. Look in Appendix E for a section with this area. The two cross-sectional dimensions should be in a 2:1 ratio in order to make efficient use of the available bracing. Select a 3×6, which has an area of 13.750 in^2. Now, evaluate the slenderness ratios for the 3×6 trial size, after orienting it to brace the weak direction at the midpoint.

$$\left(\frac{L_e}{d}\right)_{weak} = \frac{(6 \text{ ft}) \left(12 \frac{\text{in}}{\text{ft}}\right)}{2.5 \text{ in}} = 28.80$$

$$\left(\frac{L_e}{d}\right)_{strong} = \frac{(12 \text{ ft}) \left(12 \frac{\text{in}}{\text{ft}}\right)}{5.5 \text{ in}} = 26.18$$

The two slenderness ratios are nearly equal, which is efficient, but weak axis buckling will control. The maximum slenderness ratio is greater than 11, so the column is not short. To distinguish long from intermediate columns, K must be evaluated.

$$K = 0.671 \sqrt{\frac{E}{F_c}}$$
$$= 0.671 \sqrt{\frac{1,800,000 \text{ psi}}{(1.15)(1250 \text{ psi})}}$$
$$= 23.74$$

Note how the 1.15 LDF appears in the expression for K. Since the maximum slenderness ratio is greater than

K, the column is long, but not too long since L_e/d is less than 50. From Eq. 7.6,

$$F_c' = \frac{(0.3)(1,800,000 \text{ psi})}{(28.80)^2} = 651 \text{ psi}$$

The 3×6 has a capacity of

$$(651 \text{ psi})(13.75 \text{ in}^2) = 8,950 \text{ lb}$$

The capacity is much lower than the required 14,000 lb, so try the next larger size with the 2:1 dimension ratio; a 4×8.

$$\left(\frac{L_e}{d}\right)_{weak} = \frac{(6 \text{ ft}) \left(12 \frac{\text{in}}{\text{ft}}\right)}{3.5 \text{ in}} = 20.57$$

$$\left(\frac{L_e}{d}\right)_{strong} = \frac{(12 \text{ ft}) \left(12 \frac{\text{in}}{\text{ft}}\right)}{7.25 \text{ in}} = 19.86$$

The weak axis buckling still controls. K does not change with the size change, but it is larger than the slenderness ratio, so this is an intermediate column. From Eq. 7.5,

$$F_c' = (1.15)(1250 \text{ psi}) \left[1 - \left(\frac{1}{3}\right)\left(\frac{20.57}{23.74}\right)^4\right] = 1167 \text{ psi}$$

The 4×8 column capacity is

$$(1167 \text{ psi})(25.375 \text{ in}^2) = 29,600 \text{ lb}$$

This section is adequate, but significantly oversized. Try a 4×6.

$$\left(\frac{L_e}{d}\right)_{weak} = 20.57 \text{ (same as for a } 4 \times 8)$$

$$\left(\frac{L_e}{d}\right)_{strong} = \frac{(12 \text{ ft}) \left(12 \frac{\text{in}}{\text{ft}}\right)}{5.5 \text{ in}} = 26.18$$

The 26.18 slenderness ratio is greater than K (23.74), so the column is long. From Eq. 7.6,

$$F_c' = \frac{(0.3)(1,800,000 \text{ psi})}{(26.18)^2} = 788 \text{ psi}$$

The 4×6 capacity is

$$(788 \text{ psi})(19.25 \text{ in}^2) = 15,169 \text{ lb}$$

This is greater than the required 14,000 lb, but not enough to warrant further investigation of smaller sections.

Use a 4×6, no. 1 Douglas fir-larch column, with the midspan bracing in the weak direction.

Example 7.2

A column is a 10×10, dense no. 1 Douglas fir-larch, installed wet and exposed in service. The member is 25 feet long, with the bottom embedded 6 feet and the top braced against sidesway. (a) What is the dead load capacity of this column, assuming lives depend upon its not failing? (b) Find the minimum required bearing area at the top, with and without a metal bearing plate to distribute the load. (c) What would the capacity be if only 3 feet were embedded?

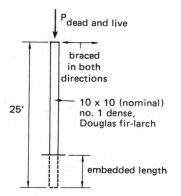

(a) To find the capacity, establish the L_e/d ratio using the effective length. Check the end grain bearing stress to establish the required bearing areas.

From Table 6.1, the exposed 19 feet of column has an effective length of

$$L_e = (19 \text{ ft})(0.8) = 15.20 \text{ ft}$$

The 0.8 factor accounts for the fixed bottom, seen in Table 6.1. The slenderness ratio is, therefore,

$$\frac{(15.20 \text{ ft}) \left(12 \frac{\text{in}}{\text{ft}} \right)}{9.5 \text{ in}} = 19.20$$

The division between intermediate and long columns, K, in dense no. 1 Douglas fir-larch is calculated using values from Appendix B.

$$K = 0.671 \sqrt{\frac{(\text{CUF})(\text{E})}{(\text{CUF})(\text{LDF})(F_c)}}$$

$$= 0.671 \sqrt{\frac{(1.0)(1,700,000 \text{ psi})(0.60)}{(0.91)(0.9)(1200 \text{ psi})}}$$

$$= 21.62$$

From Table 3.1, a load duration factor for dead load is applied to F_b, but not to E. The modulus of elasticity is multiplied by 0.6 because this is a critical column. The 0.91 and 1.0 condition of use factors come from footnote 10 of Appendix B and account for the wet use.

Since the slenderness ratio is less than K, the post acts as an intermediate column. Using Eq. 7.5,

$$F_c' = (0.9)(1200)(0.91 \text{ psi}) \left[1 - \left(\frac{1}{3} \right) \left(\frac{19.20}{21.62} \right)^4 \right]$$

$$= 779 \text{ psi}$$

This allowable stress level gives a post capacity of

$$(779 \text{ psi})(90.25 \text{ in}^2) = 70,300 \text{ lb}$$

(b) The allowable end-grain bearing stress for dense Douglas fir-larch is 1570 psi from Appendix A, assuming wet service conditions. Modifying for dead load duration with the 0.9 of Table 3.1, the minimum bearing area required is

$$\frac{70,300 \text{ lb}}{(0.9)(1570 \text{ psi})} = 49.75 \text{ in}^2$$

Note that this area is based on end-grain stresses at 100% of capacity, which requires a metal bearing plate to distribute the stress. The plate can be omitted by holding stress levels to only 75% of the allowable stress. This would require a minimum net bearing area of

$$\frac{70,300 \text{ lb}}{(0.9)(1570 \text{ psi})(0.75)} = 66.3 \text{ in}^2$$

(c) If the column were embedded only 3 feet, the slenderness ratio would be

$$\frac{L_e}{d} = \frac{(22 \text{ ft}) \left(12 \frac{\text{in}}{\text{ft}} \right)(0.8)}{9.5 \text{ in}} = 22.23$$

This is just larger than K, making the post a long column. The allowable stress is, therefore,

$$F_c' = \frac{(0.3)(1,700,000 \text{ psi})(0.60)}{(22.23)^2} = 619 \text{ psi}$$

The post capacity is

$$(619 \text{ psi})(90.25 \text{ in}^2) = 55,900 \text{ lb}$$

E. Spaced Columns

A spaced column consists of two or more solid columns connected to one another, but separated along their length by spacer blocks. The separated members act together much as an I-beam section does, gaining considerable bending stiffness in what would otherwise be the weak plane for buckling. The internal lateral bracing makes the spaced column a more efficient member. This construction method is significantly more labor intensive, and it is generally used only when the configuration is also justified by fabrication considerations.

In order to resist the shear deformations at the spacer blocks that would allow the spaced column to buckle, the connections must be stiff. Determining the spacer block connection stiffness and evaluating a variety of slenderness ratios are the essential elements of spaced column design. The National Design Specification, section 3.8, contains the necessary particulars should a spaced column seem worth the effort and expense.

F. Built-Up Columns

It is sometimes easier to build up a large column from smaller sections than to find a large or dry enough solid-sawn member. Unlike spaced or glue-laminated columns, which are connected rigidly enough to achieve full composite member action, built-up columns require reduced capacities to account for the semi-rigid connection between the individual pieces. Table 7.1 gives these reductions as they vary with the slenderness ratio of the built-up section.

Table 7.1
Percent Reductions in Strength
for Built-Up Columns

L/d ratio	percent reduction
6	18
10	23
14	29
18	35
22	26
26	18

Reproduced from Wood Handbook: Wood as an Engineering Material, Agriculture Handbook No. 72, by Forest Products Laboratory, Forest Service, U.S. Department of Agriculture, 1974.

Part 8
Design of Timber Structural Members—Bending Members

Timber bending members are designed with the allowable stress method. Four separate concerns are dealt with in these designs: bending stresses, shear stresses, deflections, and bearing stresses at supports and loads. Differences in designing solid-sawn and glue-laminated members will be covered as they arise.

1 BENDING STRESSES

Actual bending stresses are evaluated with Eq. 8.1, and they should be less than the adjusted allowable bending stress.

$$f_b = \frac{Mc}{I} = \frac{M}{S} \leq F_b' \qquad 8.1$$

The bending moment, M, is determined in the normal manner. The section modulus, S, is found in Appendix E for nominal lumber sizes. The section modulus for the net section must be calculated at connections and notches. When calculating the moments in beams, the most correct span to use is the clear distance between support faces, plus one-half the required bearing length at each support.

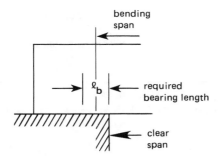

Figure 8.1 Beam Span Measurement

There are two ways that a beam fails under high bending stresses: a beam can either buckle laterally, or the extreme fibers can fail. Since these are two distinct phenomena, there are two separate allowable bending stresses to be evaluated, with the lesser controlling.

A. Allowable Bending Stresses, Lateral Buckling

The allowable bending stress considering lateral buckling is a function of the beam's slenderness. If a beam is no deeper than its thickness, or if the beam is supported full length along its compression edge, lateral buckling

is ignored. Otherwise, the beam slenderness factor, C_s, must be calculated.

$$C_s = \sqrt{\left(\frac{\ell_e d}{b^2}\right)} \qquad 8.2$$

The d and b dimensions are specific to the beam cross section, while the effective length, ℓ_e, is a function of an unbraced length, ℓ_u, and the beam/loading configuration.

The unbraced length, ℓ_u, is the distance between lateral supports or points where rotation is prevented. The effective length is obtained by multiplying the unbraced length by the appropriate factor of Fig. 8.2. If a single beam, continuous over supports, has more than one slenderness factor along its length, the maximum one controls.

B. Beam Slenderness Categories

Once the slenderness factor, C_s, is determined, the beam can be classified as short, intermediate, or long. Each beam category has its own allowable stress levels.

- *Short Beams:* If $C_s \leq 10$, the beam is short and $F_b' = (F_b)(\text{CUF})(\text{LDF})(FF)(DF)$

- *Intermediate Beams:* If $10 < C_s \leq C_k = (0.811) \times \sqrt{(E/F_b)}$, the beam is intermediate. Glulam members (with at least six laminae) are less variable and can be assumed to act as intermediate beams up to a $C_k = 0.956\sqrt{\frac{E}{F_b}}$.

$$F_b' = F_b \left[1 - \left(\frac{1}{3}\right)\left(\frac{C_s}{C_k}\right)^4\right] \qquad 8.3$$

- *Long Beams:* If $C_k < C_s$ and no greater than the upper limit of 50, the beam is a long one.

$$F_b' = (0.438)\left(\frac{E}{C_s^2}\right) \qquad 8.4$$

As with C_k, glulam beams are sufficiently predictable to justify an increase in F_b' in long beams to $(0.609)(E/C_s^2)$. Apply the load duration factor to F_b and the condition of use factor to E and F_b wherever they appear in the above equations.

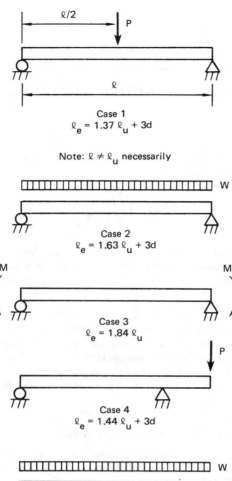

Case 1
$\ell_e = 1.37 \, \ell_u + 3d$

Note: $\ell \neq \ell_u$ necessarily

Case 2
$\ell_e = 1.63 \, \ell_u + 3d$

Case 3
$\ell_e = 1.84 \, \ell_u$

Case 4
$\ell_e = 1.44 \, \ell_u + 3d$

Case 5
$\ell_e = 0.90 \, \ell_u + 3d$

Case 6
any other configuration conservatively use

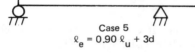

$\ell_e = 1.84 \, \ell_u$, if $\dfrac{\ell_u}{d} > 14.3$

$\ell_e = 1.63 \, \ell_u + 3d$, if $\dfrac{\ell_u}{d} < 14.3$

Figure 8.2 Effective Beam Lengths

C. Allowable Bending Stresses, Limited by Extreme Fiber Failure

There are two other adjustments that apply to the allowable bending stress as limited by fiber failure, or in short beams only. These factors do not apply to intermediate and long beams.

Form Factor

The bending stress design equation assumes a rectangular timber section. The allowable bending stress in other shapes must be modified with the form factor, C_f.

With a circular cross section, F_b is multiplied by 1.18. If a square section is used on edge, as a diamond, F_b is multiplied by 1.414, so long as the load is applied along a diagonal. Note that when dimensional lumber is used flat, as a plank, footnotes to the allowable stress table describe increased allowable stresses.

Size Factor

Deeper timber beams behave less in accordance with the bending stress equation assumptions. The modification made to F_b to account for this difference, C_F, depends on whether the beam is solid-sawn or glue-laminated.

In solid-sawn beams wider than 4 inches and deeper than 12 inches, F_b is multiplied by the size factor, C_F.

$$C_F = \left(\frac{12}{d}\right)^{1/9} \qquad 8.5$$

The size factor, C_F, when used with glue-laminated beams, is also a function of the load type. See Table 8.1 for these factors, which may be interpolated for intermediate beam depths.

Table 8.1
Size Factor, C_F, for Glue-Laminated Beams

span-to-depth ratio, L/d	change %	loading conditions for simply supported beams	change %
7	+6.2	single concentrated load	+7.8
14	+2.3		
		uniform load	0
21	0		
		third-point load	−3.2
28	−1.6		
35	−2.8		

Reproduced from Wood Handbook: Wood as an Engineering Material, Agriculture Handbook No. 72, by Forest Products Laboratory, Forest Service, U.S. Department of Agriculture, 1974.

D. Curved Bending Members

There are two additional concerns with stresses induced by bending in glue-laminated beams fabricated with an in-plane curvature more pronounced than simple camber.

Curvature Factor

For only those regions that contain bent laminae, the allowable bending stress is multiplied by the curvature factor, C_c.

$$C_c = 1 - (2000)\left(\frac{t}{R}\right)^2 \qquad 8.6$$

The radius, R, is measured in inches to the member inside face. The thickness of the individual laminations, t, is in inches. The t/R ratio is empirically limited by splitting concerns to $1/100$ for southern pine, and $1/125$ for other softwoods.

Radial Tension or Compression

Bending moments that tend to straighten a bent member cause radial tension. Bending moments that tend to increase a bent member's curvature cause radial compression. In either case, the radial stress in a member with constant cross section is

$$f_r = \frac{3M}{2Rbd} \qquad 8.7$$

The radius, R, is measured in inches to the member centerline.

For curved beams with varying cross sections (non-prismatic), see the National Design Specification, section 5.4.1.

The allowable radial tension, F_{rt}, is one-third the F_v for southern pine and Douglas fir-larch with wind and seismic loads. For other load types in Douglas fir-larch, F_{rt} is only 15 psi. These stress levels are so low that mechanical radial reinforcement, such as bolts or lag screws, may be required.

The allowable radial compression, F_{rc}, should be limited to the allowable compression perpendicular to the grain, $F_{c\perp}$, for the species involved.

2 SHEAR STRESSES IN BENDING MEMBERS

The design equation for shear stresses in rectangular section beams is

$$f_v = \frac{1.5V}{A} \leq F_v'$$
$$= (F_v)(LDF)(CUF) \qquad 8.8$$

The tabulated allowable shear stress for sawn lumber, F_v, is conservatively based on an assumed worst-case split at the member's end. The National Design Specification recognizes how restrictive this assumption is and essentially allows the tabulated F_v to be increased by up to 100 percent, if the maximum possible shear force is carefully evaluated (NDS 4.2.6.3). This NDS section also provides alternative methods of calculating shear stresses. Finally, footnote 11 in the allowable stress tables also allows shear stress increases, but only if the given piece of wood has limited checks at its ends. These increases do not apply to glue-laminated members.

There are several special circumstances in shear calculations that deserve mention.

Shear with Loads Near Supports

Most materials used in bending members are so stiff through the member depth that transverse loads applied very near the supports are really transferred directly to the support by arching compression action, rather than through bending. Because shear often controls in timber design, the engineer can benefit from accurately determining the shear by neglecting all loads applied to the beam within the depth of the member from the support (NDS 3.4.4.1a).

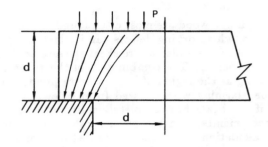

Figure 8.3 Loads Near Supports

Shear in Notched Beams

It is temptingly easy to solve many clearance problems by notching timber beams. Unfortunately, this not only reduces the cross section resisting shear, but also induces significant stress concentrations. Shear stresses at a notch are calculated by including a factor that reflects the severity of the notching.

$$f_v = \left(\frac{3}{2}\right)\left(\frac{V}{bd'}\right)\left(\frac{d}{d'}\right) \qquad 8.9$$

The stress concentration factor, d/d', can be neglected if the notch has a gradual change in cross section (NDS 3.4.5.2). This means, anomalously, that a notched beam can be strengthened by removing material, if the abrupt notch is smoothed. Notched beams are a common source of problems, and should be used only if there is no other reasonable option.

Shear in Connections

If a connection is more than five member depths from the end of the member, splits and their effects are reduced. Therefore, tabulated allowable shear stresses can be increased 50 percent at such connections (NDS 3.4.7.1a). However, the shear stress must be evaluated on the basis of the effective depth of the member at the connection. This is often equal to the member depth minus the unloaded edge distance, but the National Design Specification should be consulted in questionable cases (NDS 3.4.7.1b).

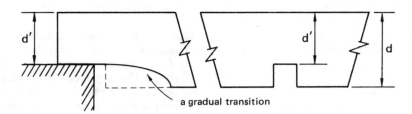

Figure 8.4 Shear Stresses in Notched Beams

Shear in Checked Beams

Large splits in wood are most often found at the ends of members, where drying defects can initiate and propagate. The ends are also where shear stresses are highest in simple beams. The combination of the worst defect appearing at the region of highest corresponding stress can be alarming when viewed from below. However, even if the beam has completely split and acts as two separate members on top of each other, it is stronger than calculations might show because the shear stress in the two pieces seems to be redistributed nearly equally throughout the cross section. See Appendix E of the National Design Specification for more information on this phenomenon, known as *two beam shear action.*

3   BEAM DEFLECTIONS

The deflections of wood beams under loads are calculated almost exactly as they are with other materials. The modulus of elasticity is given in Appendix B for the appropriate species, size, and grade.

The only difference in calculating timber beam deflections arises with long term or permanent loads. Timber will relax under long term loads and acquire a nonelastic set. The standard method of accounting for this long term deflection is to double the calculated deflection for unseasoned members and those that will dry in place, and to increase the deflections by 50 percent for seasoned lumber and glue-laminated members (NDS 3.5.2).

4   BEARING STRESSES AT LOADS AND SUPPORTS

The allowable bearing stress perpendicular to the grain, $F_{c\perp}$, is limited by deformations, not failure. Therefore, the load duration factors of Table 3.1 do not apply to this allowable stress. The required length of bearing is a simple function of the load being resisted, the bearing width (often b), and the allowable compression perpendicular to grain stress.

$$\ell_b = \frac{\text{load}}{(b)(F_{c\perp})} \qquad 8.10$$

When the load is applied at least 3 inches from a member end, and over a length less than 6 inches (along the grain), the allowable bearing stress can be multiplied by the factor in Eq. 8.11.

$$\text{non-end bearing stress factor} = \frac{\ell_b + 0.375}{\ell_b} \qquad 8.11$$

This increase in allowable bearing stress can be applied to the contact area under washers by using a bearing length equal to the washer diameter (NDS 3.11.2.3).

Example 8.1

Check the capacity of the glue-laminated crane beam used to carry ore carts. The beam is outdoors and stays wet in service. The supports also provide lateral and torsional restraint. Neglect deflections and assume a normal load duration.

To solve this problem, determine the maximum expected bending and shear stresses. Compare these with the controlling allowable bending stress and the allowable shear stress. Check the bearing stresses at supports.

The maximum bending moment will occur either at B with the load at the end of the cantilever, or under the load at some point between A and B. In glulam beams, unlike solid-sawn, certain laminae configurations will have allowable tension bending stresses that differ from the allowable compression bending stresses. With the cart at the end, the maximum moment is

$$M_{\max} = (6\text{ ft})(5000\text{ lb}) + (6\text{ ft} - 5\text{ ft})(5000\text{ lb})$$
$$= 35,000\text{ ft-lb}$$

Using the formula for maximum bending moment with two equal point loads found in most structural handbooks, the maximum moment between the supports is

$$M_{\max} = \frac{P}{2L}\left(L - \frac{a}{2}\right)^2$$
$$= \left[\frac{5000\text{ lb}}{(2)(34\text{ ft})}\right]\left(34\text{ ft} - \frac{5\text{ ft}}{2}\right)^2$$
$$= 72,960\text{ ft-lb}$$

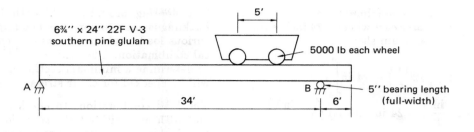

Section properties are calculated for glue-laminated members, whose nominal dimensions are also actual. The section modulus, S, is

$$S = \frac{bd^2}{6} = \frac{(6.75 \text{ in})(24 \text{ in})^2}{6}$$
$$= 648 \text{ in}^3$$

The design bending stresses, therefore, are

$$\frac{(35,000 \text{ ft-lb})(12 \frac{\text{in}}{\text{ft}})}{648 \text{ in}^3} = 648 \text{ psi at B}$$

$$\frac{(72,960 \text{ ft-lb})\left(12 \frac{\text{in}}{\text{ft}}\right)}{648 \text{ in}^3} = 1,350 \text{ psi between supports}$$

The allowable bending stress is the smaller of the stresses limited by lateral buckling and the extreme fiber stress. Lateral buckling is a function of the unbraced length, ℓ_u (here equal to 34 feet), and the beam configuration. This beam falls in case 4 of Fig. 8.2.

Thus, the effective length, ℓ_e, is

$$(1.44)(34 \text{ ft})\left(12 \frac{\text{in}}{\text{ft}}\right) + (3)(24 \text{ in}) = 659.5 \text{ in}$$

The slenderness factor is

$$C_s = \sqrt{\frac{\ell_e d}{b^2}} = \sqrt{\frac{(659.5 \text{ in})(24 \text{ in})}{(6.75 \text{ in})^2}}$$
$$= 18.64$$

This is larger than 10, so the beam is not short. C_k must be calculated to distinguish between long and intermediate beams.

$$C_k = 0.811\sqrt{\frac{(E)(\text{CUF})}{(F_b)(\text{CUF})(\text{LDF})}}$$

$$= 0.811\sqrt{\frac{(0.833)(1,600,000 \text{ psi})}{(0.8)(1.0)(2200 \text{ psi})}}$$

$$= 22.32 > C_s$$

Therefore, the beam is intermediate. The material properties and condition of use factors (called *wet use factors* in glulam parlance and found in the last row of the allowable stress tables) are found in Appendix B. An adjustment is made for condition of use and load duration when considering lateral buckling. The allowable stress considering lateral buckling is

$$F_b' = F_b(1.0)(0.8)\left[1 - \left(\frac{1}{3}\right)\left(\frac{18.64}{22.32}\right)^4\right]$$
$$= (0.6703)F_b \text{ psi}$$

Now, determine the allowable bending stress considering extreme fiber failure. The load duration factor for normal durations is 1.0. The condition of use factor for wet use is 0.8, from Appendix B. The size factor, C_F, is 1.0 (interpolating for $d = 24$ inches in the single point load case in Table 8.1).

The allowable bending stress for extreme fiber failure is, therefore,

$$F_b(1.0)(0.8)(1.0) = (0.80)F_b \text{ psi}$$

Lateral buckling controls. The allowable bending stress is left in terms of F_b because there will be both tension and compression bending stresses to evaluate.

The allowable bending stress at B is $(0.6703)(1100 \text{ psi})$ = 737 psi, because the bending causes tension at the top of the beam—normally its compression zone (footnote 8). This is more than the actual 648 psi, so the beam is adequate in bending at B.

The allowable stress between supports is $(0.6703) \times (2200 \text{ psi})$ = 1475 psi. In this case, the tension is in the tension zone of the beam, resulting in the higher tabulated allowable stress. Again, the actual stress, 1350 psi, is lower than the allowable stress.

When evaluating the maximum shear force, remember that loads within a beam depth of supports flow directly to the support through compression. The shear force is not maximum, therefore, when the left wheel moves to the left of point B. When the right wheel is at the right beam end, the left wheel is still too close to B to cause shear in the cantilever. The maximum shear, therefore, is calculated with the nearer cart wheel is 24 inches from either support. This maximum shear is

$$(5000 \text{ lb})\left[(34 \text{ ft})\left(12 \frac{\text{in}}{\text{ft}}\right) - 24 \text{ in}\right] +$$
$$\left[(34 \text{ ft})\left(12 \frac{\text{in}}{\text{ft}}\right) - 24 \text{ in} - (5 \text{ ft})\left(12 \frac{\text{in}}{\text{ft}}\right)\right]$$
$$= 8676 \text{ lb}$$

The shear stress is

$$f_v = \frac{3V}{2A}$$
$$= \frac{(3)(8676 \text{ lb})}{(2)(6.75 \text{ in})(24 \text{ in})}$$
$$= 80.3 \text{ psi}$$

The allowable shear stress, F_v', uses the load duration factor (1.0) of Table 3.1 and the condition of use factor (0.875) from Appendix B.

$$(200 \text{ psi})(0.875)(1.0) = 175 \text{ psi}$$

The allowable shear stress is significantly larger than required.

The maximum support reaction occurs at B when the cart is at the end of the cantilever, and is

$$(5000 \text{ lb})\left[\frac{(34 \text{ ft} + 6 \text{ ft}) + (34 \text{ ft} + 6 \text{ ft} - 5 \text{ ft})}{34 \text{ ft}}\right]$$
$$= 11,030 \text{ lb}$$

No load duration factors are applied to compression perpendicular to the grain, but the condition of use factor is 0.53, found in Appendix B. The allowable bearing stress can be increased because the bearing length is less than 6 inches. The maximum bearing stress is

$$\frac{11,030 \text{ lb}}{(5 \text{ in })(6.75 \text{ in})} = 327 \text{ psi}$$

The allowable bearing stress, considering Eq. 8.11, is

$$(650 \text{ psi})(0.53)\left(\frac{5 \text{ in} + 0.375 \text{ in}}{5 \text{ in}}\right) = 370 \text{ psi}$$

The beam is adequate in bending, shear, and bearing stresses.

Example 8.2

Design a floor girder to carry the loads shown. Use kiln-dried no. 2 southern pine. Flooring is nailed to the top of the girder. For occupant satisfaction, deflections are limited to span/360 for live loads. Total deflections should be less than span/240.

The flooring provides full-length lateral support, so buckling is not a factor. The bending stresses caused by various load combinations will be checked for the critical combination. The critical combination will be used to determine a minimum section modulus. The section will be checked for shear stresses and deflections.

The load combinations to check are dead load alone, and with and without the snow load. With the snow load included, the maximum moment is

$$\left[(50 \text{ plf} + 200 \text{ plf})\left[\frac{(16 \text{ ft})^2}{8}\right] + (400 \text{ lb} + 600 \text{ lb})\left(\frac{16 \text{ ft}}{4}\right)\right]$$
$$\times \frac{12 \frac{\text{in}}{\text{ft}}}{1.15} = 125,217 \text{ in-lb}$$

The 1.15 load duration factor of Table 3.1 is applied because the load combination includes the snow load. The net moment without the snow load is

$$\left[(50 \text{ plf} + 200 \text{ plf})\left[\frac{(16 \text{ ft})^2}{8}\right] + (400 \text{ lb})\left(\frac{16 \text{ ft}}{4}\right)\right]$$
$$\times 12 \frac{\text{in}}{\text{ft}} = 115,200 \text{ in-lb}$$

With dead load alone,

$$\text{net moment} = \left[(50 \text{ ft})\left(\frac{(16 \text{ ft})^2}{8}\right) + \left(\frac{(400 \text{ lb})(16 \text{ ft})}{4}\right)\right]$$
$$\times \left(12 \frac{\text{in}}{\text{ft}}\right)\left(\frac{1}{0.9}\right)$$
$$= 42,667 \text{ in-lb}$$

Even though the snow load combination controls, the stresses are nearly as critical with the snow load left off because the lower load has a longer duration.

Appendix B gives a single-use F_b of 1300 psi for no. 2 K-D southern pine. Thus, the required section modulus is

$$S_{\text{required}} = \frac{125,217 \text{ in-lb}}{1300 \text{ psi}} = 96.32 \text{ in}^3$$

Note that the load duration factor is not included in this calculation—it is already in the design bending moment.

Using the section properties of Appendix E, the required section modulus can be obtained in various ways.

$$\frac{96.32 \text{ in}^3}{21.391 \text{ in}^3} = 4.50; \text{ five } 2 \times 10\text{'s}$$

or

$$\frac{96.32 \text{ in}^3}{31.641 \text{ in}^3} = 3.04; \text{ three } 2 \times 12\text{'s}$$

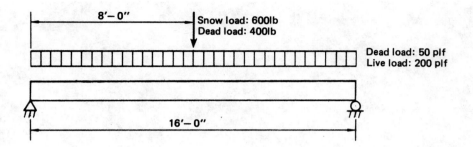

However, with three interconnected side-by-side members, the repetitive-use allowable bending stress is justified. Appendix B gives 1500 psi for these conditions. Therefore, the required section modulus is only

$$S_{\text{required}} = \frac{125,217 \text{ in-lb}}{1500 \text{ psi}} = 83.48 \text{ in}^3$$

This section modulus is available in various forms.

$$\frac{83.48 \text{ in}^3}{21.391 \text{ in}^3} = 3.90; \text{ four } 2 \times 10\text{'s}$$

or

$$\frac{83.48 \text{ in}^3}{31.641 \text{ in}^3} = 2.64; \text{ three } 2 \times 12\text{'s}$$

The three 2×12's represent less cross-sectional area, and therefore less lumber, than the four 2×10's. If the shear stress is not too high, and if the cost is not higher with the larger size, pick the 2×12's. They should also provide greater stiffness.

To check the shear stress, determine the critical shear force. Neglect the distributed load within a beam depth of the supports. First, calculate the shear force with the snow load.

$$V_{\text{max}} = \frac{600 \text{ lb} + 400 \text{ lb}}{2} + (50 \text{ plf} + 200 \text{ plf})$$
$$\times \left(\frac{16}{2} \text{ ft} - \frac{11.25}{12} \text{ ft}\right)$$
$$= \frac{2266 \text{ lb}}{1.15}$$
$$= 1970 \text{ lb}$$

Now, calculate the shear without the snow load

$$V_{\text{max}} = \frac{400 \text{ lb}}{2} + (50 \text{ plf} + 200 \text{ plf})$$
$$\times \left(\frac{16}{2} \text{ ft} - \frac{11.25}{12} \text{ ft}\right)$$
$$= 1966 \text{ lb}$$

The maximum shear stress is

$$f_v = \frac{(1.5)(1970 \text{ lb})}{(3)(16.875 \text{ in}^2)}$$
$$= 58.4 \text{ psi}$$

The allowable stress is 95 psi, so the three 2×12's are adequate. The allowable shear stress could have been increased by 50% with the carefully checked maximum shear forces, but this was not required.

Now check the deflections. Use tabled formulae for maximum deflections in simple spans. Use half the modulus of elasticity for the dead load component to account for long term creep effects.

$$D_{\text{live}} = \frac{\dfrac{(5)\left(\dfrac{200}{12}\right)[(16)(12)]^4}{348} + \dfrac{(600)[(16)(12)]^3}{48}}{(1,600,000)(3)(177.979)}$$
$$= 0.45 \text{ in}$$
$$= \frac{\text{span }(\ell)}{\dfrac{(16 \text{ ft})\left(12\dfrac{\text{in}}{\text{ft}}\right)}{0.45 \text{ in}}}$$
$$= \frac{\text{span}}{457} < \frac{1}{360}$$

$$D_{\text{dead}} = \frac{\dfrac{(5)\left(\dfrac{50}{12}\right)[(16)(12)]^4}{384} + \dfrac{(400)[(16)(12)]^3}{48}}{\left(\dfrac{1,600,000}{2}\right)(3)(177.979)}$$
$$= 0.31 \text{ in}$$

The total deflection is 0.31 + 0.45 = 0.76″, equal to span/250, slightly less than the maximum allowable deflection of span/240. So the three 2×12, no. 2 southern pine girder is adequate.

Part 9
Plywood

1 INTRODUCTION

Plywood has many varied structural applications. Plywood is valuable because of its size and physical properties. A piece of solid-sawn wood $\frac{1}{2}$ inch $\times$ 48 inches $\times$ 96 inches would be very expensive and absolutely useless structurally, but the same size piece of plywood is much cheaper and, in some ways, stronger than the wood of which it is made.

Virtually any softwood species can be used in plywood. Plywood is made by peeling logs into veneer and laminating layers of this veneer with glue. The strength results from cutting up and spreading out the knots and other defects, and cross-banding the laminae. Cross-banding means that alternate laminae are perpendicular to each other. The result is that plywood has two strong (parallel-to-grain) directions instead of one, as in solid timber.

A. Plywood Grades and Types

Plywood is available in many forms and grades. The variables in plywood composition are veneer grade and species, veneer configuration, and glue type. Structural plywood veneers are graded for quality from A to D. Plywood is designated by the veneer grades that appear in the outer or face plies. C-D plywood, for example, has a D grade veneer on the back face and a C grade front face with smaller knot holes.

With all the potential variations in plywood composition, it is only through the standards established by the American Plywood Association[3] that the end users can know what to expect from a given sheet. The performance-based standards are written as fabrication limits for equivalent plywood designations.

A given plywood thickness can have various combinations of the number of plies and their individual thicknesses. In marine grade plywood, the veneers are oriented at angles other than just the two perpendicular ones, giving the product an even more uniform performance in all directions. The two major glue types used in plywood are interior and exterior, which have varying degrees of resistance to wet-dry cycles.

B. Plywood Structural Applications

The most common plywood applications are flooring, roofing, and siding. The plywood spans the space between joists, rafters, or studs, and distributes loads to those members. Engineering calculations can be used to investigate the plywood stresses under these conditions,

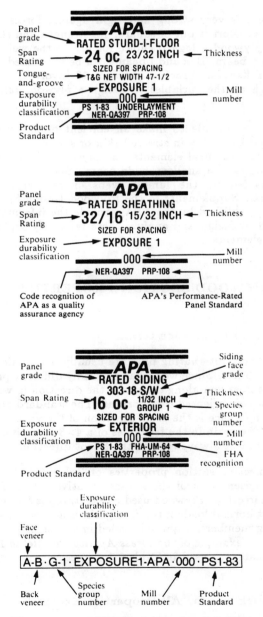

Figure 9.1 APA Grade-Trademark Stamp

Used with permission of the American Plywood Association, Tacoma, WA.

---

[3] American Plywood Association, 7011 South 19th St., Tacoma, Washington 98411-0700.

but it is much simpler to follow the allowable span recommendations found in the certification stamp for most common decking plywoods. Figure 9.1 is an example plywood stamp. The 24/0 means that the maximum roof rafter spacing is 24 inches, and that the plywood is not recommended for floor decking, no matter what the joist spacing.

Plywood sheathing on walls, roofs, and floors can resist more than just loads normal to the surface. If the plywood is sized and connected adequately, the walls, roofs, and floors can act as shear diaphragms in resisting lateral loads on a building. Practice problem 17 deals with diaphragm design.

Plywood is very strong and rigid against forces that tend to distort it out of square. Its strength and shape make plywood a logical choice for use as the web of a built-up beam. Box and I beams can be fabricated with lumber flanges. Practice problem 18 involves sorting through all the variables to design a plywood-lumber beam.

It is also possible to make an efficient double use of plywood sheathing in stressed-skin or sandwich panels. In these structural elements, the plywood skin acts as the flanges of a shallow, wide beam. Shear resistance is provided by the lumber webs or sandwich core material. Supplements to the Plywood Design Specification, published by the APA, provide the information needed to design and analyze these relatively sophisticated elements.

2   PLYWOOD SECTION PROPERTIES

A. Direction of Face Grain

In plywood, alternating plies are usually perpendicular to each other. Since wood has markedly different properties across and along the grain, the direction in which the plies are oriented is important. The standard orientation reference is the grain direction of the visible face plies. The grain in the face plies of a 4×8 foot plywood panel almost always runs in the 8 foot direction.

The effective section properties of Table 9.1 depend on the orientation of the stresses relative to this face-grain direction. Plywood used as sheathing is strongest against normal loads if the face grain is across the supporting members. Plywood loaded in this strong direction is an example of the *Stress Applied Parallel to Face Grain* category used in Table 9.1.

B. Thickness for All Properties Except Shear

For all calculations other than those involving shear, the nominal thickness found in column 1 of Table 9.1 is used.

C. Thickness for Shear

For calculating shear stresses, the effective thicknesses of column 3 in Table 9.1 are used. For structural plywood grades, this effective thickness can be larger than the actual, nominal thickness.

D. Cross-Sectional Area

The effective areas of columns 4 and 8 in Table 9.1 reflect the differences in grain orientation. Those plies with fibers perpendicular to the direction of stress application are neglected as having essentially no stiffness or strength. Note that the effective areas are much larger when the stress is applied parallel to the face.

The effective area is given in units of in^2/ft. This per-foot basis treats the membrane of plywood as a series of interconnected, one foot wide beams and is common to the rest of the section properties. The foot represents a twelve inch wide strip of the specific piece of plywood, measured perpendicular to the direction of stress application. A 4×8 foot panel with the stress parallel to the face grain would, therefore, have an effective area resisting that stress of four times the value found in column 4 of Table 9.1.

E. Moment of Inertia

Only those plies whose fibers are parallel to the stress direction are included in the values of columns 5 and 10 of Table 9.1. The per-foot unit means the same as it does for effective area.

F. Section Modulus

The effective section modulus, KS, includes the empirical factor, K. This KS value should always be used for bending stress calculations when the plywood is installed as sheathing and loaded normal to the surface. Specifically, the apparently valid I/c value for an effective section modulus should not be used. Figure 9.2 illustrates the difference between loading in the plane of the plywood and loading normal to that plane.

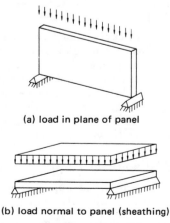

(a) load in plane of panel

(b) load normal to panel (sheathing)

Figure 9.2 Plywood in Bending

Table 9.1
Effective Plywood Section Properties

Face Plies of Different Species Group from Inner Plies

Nominal Thickness (in.)	Approximate Weight (psf)	t_s Effective Thickness For Shear (in.)	Stress Applied Parallel to Face Grain				Stress Applied Perpendicular to Face Grain			
			A Area (in.^{2}/ft)	I Moment of Inertia (in.^{4}/ft)	KS Effective Section Modulus (in.^{3}/ft)	Ib/Q Rolling Shear Constant (in.^{2}/ft)	A Area (in.^{2}/ft)	I Moment of Inertia (in.^{4}/ft)	KS Effective Section Modulus (in.^{3}/ft)	Ib/Q Rolling Shear Constant (in.^{2}/ft)
UNSANDED PANELS										
5/16-U	1.0	0.268	1.491	0.022	0.112	2.569	0.660	0.001	0.023	4.497
3/8 -U	1.1	0.278	1.866	0.039	0.152	3.110	0.799	0.002	0.033	5.444
15/32&1/2 -U	1.5	0.298	2.292	0.067	0.213	3.921	1.007	0.004	0.056	2.450
19/32&5/8 -U	1.8	0.319	2.330	0.121	0.379	5.004	1.285	0.010	0.091	3.106
23/32&3/4 -U	2.2	0.445	3.247	0.234	0.496	6.455	1.563	0.036	0.232	3.613
7/8 -U	2.6	0.607	3.509	0.340	0.678	7.175	1.950	0.112	0.397	4.791
1 -U	3.0	0.842	3.916	0.493	0.859	9.244	3.145	0.210	0.660	6.533
1-1/8 -U	3.3	0.859	4.725	0.676	1.047	9.960	3.079	0.288	0.768	7.931
SANDED PANELS										
1/4 -S	0.8	0.267	0.996	0.008	0.059	2.010	0.348	0.001	0.009	2.019
11/32-S	1.0	0.284	0.996	0.019	0.093	2.765	0.417	0.001	0.016	2.589
3/8 -S	1.1	0.288	1.307	0.027	0.125	3.088	0.626	0.002	0.023	3.510
15/32-S	1.4	0.421	1.947	0.066	0.214	4.113	1.204	0.006	0.067	2.434
1/2 -S	1.5	0.425	1.947	0.077	0.236	4.466	1.240	0.009	0.087	2.752
19/32 -S	1.7	0.546	2.423	0.115	0.315	5.471	1.389	0.021	0.137	2.861
5/8 -S	1.8	0.550	2.475	0.129	0.339	5.824	1.528	0.027	0.164	3.119
23/32-S	2.1	0.563	2.822	0.179	0.389	6.581	1.737	0.050	0.231	3.818
3/4 -S	2.2	0.568	2.884	0.197	0.412	6.762	2.081	0.063	0.285	4.079
7/8 -S	2.6	0.586	2.942	0.278	0.515	8.050	2.651	0.104	0.394	5.078
1 -S	3.0	0.817	3.721	0.423	0.664	8.882	3.163	0.185	0.591	7.031
1-1/8 -S	3.3	0.836	3.854	0.548	0.820	9.883	3.180	0.271	0.744	8.428
TOUCH-SANDED PANELS										
1/2 -T	1.5	0.342	2.698	0.083	0.271	4.252	1.159	0.006	0.061	2.746
19/32&5/8 -T	1.8	0.408	2.354	0.123	0.327	5.346	1.555	0.016	0.135	3.220
23/32&3/4 -T	2.2	0.439	2.715	0.193	0.398	6.589	1.622	0.032	0.219	3.635
1-1/8 -T	3.3	0.839	4.548	0.633	0.977	11.258	4.067	0.272	0.743	8.535

Structural I and Marine

Nominal Thickness (in.)	Approximate Weight (psf)	t_s Effective Thickness For Shear (in.)	Stress Applied Parallel to Face Grain				Stress Applied Perpendicular to Face Grain			
			A Area (in.^{2}/ft)	I Moment of Inertia (in.^{4}/ft)	KS Effective Section Modulus (in.^{3}/ft)	Ib/Q Rolling Shear Constant (in.^{2}/ft)	A Area (in.^{2}/ft)	I Moment of Inertia (in.^{4}/ft)	KS Effective Section Modulus (in.^{3}/ft)	Ib/Q Rolling Shear Constant (in.^{2}/ft)
UNSANDED PANELS										
5/16-U	1.0	0.356	1.619	0.022	0.126	2.567	1.188	0.002	0.029	6.037
3/8 -U	1.1	0.371	2.226	0.041	0.195	3.107	1.438	0.003	0.043	7.307
15/32&1/2 -U	1.5	0.535	2.719	0.074	0.279	4.157	2.175	0.012	0.116	2.408
19/32&5/8 -U	1.8	0.707	3.464	0.154	0.437	5.685	2.742	0.045	0.240	3.072
23/32&3/4 -U	2.2	0.739	4.219	0.236	0.549	6.148	2.813	0.064	0.299	3.540
7/8 -U	2.6	0.776	4.388	0.346	0.690	6.948	3.510	0.131	0.457	4.722
1 -U	3.0	1.088	5.200	0.529	0.922	8.512	5.661	0.270	0.781	6.435
1-1/8 -U	3.3	1.118	6.654	0.751	1.164	9.061	5.542	0.408	0.999	7.833
SANDED PANELS										
1/4 -S	0.8	0.342	1.280	0.012	0.083	2.009	0.626	0.001	0.013	2.723
11/32-S	1.0	0.365	1.280	0.026	0.133	2.764	0.751	0.001	0.023	3.397
3/8 -S	1.1	0.373	1.680	0.038	0.177	3.086	1.126	0.002	0.033	4.927
15/32-S	1.4	0.537	1.947	0.067	0.246	4.107	2.168	0.009	0.093	2.405
1/2 -S	1.5	0.545	1.947	0.078	0.271	4.457	2.232	0.014	0.123	2.725
19/32 -S	1.7	0.709	3.018	0.116	0.338	5.566	2.501	0.034	0.199	2.811
5/8 -S	1.8	0.717	3.112	0.131	0.361	5.934	2.751	0.045	0.238	3.073
23/32-S	2.1	0.741	3.735	0.183	0.439	6.109	3.126	0.085	0.338	3.780
3/4 -S	2.2	0.748	3.848	0.202	0.464	6.189	3.745	0.108	0.418	4.047
7/8 -S	2.6	0.778	3.952	0.288	0.569	7.539	4.772	0.179	0.579	5.046
1 -S	3.0	1.091	5.215	0.479	0.827	7.978	5.693	0.321	0.870	6.981
1-1/8 -S	3.3	1.121	5.593	0.623	0.955	8.841	5.724	0.474	1.098	8.377
TOUCH-SANDED PANELS										
1/2 -T	1.5	0.543	2.698	0.084	0.282	4.511	2.486	0.020	0.162	2.720
19/32&5/8 -T	1.8	0.707	3.127	0.124	0.349	5.500	2.799	0.050	0.259	3.183
23/32&3/4 -T	2.2	0.739	4.059	0.201	0.469	6.592	3.625	0.078	0.350	3.596

Used with permission of the American Plywood Association, Tacoma, WA.

When plywood is used as the web of a plywood-lumber beam, the loads are in the plane of the panel and bending stresses in the plywood are more like axial forces. A different section modulus will be used in those calculations.

G. Rolling Shear Constant

When plywood is loaded in shear through the thickness (Fig. 9.3), it is tremendously strong because the cross plies are being sheared across the grain. When the shear stresses lie in the plane of the plies, however, plywood is not nearly as strong. The rolling shear that develops (Fig. 9.3) tends to roll the fibers of the cross plies over each other, a tendency against which wood has little resistance. Rolling shear stresses arise in plywood used as sheathing, and at the connection between plywood webs and lumber flanges in plywood-lumber beams.

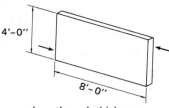

shear through thickness

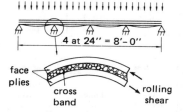

Figure 9.3 Shear Stress Orientations

3 ALLOWABLE STRESSES—PLYWOOD

There are two basic factors that determine the allowable stresses in plywood: the species used in the laminae; and how those laminae are assembled. The allowable stresses are further subject to modification for load duration and conditions of use.

A. Grade Stress Levels

The first distinction drawn in the allowable plywood stress tables is the grades of the laminae used in the plywood. Plywood is classified into three grade stress levels: S-1, S-2, and S-3. The highest grade stress level, S-1, is associated with plywood using only exterior glue and top grade veneers. The lowest grade stress level, S-3, is reserved for plywood with interior glue. The intermediate grade stress level, S-2, incorporates all the

other plywoods. Table 9.2 is a listing of the most common structural plywood types. Once the plywood type is specified, Table 9.2 will give the grade stress level.

B. Plywood Species Groups

The next distinction required in order to determine the allowable stress is the species used to make the laminae. The seventy-plus wood species commonly used in plywood are divided into five groups. For certain plywoods, Table 9.2 contains the species group information. If Table 9.2 does not specify the group number used in a plywood, there are two other ways to determine the information.

If the species is known, Table 9.3 provides the classification information.

Very often, however, the plywood manufacturer will not stamp the plywood with the species. The stamp could include an allowable roof/floor span rating which can be used to indirectly determine the species. Figure 9.4 gives the species group as a function of the plywood thickness and span rating. For example, a $\frac{5}{8}$ inch piece of plywood with group III species plies, and a $\frac{1}{2}$ inch sheet of group I species plywood will both handle 32 inch rafter spacings and 16 inch joist spacings.

For panels with "Span Rating" as across top, and thickness as at left, use stress for species group given in table.

Thickness (in.)	Span Rating (APA RATED SHEATHING grades)							
	12/0	16/0	20/0	24/0	32/16	40/20	48/24	
					Span Rating (STURD-I-FLOOR grades)			
					16 o.c.	20 o.c.	24 o.c.	48 o.c.
5/16	4	3	1					
3/8			4(3)	1				
15/32 & 1/2				4(3)	1(1)			
19/32 & 5/8					4(3)	1		
23/32 & 3/4						4(3)	1	
7/8							3(2)	
1-1/8								1

(1) Thicknesses not applicable to APA RATED STURD-I-FLOOR.
(2) For APA RATED STURD-I-FLOOR 24 oc, use Group 4 stresses.
(3) For STRUCTURAL II, use Group 3 stresses.

Figure 9.4 Species Group-Span Rating Relationship

Used with permission of the American Plywood Association, Tacoma, WA.

C. Conditions of Use

There are only two conditions of use that apply to plywood allowable stresses: wet and dry. If the equilibrium moisture content will be less than 16 percent in service, the dry use values should be used. As long as the plywood is not directly exposed to the weather, this dry condition can be assumed.

Table 9.2A
Plywood Specifications—Abbreviated

	Plywood Grade	Description and Use	Typical Trademarks	Veneer Grade			Common Thicknesses	Grade Stress Level (Table 3)	Species Group	Section Property Table
				Face	Back	Inner				
INTERIOR OR PROTECTED APPLICATIONS	APA RATED SHEATHING EXP 1 or 2[3]	Unsanded sheathing grade for wall, roof, sub-flooring, and industrial applications such as pallets and for engineering design, with proper stresses. Manufactured with intermediate and exterior glue (1). For permanent exposure to weather or moisture only Exterior type plywood is suitable.	APA RATED SHEATHING 32/16 15/32 INCH SIZED FOR SPACING EXPOSURE 1 000 PS 1-83 C-D NER-QA397 PRP-108	C	D	D	5/16, 3/8, 15/32, 1/2, 19/32, 5/8, 23/32, 3/4	S-3 (1)	See "Key to Span Rating"	Table 1 (unsanded)
	APA STRUCTURAL I RATED SHEATHING EXP 1[3] or APA STRUCTURAL II[2] RATED SHEATHING EXP 1	Plywood grades to use where strength properties are of maximum importance, such as plywood-lumber components. Made with exterior glue only. STRUCTURAL I is made from all Group 1 woods. STRUCTURAL II allows Group 3 woods.	APA RATED SHEATHING STRUCTURAL I 24/0 3/8 INCH SIZED FOR SPACING EXPOSURE 1 000 PS 1-83 C-D NER-QA397 PRP-108	C	D	D	5/16, 3/8, 15/32, 1/2, 19/32, 5/8, 23/32, 3/4	S-2	Structural I use Group 1 / Structural II See "Key to Span Rating"	Table 2 (unsanded) / Table 1 (unsanded)
	APA RATED STURD-I-FLOOR EXP 1 or 2[3]	For combination subfloor-underlayment. Provides smooth surface for application of carpet. Possesses high concentrated and impact load resistance during construction and occupancy. Manufactured with intermediate and exterior glue. Touch-sanded (4). Available with tongue and groove.(5)	APA RATED STURD-I-FLOOR 20 oc 19/32 INCH SIZED FOR SPACING T&G NET WIDTH 47-1/2 EXPOSURE 1 000 PS 1-83 UNDERLAYMENT NER-QA397 PRP-108	C plugged	D	C & D	19/32, 5/8, 23/32, 3/4, 1-1/8 (2-4-1)	S-3 (1)	See "Key to Span Rating"	Table 1 (touch-sanded)
	APA UNDERLAYMENT EXP 1, 2 or INT	For underlayment under carpet. Available with exterior glue. Touch-sanded. Available with tongue and groove.(5)	APA UNDERLAYMENT GROUP 1 EXPOSURE 1 000 PS 1-83	C plugged	D	C & D	1/2, 19/32, 5/8, 23/32, 3/4	S-3 (1)	As Specified	Table 1 (touch-sanded)
	APA C-D PLUGGED EXP 1, 2 or INT	For built-ins, wall and ceiling tile backing, NOT for underlayment. Available with exterior glue. Touch-sanded.(5)	APA C-D PLUGGED GROUP 2 EXPOSURE 1 000 PS 1-83	C plugged	D	D	1/2, 19/32, 5/8, 23/32, 3/4	S-3 (1)	As Specified	Table 1 (touch-sanded)
	APA APPEARANCE GRADES EXP 1, 2 or INT	Generally applied where a high quality surface is required. Includes APA N-N, N-A, N-B, N-D, A-A, A-B, A-D, B-B, and B-D INT grades.(5)	APA A-D GROUP 1 EXPOSURE 1 000 PS 1-83	B or better	D or better	C & D	1/4, 11/32, 3/8, 15/32, 1/2, 19/32, 5/8, 23/32, 3/4	S-3 (1)	As Specified	Table 1 (sanded)

Used with permission of the American Plywood Association, Tacoma, WA.

D. Allowable Stress Tables

Table 9.4 lists the allowable stresses and stiffnesses that should be used in plywood design.

E. Duration of Load Factors

Plywood is a wood product, so its load capacity is time-dependent. The load duration factors of Table 3.1 also apply to the allowable plywood stresses of Table 9.4.

The allowable stresses of Table 9.4 apply to plywood panels that are at least 24 inches wide. If the plywood is used in narrower strips, there is an increased possibility of a defect appearing in a critical section. Allowable stresses should be linearly decreased from full strength at 24 inches wide to half strength at 8 inches wide.

4 DIAPHRAGMS AND SHEAR WALLS

Wind and earthquakes are the principal lateral forces a structure must resist. With relatively minor modifications, building walls can act as shear walls to efficiently resist these lateral loads. The floors and roof can also act as diaphragms to redistribute or gather forces and transmit them to the shear walls. Problems involving complex layout or critical diaphragm loading require analyses that are well beyond the scope of this review text (and most P.E. exams). Other sources, such as those listed as references for this book, should be consulted.

Table 9.2B
Plywood Specifications—Abbreviated

Plywood Grade	Description and Use	Typical Trademarks	Veneer Grade			Common Thicknesses	Grade Stress Level (Table 3)	Species Group	Section Property Table
			Face	Back	Inner				
APA RATED SHEATHING EXT[3]	Unsanded sheathing grade with waterproof glue bond for wall, roof, subfloor and industrial applications such as pallet bins.	APA RATED SHEATHING 48/24 23/32 INCH SIZED FOR SPACING EXTERIOR 000 PS 1-83 C-C NER-QA397 PRP-108	C	C	C	5/16, 3/8, 15/32, 1/2, 19/32, 5/8, 23/32, 3/4	S-1 [6]	See "Key to Span Rating"	Table 1 (unsanded)
APA STRUCTURAL I RATED SHEATHING EXT[3] or APA STRUCTURAL II[2] RATED SHEATHING EXT	"Structural" is a modifier for this unsanded sheathing grade. For engineered applications in construction and industry where full exterior-type panels are required. STRUCTURAL I is made from Group 1 woods only.	APA RATED SHEATHING STRUCTURAL I 24/0 3/8 INCH SIZED FOR SPACING EXTERIOR 000 PS 1-83 C-C NER-QA397 PRP-108	C	C	C	5/16, 3/8, 15/32, 1/2, 19/32, 5/8, 23/32, 3/4	S-1 [6]	Structural I use Group 1 ——— Structural II See "Key to Span Rating"	Table 2 (unsanded) ——— Table 1 (unsanded)
APA RATED STURD-I-FLOOR EXT[3]	For combination subfloor-underlayment where severe moisture conditions may be present, as in balcony decks. Possesses high concentrated and impact load resistance during construction and occupancy. Touch-sanded (4). Available with tongue and groove.(5)	APA RATED STURD-I-FLOOR 20 oc 19/32 INCH SIZED FOR SPACING EXTERIOR 000 PS 1-83 C-C PLUGGED NER-QA397 PRP-108	C plugged	C	C	19/32, 5/8, 23/32, 3/4	S-2	See "Key to Span Rating"	Table 1 (touch-sanded)
APA UNDERLAYMENT EXT and APA C-C PLUGGED EXT	Underlayment for floor under where severe moisture conditions may exist. Also for controlled atmosphere rooms and many industrial applications. Touch-sanded. Available with tongue and groove.(5)	APA C-C PLUGGED GROUP 2 EXTERIOR 000 PS 1-83	C plugged	C	C	1/2, 19/32, 5/8, 23/32, 3/4	S-2	As Specified	Table 1 (touch-sanded)
APA B-B PLYFORM CLASS I or II[2]	Concrete-form grade with high reuse factor. Sanded both sides, mill-oiled unless otherwise specified. Available in HDO. For refined design information on this special-use panel see APA Design/Construction Guide: Concrete Forming, Form No. V345. Design using values from this specification will result in a conservative design.(5)	APA PLYFORM B-B CLASS I EXTERIOR 000 PS 1-83	B	B	C	19/32, 5/8, 23/32, 3/4	S-2	Class I use Group 1; Class II use Group 3	Table 1 (sanded)
APA MARINE EXT	Superior Exterior-type plywood made only with Douglas Fir or Western Larch. Special solid-core construction. Available with MDO or HDO face. Ideal for boat hull construction.	MARINE · A-A · EXT APA · 000 · PS1-83	A or B	A or B	B	1/4, 3/8, 1/2, 5/8, 3/4	A face & back use S-1 B face or back use S-2	Group 1	Table 2 (sanded)
APA APPEARANCE GRADES EXT	Generally applied where a high quality surface is required. Includes APA A-A, A-B, A-C, B-B, B-C, HDO and MDO EXT.(5)	APA A-C GROUP 1 EXTERIOR 000 PS 1-83	B or better	C or better	C	1/4, 11/32, 3/8, 15/32, 1/2, 19/32, 5/8, 23/32, 3/4	A or C face and back use S-1 [6] B face or back use S-2	As Specified	Table 1 (sanded)

(Left margin vertical label: EXTERIOR APPLICATIONS)

(1) When exterior glue is specified, i.e. Exposure 1, stress level 2 (S-2) should be used.
(2) Check local suppliers for availability before specifying STRUCTURAL II and PLYFORM Class II grades.
(3) Properties and stresses apply only to APA RATED STURD-I-FLOOR and APA RATED SHEATHING manufactured entirely with veneers.
(4) APA RATED STURD-I-FLOOR 2-4-1 may be produced unsanded.
(5) May be available as STRUCTURAL I. For such designation use Group 1 stresses and Table 2 section properties.
(6) C face and back must be natural unrepaired; if repaired, use stress level 2 (S-2).

Used with permission of the American Plywood Association, Tacoma, WA.

Table 9.3
Plywood Species Classifications

Group 1	Group 2		Group 3	Group 4	Group 5[a]

Apitong[b][c]
Beech, American
Birch
  Sweet
  Yellow
Douglas Fir 1[d]
Kapur[b]
Keruing[b][c]
Larch, Western
Maple, Sugar
Pine
  Caribbean
  Ocote
Pine, Southern
  Loblolly
  Longleaf
  Shortleaf
  Slash
Tanoak
	Cedar, Port Orford
	Cypress
	Douglas Fir 2[d]
	Fir
	  Balsam
	  California Red
	  Grand
	  Noble
	  Pacific Silver
	  White
	Hemlock, Western
	Lauan
	  Almon
	  Bagtikan
	  Mayapis
	  Red Lauan
	  Tangile
	  White Lauan
		Maple, Black
		Mengkulang[b]
		Meranti, Red[b][e]
		Mersawa[b]
		Pine
		  Pond
		  Red
		  Virginia
		  Western White
		Spruce
		  Black
		  Red
		  Sitka
		Sweetgum
		Tamarack
		Yellow-poplar
			Alder, Red
			Birch, Paper
			Cedar, Alaska
			Fir, Subalpine
			Hemlock, Eastern
			Maple, Bigleaf
			Pine
			  Jack
			  Lodgepole
			  Ponderosa
			  Spruce
			Redwood
			Spruce
			  Engelmann
			  White
				Aspen
				  Bigtooth
				  Quaking
				Cativo
				Cedar
				  Incense
				  Western Red
				Cottonwood
				  Eastern
				  Black (Western
				     Poplar)
				Pine
				  Eastern White
				  Sugar
					Basswood
					Poplar, Balsam

(a) Design stresses for Group 5 not assigned.

(b) Each of these names represents a trade group of woods consisting of a number of closely related species.

(c) Species from the genus Dipterocarpus are marketed collectively: Apitong if originating in the Philippines; Keruing if originating in Malaysia or Indonesia.

(d) Douglas fir from trees grown in the states of Washington, Oregon, California, Idaho, Montana, Wyoming, and the Canadian Provinces of Alberta and British Columbia shall be classed as Douglas fir No. 1. Douglas fir from trees grown in the states of Nevada, Utah, Colorado, Arizona and New Mexico shall be classed as Douglas fir No. 2.

(e) Red Meranti shall be limited to species having a specific gravity of 0.41 or more based on green volume and oven dry weight.

Used with permission of the American Plywood Association, Tacoma, WA.

A. Diaphragms

Floors and roofs can be designed to act as very deep, horizontal beams that carry the lateral forces applied to the walls between the floors and roof. These deep beams, or diaphragms, span between shear walls and other structural elements carrying the lateral loads to the building foundation.

Just as with other beams, diaphragms are designed to resist the imposed shear and bending stresses. The shear stress is carried by the plywood decking, and is assumed to be uniformly distributed across the depth. The nailing schedule and panel splicing details required for a given design shear force are determined from Table 9.5.

In both Tables 9.5 and 9.6, blocking the unsupported plywood edges between the principal framing members significantly increases the capacity. Blocking means installing short pieces of lumber to which all abutting free edges are attached.

The bending forces in diaphragms are usually resisted by the roof or floor perimater framing, which acts as the diaphragm chords—comparable to the chords of a truss. The chord is sized to resist the calculated bending forces. Since diaphragms are commonly much longer than available or manageable lumber lengths, the chords must be spliced adequately.

B. Shear Walls

Building walls that are parallel to an applied lateral force can carry that force down to the foundation as do short, deep cantilevers. Once the shear forces along the shear wall-diaphragm intersection are determined, Table 9.6 can be used to determine the plywood thickness, panel layout, and nailing schedule required to provide the design capacity.

C. Design Methods—Shear Walls and Diaphragms

The basic design procedure is to determine the applied loads and detail the respective elements to carry the loads.

step 1: Calculate the applied loads as shears (lb/ft) along the supported edge of diaphragms or the loaded edge of shear walls.

step 2: Determine panel layout, plywood thickness, and nailing schedule from Table 9.5 or 9.6.

step 3: Determine diaphragm chord size and detail splices.

step 4: Check deflections by comparing length-width ratios to allowable ones.

step 5: Detail connection between elements and to the foundation.

Table 9.4
Plywood Allowable Stresses

Allowable Stresses for Plywood (psi) conforming to U.S. Product Standard PS 1-83 for Construction and Industrial Plywood. Stresses are based on normal duration of load, and on common structural applications where panels are 24″ or greater in width. For other use conditions, see Section 3.3 for modifications.

Type of Stress	Species Group of Face Ply	Grade Stress Level[1]				
		S-1		S-2		S-3
		Wet	Dry	Wet	Dry	Dry Only
EXTREME FIBER STRESS IN BENDING (F_b) F_b	1	1430	2000	1190	1650	1650
TENSION IN PLANE OF PLIES (F_t) &	2, 3	980	1400	820	1200	1200
Face Grain Parallel or Perpendicular to Span F_t	4	940	1330	780	1110	1110
(At 45° to Face Grain Use 1/6 F_t)						
COMPRESSION IN PLANE OF PLIES	1	970	1640	900	1540	1540
	2	730	1200	680	1100	1100
Parallel or Perpendicular to Face Grain F_c	3	610	1060	580	990	990
(At 45° to Face Grain Use 1/3 F_c)	4	610	1000	580	950	950
SHEAR THROUGH THE THICKNESS[3]	1	155	190	155	190	160
Parallel or Perpendicular to Face Grain F_v	2, 3	120	140	120	140	120
(At 45° to Face Grain Use 2 F_v)	4	110	130	110	130	115
ROLLING SHEAR (IN THE PLANE OF PLIES)	MARINE & STRUCTURAL I	63	75	63	75	—
Parallel or Perpendicular to Face Grain F_s (At 45° to Face Grain Use 1-1/3 F_s)	ALL OTHER[2]	44	53	44	53	48
MODULUS OF RIGIDITY (OR SHEAR MODULUS)	1	70,000	90,000	70,000	90,000	82,000
	2	60,000	75,000	60,000	75,000	68,000
Shear in Plane Perpendicular G	3	50,000	60,000	50,000	60,000	55,000
to Plies (through the thickness) (At 45° to Face Grain Use 4G)	4	45,000	50,000	45,000	50,000	45,000
BEARING (ON FACE)	1	210	340	210	340	340
Perpendicular to Plane $F_c \perp$	2, 3	135	210	135	210	210
of Plies	4	105	160	105	160	160
MODULUS OF ELASTICITY IN BENDING IN PLANE OF PLIES	1	1,500,000	1,800,000	1,500,000	1,800,000	1,800,000
	2	1,300,000	1,500,000	1,300,000	1,500,000	1,500,000
E	3	1,100,000	1,200,000	1,100,000	1,200,000	1,200,000
Face Grain Parallel or Perpendicular to Span	4	900,000	1,000,000	900,000	1,000,000	1,000,000

(1) See pages 12 and 13 for Guide.
   To qualify for stress level S-1, gluelines must be exterior and only veneer grades N, A, and C (natural, not repaired) are allowed in either face or back.
   For stress level S-2, gluelines must be exterior and veneer grade B, C-Plugged and D are allowed on the face or back.
   Stress level S-3 includes all panels with interior or intermediate (IMG) gluelines.

(2) Reduce stresses 25% for 3-layer (4- or 5-ply) panels over 5/8″ thick. Such layups are possible under PS 1-83 for APA RATED SHEATHING, APA RATED STURD-I-FLOOR, UNDERLAYMENT, C-C Plugged and C-D Plugged grades over 5/8″ through 3/4″ thick.

(3) Shear-through-the-thickness stresses for MARINE and SPECIAL EXTERIOR grades may be increased 33%. See Section 3.8.1 for conditions under which stresses for other grades may be increased.

Used with permission of the American Plywood Association, Tacoma, WA.

Table 9.5
Required Panel Details—Diaphragms

Recommended Shear (pounds per foot) for Horizontal APA Panel Diaphragms with Framing of Douglas Fir, Larch or Southern Pine[a] for Wind or Seismic Loading

Panel Grade	Common Nail Size	Minimum Nail Penetration in Framing (inches)	Minimum Nominal Panel Thickness (inch)	Minimum Nominal Width of Framing Member (inches)	Blocked Diaphragms				Unblocked Diaphragms	
					Nail Spacing (in.) at diaphragm boundaries (all cases), at continuous panel edges parallel to load (Cases 3 & 4), and at all panel edges (Cases 5 & 6)[b]				Nails Spaced 6" max. at Supported Edges[b]	
					6	4	2½[c]	2[c]	Case 1 (No unblocked edges or continuous joints parallel to load)	All other configurations (Cases 2, 3, 4, 5 & 6)
					Nail Spacing (in.) at other panel edges (Cases 1, 2, 3 & 4)					
					6	6	4	3		
APA STRUCTURAL I RATED SHEATHING EXP 1 or EXT	6d	1-1/4	5/16	2	185	250	375	420	165	125
				3	210	280	420	475	185	140
	8d	1-1/2	3/8	2	270	360	530	600	240	180
				3	300	400	600	675	265	200
	10d[d]	1-5/8	15/32	2	320	425	640	730	285	215
				3	360	480	720	820	320	240
APA RATED SHEATHING, APA RATED STURD-I-FLOOR EXP 1, EXP 2 or EXT; and other APA grades except Species Group 5	6d	1-1/4	5/16	2	170	225	335	380	150	110
				3	190	250	380	430	170	125
			3/8	2	185	250	375	420	165	125
				3	210	280	420	475	185	140
	8d	1-1/2	3/8	2	240	320	480	545	215	160
				3	270	360	540	610	240	180
			7/16	2	255	340	505	575	230	170
				3	285	380	570	645	255	190
			15/32	2	270	360	530	600	240	180
				3	300	400	600	675	265	200
	10d[d]	1-5/8	15/32	2	290	385	575	655	255	190
				3	325	430	650	735	290	215
			19/32	2	320	425	640	730	285	215
				3	360	480	720	820	320	240

(a) For framing of other species: (1) Find species group of lumber in NFPA National Design Spec. (2) Find shear value from table above for nail size for Structural I panels (regardless of actual grade). (3) Multiply value by 0.82 for Lumber Group III or 0.65 for Lumber Group IV.

(b) Space nails 12 in. oc along intermediate framing members (Applicable building codes may require 10 in. oc nail spacing at intermediate supports for floors).

(c) Framing at adjoining panel edges shall be 3-in. nominal or wider, and nails shall be staggered where nails are spaced 2 inches oc or 2-1/2 inches oc.

(d) Framing at adjoining panel edges shall be 3-in. nominal or wider, and nails shall be staggered where 10d nails having penetration into framing of more than 1-5/8 inches are spaced 3 inches oc.

Notes: Design for diaphragm stresses depends on direction of continuous panel joints with reference to load, not on direction of long dimension of sheet. Continuous framing may be in either direction for blocked diaphragms.

Used with permission of the American Plywood Association, Tacoma, WA.

Example 9.1

Determine the design shear on the diaphragms and shear walls of the building shown. Design and detail the roof as a diaphragm and the first-floor interior wall as a shear wall. Assume a wind load of 25 psf and consider only wind against the long side of the building. Use K-D southern pine for the framing. Determine the wind loads applied to the long edges of the roof and floor from the wall that frames between them. Assume a tributary area distribution of the uniform load.

load on the 120 ft length of the roof

$$= \frac{(25 \text{ psf})(10 \text{ ft})}{2}$$
$$= 125 \text{ plf}$$

load on the 120 ft length of the second floor

$$= \frac{(25 \text{ psf})(10 \text{ ft} + 12 \text{ ft})}{2}$$
$$= 275 \text{ plf}$$

Table 9.6
Plywood Shear Wall Capacities

Recommended Shear (pounds per foot) for APA Panel Shear Walls with Framing of Douglas Fir, Larch, or Southern Pine [a] for Wind or Seismic Loading [b]

Panel Grade	Minimum Nominal Panel Thickness (in.)	Minimum Nail Penetration in Framing (in.)	Panels Applied Direct to Framing					Panels Applied Over 1/2" Gypsum Sheathing				
			Nail Size (common or galvanized box)	Nail Spacing at Panel Edges (in.)				Nail Size (common or galvanized box)	Nail Spacing at Panel Edges (in.)			
				6	4	3	2[e]		6	4	3	2[e]
APA STRUCTURAL I RATED SHEATHING EXP 1 or EXT	5/16	1-1/4	6d	200	300	390	510	8d	200	300	390	510
	3/8		8d	230[d]	360[d]	460[d]	610[d]		280	430	550	730
	7/16	1-1/2		255[d]	395[d]	505[d]	670[d]	10d[f]	—	—	—	—
	15/32			280	430	550	730		—	—	—	—
	15/32	1-5/8	10d[f]	340	510	665	870	—				
APA RATED SHEATHING EXP 1, EXP 2 or EXT; APA RATED SIDING 303[g] and other APA grades except species Group 5.	5/16 or 1/4[c]	1-1/4	6d	180	270	350	450	8d	180	270	350	450
	3/8			200	300	390	510		200	300	390	510
	3/8	1-1/2	8d	220[d]	320[d]	410[d]	530[d]	10d[f]	260	380	490	640
	7/16			240[d]	350[d]	450[d]	585[d]		—	—	—	—
	15/32			260	380	490	640		—	—	—	—
	15/32	1-5/8	10d[f]	310	460	600	770	—				
	19/32			340	510	665	870	—				
APA RATED SIDING 303[g] and other APA grades except species Group 5	5/16[c]	1-1/4	Nail Size (galvanized casing) 6d	140	210	275	360	Nail Size (galvanized casing) 8d	140	210	275	360
	3/8	1-1/2	8d	160	240	310	410	10d[f]	160	240	310	410

(a) For framing of other species: (1) Find species group of lumber in the NFPA National Design Spec. (2) (a) For common or galvanized box nails, find shear value from table above for nail size for STRUC-TURAL I panels (regardless of actual grade). (b) For galvanized casing nails, take shear value directly from table above. (3) Multiply this value by 0.82 for Lumber Group III or 0.65 for Lumber Group IV.

(b) All panel edges backed with 2-inch nominal or wider framing. Install panels either horizontally or vertically. Space nails 6 inches oc along intermediate framing members for 3/8-inch and 7/16-inch panels installed on studs spaced 24 inches oc. For other conditions and panel thicknesses, space nails 12 inches oc on intermediate supports.

(c) 3/8-inch or 303 - 16 oc is minimum recommended when applied direct to framing as exterior siding.

(d) Shears may be increased to values shown for 15/32-inch sheathing with same nailing provided (1) studs are spaced a maximum of 16 inches oc, or (2) if panels are applied with long dimension across studs.

(e) Framing at adjoining panel edges shall be 3-inch nominal or wider, and nails shall be staggered where nails are spaced 2 inches oc.

(f) Framing at adjoining panel edges shall be 3-inch nominal or wider, and nails shall be staggered where 10d nails having penetration into framing of more than 1-5/8 inches are spaced 3 inches o.c.

(g) Values apply to all-veneer plywood APA RATED SIDING 303 panels only. 303 - 16 oc plywood may be 11/32-inch, 3/8-inch or thicker. Thickness at point of nailing on panel edges governs shear values.

Typical Layout for Shear Walls

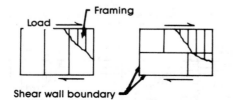
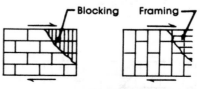

Used with permission of the American Plywood Association, Tacoma, WA.

Note that the wind load on the lower 6 feet of the wall is carried directly to the foundation and represents a relatively small shear force.

Determine the shears along the supported edges of the diaphragms (where they are connected to the shear walls).

roof-to-end walls connection shear

$$= \frac{(125 \text{ plf})\left(\frac{120 \text{ ft}}{2}\right)}{50 \text{ ft}}$$
$$= 150 \text{ plf}$$

floor-to-end walls shear

$$= \frac{(275 \text{ plf})\left(\frac{60 \text{ ft}}{2}\right)}{50 \text{ ft}}$$
$$= 165 \text{ plf}$$

floor-to-centerline walls

$$= \frac{\left(\frac{5}{8}\right)(120 \text{ ft})(275 \text{ plf})}{40 \text{ ft}}$$
$$= 516 \text{ plf}$$

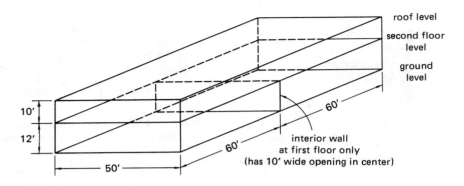

Note that the last shear calculation includes the $\frac{5}{8}$ factor applicable to the center support of a beam continuous over three supports, even though the end-wall calculation is based on a simple tributary area calculation.

This assumed behavior is conservative and indicative of the simplified analyses justified in load distribution calculations. Note also that the 10 ft opening is considered by loading only 40 feet of the interior wall.

To design the roof as a diaphragm, first find an adequate configuration in Table 9.4. Since installing complete blocking is expensive, first try to find an option with unblocked edges. The lower group of plywood grades is the cheaper, so also try to find a layout in that section of Table 9.4. Several layouts meet the design requirement for 150 plf. In practice, the choice might be influenced by snow loads, local practice, or other architectural considerations. For this case, assume 2″ nominal framing will be adequate and that $\frac{3}{8}$″ plywood will be adequate for the snow load. A 160 plf capacity is provided by the following configuration:

C-C EXT-APA, $\frac{3}{8}$″ plywood, 8d nails on 6″ centers along the end wall and on 12″ centers along the other framing. The edges can be unblocked, and 2″ nominal framing members are adequate. The panel layout can be case 2, 3, 4, 5, or 6.

The chord force is determined by finding the maximum bending moment and dividing by the diaphragm depth—the moment arm of the chord forces.

The maximum moment is

$$M_{\max} = \frac{w\ell^2}{8}$$
$$= \frac{(125\text{ plf})(120\text{ ft})^2}{8}$$
$$= 225,000\text{ ft-lb}$$

The bending force in the chords is, therefore,

$$\frac{M_{\max}}{d} = \frac{225,000\text{ ft-lb}}{50\text{ ft}}$$
$$= 4500\text{ lb}$$

Since one chord will be in tension and the other in compression, the smaller of the two allowable axial stresses will control the chord size. Appendix B gives $F_c = 1200$ psi and $F_t = 675$ psi, so that the tension chord controls the design size. Furthermore, footnote 3 specifies a 40% reduction in F_t for an assumed 10″ or deeper member. The required chord area is, therefore,

$$\frac{4500\text{ lb}}{(675\text{ psi})(0.60)(1.33)} = 8.35\text{ in}^2$$

1.33 is the load duration factor for wind loads. Assuming a doubled 2″ nominal chord, splices will have a 1.5″ wide continuous member. The required depth of the chord is

$$\frac{8.35\text{ in}^2}{1.5\text{ in}} = 5.57\text{ in}$$

Even after removing some of the chord section for the splice fasteners, any chord of doubled 2×8's or larger will be adequate. The splices should be designed to handle the maximum chord force.

The diaphragm is only as good as the connection supports it at the shear walls. This connection should have a design capacity of 160 plf, the capacity of the diaphragm—not the 150 plf design load. There are several ways to achieve this capacity. One efficient way is to have the plywood wall sheathing overlap the roof perimeter framing.

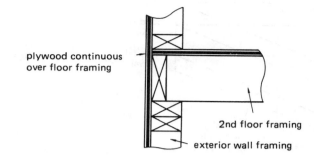

plywood continuous over floor framing

2nd floor framing

exterior wall framing

The Uniform Building Code (and most other codes) specifies a maximum length-width ratio of 4:1 for horizontal diaphragms sheathed with plywood. This ratio is intended to eliminate excessive deflection. The ratio in this example is 120 ft : 50 ft = 2.4 : 1, so the criterion is satisfied.

The interior wall has a shear load of 516 plf, applied on the top by the second floor and transmitted down to the foundation. Table 9.6 distinguishes between walls with the plywood applied directly to the framing and plywood applied over $\frac{1}{2}''$ gypsum sheathing intended as fire walls. Assuming this is not a fire wall, a 570 plf load can be carried in a shear wall with the following specifications:

C-D INT-APA $\frac{3}{8}''$ sheathing, with 8d nails $2\frac{1}{2}''$ on center at the boundary framing members and $12''$ on center at all other framing. Any of the panel layouts illustrated at the bottom of Table 9.5 are acceptable.

The chords of shear walls are the vertical framing members at the corners and around openings. Since standard framing practice results in triple members at corners and double members at openings, the chords at the openings control. The load at the top of each half of the shear wall is

$$(515 \text{ plf})(20 \text{ ft}) = 10,030 \text{ lb}$$

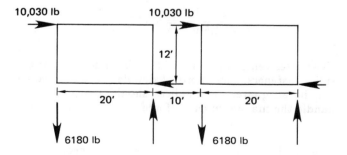

This force creates a bending moment that is maximum at the bottom of the wall, where it is equal to

$$(10,030 \text{ lb})(12 \text{ ft}) = 123,600 \text{ ft-lb}$$

The height of the wall is 12 feet. This causes a bending force in the vertical chords equal to the applied moment divided by the chord separation, or shear wall length:

$$\text{chord force} = \frac{123,600 \text{ ft-lb}}{20 \text{ ft}} = 6180 \text{ lb}$$

Using the allowable tension stress calculated for the roof diaphragm, this chord force requires an area of

$$\frac{6180 \text{ lb}}{(0.60)(1.33)(675 \text{ psi})} = 11.47 \text{ in}^2$$

Assuming the verticals will be short enough to be one piece, the full $3''$ width will be available. This requires a vertical framing member depth of

$$\frac{11.47 \text{ in}^2}{3 \text{ in}} = 3.82 \text{ in}$$

This is wider than the 3.5 inches of a 2×4, so a 2×6 wall is required. If 2×6's cannot be used, a higher grade framing in this wall will be necessary.

The wall must be connected to the foundation to resist both the shear load of 570 plf and the uplift load in the chords of 6180 pounds at each corner and side of the opening. Anchor bolts at closer than standard spacings or special steel fittings can be used to provide this connection capacity.

The height-width ratio for this shear wall is 12 ft : 40 ft, or 0.30 : 1, less than the 1 : 1 ratio for which deflections should be calculated. Both 20 foot sections of the interior wall are taken into account. This issue of openings in plywood diaphragms and shear walls is very complex and is at the cutting edge of the research in the field. This text has necessarily treated this subject lightly.

5 PLYWOOD-LUMBER BUILT-UP BEAMS

With its alternating grain directions, plywood is very strong in shear. Its panel configuration also makes plywood convenient to use for webs of built-up beams. Lumber, with all its fibers oriented in the same direction, can efficiently resist the axial forces found in the flanges of built-up beams. For spans longer or loads heavier than dimension lumber beams can handle, plywood-lumber beams can be cheaper and easier to obtain than glue-laminated members.

There are many design variables involved in designing a plywood-lumber beam. The beam depth and configuration can be changed. The size, number, species, and grade of the lumber flanges are variable. Finally, the webs can be any number of any thickness and type plywood.

With all these available design variables, there are two basic design methodologies. Several manufacturers' groups and government agencies publish tables of plywood-lumber beam capacities, spans, and details.

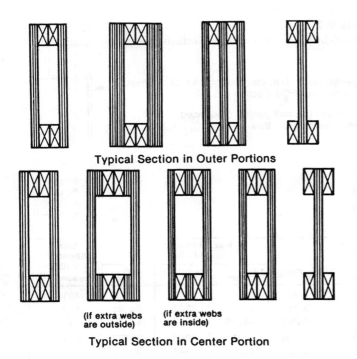

Typical Section in Outer Portions

(if extra webs   (if extra webs
are outside)   are inside)

Typical Section in Center Portion

Figure 9.5 Plywood-Lumber Beam Cross Sections

*Used with permission of the American Plywood Association, Tacoma,
WA.*

The other choice is to pick a trial section based on experience and available material. The shear stresses, bending stresses, and deflections are then checked. If the
trial section is adequate without being unreasonably
understressed, the design is completed by detailing the
connections.

Trying to achieve an optimal built-up beam design with
all the design variables could be a long task. Unless the
beams are to be mass-produced, it is generally uneco-
nomical to spend a lot of time trying to optimize design.
A more important consideration is material availability.

The following design procedure is based on Supplement
2 of the Plywood Design Specification, published by
the American Plywood Association. This publication
contains much valuable information on fabrication detailing, asymmetrical sections, and detailing. Its use is
highly recommended.

A. Design Considerations

The two basic configuration layouts used in plywood-
lumber beams are the I beam and box beam.

The allowable stresses for the lumber flanges are found
in the National Design Specification, excerpted in Appendix B. Table 9.4 provides the allowable stresses in
the plywood webs.

Deflections are calculated through standard mechanics
procedures, and should be limited to the same values as
solid beams. Since these beams tend to be long and/or
heavily loaded, and are fabricated instead of sawn, camber is a design consideration. The recommended camber is 1.5 times the dead load deflection.

B. Trial Section

To determine a trial section, choose the beam depth
as one-eighth to one-twelfth of the span, with a depth
that makes efficient use of the 4 foot module of com-
mercially available plywood. Table 9.7 gives very approximate values for the shear and moment capacities
of various cross sections. These are only preliminary
cross sections, and they must be checked against the
actual design and allowable stresses.

C. Lumber Flanges

Since the lumber flanges are primarily loaded axially by
the bending stresses, F_c and F_t are the considered allowable stresses. If the beam is symmetrical, the smaller of
the two allowable axial stresses will control. The bending stress equation (8.1) is used with the net moment of
inertia, I_n, which is calculated neglecting those longitudinal fibers in the plywood webs and lumber flanges
that are interrupted by butt splices.

When calculating I_n, three reductions in the lumber
flange area must be considered. The first is due to the
resurfacing required for a competent glue joint at the
web/flange connection. Assume this is a $\frac{1}{8}$ inch reduction in width across the beam cross section. The second
area reduction is due to resurfacing the depth of the
assembled beam and is intended to smooth out irregularities in the fit along the top and bottom of the beam.
Assume this reduction in beam and flange depth to be
$\frac{3}{8}$ inch for beams less than 24 inches deep, and $\frac{1}{2}$ inch
for beams 24 inches deep or deeper.

The last flange area reduction results from butt-splicing
the lumber to achieve the required beam length. The
reduction is a function of the butt-joint spacings. The
butt-jointed flange members are neglected in any I_n calculation. If two flange pieces are butt jointed at a spacing less than ten times the thickness of the flange pieces,
both flange pieces are neglected at the more critical of
the two locations. Unless the splices are spaced more
than 50 times the flange member width, the unjointed
flange members also have their areas reduced according
to the factor of Table 9.8. When checking flange tension stresses, the jointed members are neglected, the
unjointed members reduced with Table 9.8, and the
allowable stress is further reduced by 20 percent.

The plywood webs contribute some bending resistance.
This is accounted for in the I_n calculation by including
only the plywood plies parallel to the longitudinal beam
axis. Butt-spliced web members must be neglected in
this calculation, unless they are spliced full depth with
a plywood scab.

Table 9.7
Preliminary Capacities of Plywood-Lumber Beam Cross Sections

Plywood webs, butt joints staggered 24″ minimum,
spliced per PDS Section 5.6.3.2

Continuous lumber flanges (no butt joints), resurfaced
for gluing per Part 1, Section 4.1.2

Depth, Flange	Max. Moment,[1][2] M (ft-lb)			Max. Shear,[1] V (lb)
	M_{flange}	M_{web}[3][4]	M_{total}	$V_{horizontal}$[5][6]
12″ 1-2x4	2375	358	2733	1145
2-2x4	4751	358	5109	1159
3-2x4	7126	358	7484	1165
16″ 1-2x4	3771	648	4419	1612
2-2x4	7543	648	8191	1648
3-2x4	11314	648	11962	1663
1-2x6	4510	648	5158	1486
2-2x6	9019	648	9667	1497
3-2x6	13529	648	14177	1502
20″ 1-2x4	5217	1022	6239	2073
2-2x4	10434	1022	11456	2135
3-2x4	15652	1022	16674	2162
1-2x6	6646	1022	7668	1950
2-2x6	13291	1022	14313	1978
3-2x6	19937	1022	20959	1990
1-2x8	7193	1022	8215	1845
2-2x8	14386	1022	15408	1856
3-2x8	21580	1022	22602	1861
24″ 1-2x4	6554	1465	8019	2515
2-2x4	13108	1465	14573	2606
3-2x4	19662	1465	21127	2647
1-2x6	8761	1465	10226	2407
2-2x6	17522	1465	18987	2457
3-2x6	26283	1465	27748	2477
1-2x8	9850	1465	11315	2295
2-2x8	19699	1465	21164	2321
3-2x8	29549	1465	31014	2331
1-2x10	10411	1465	11876	2183
2-2x10	20822	1465	22287	2192
3-2x10	31234	1465	32699	2196
30″ 2-2x4	17486	2309	19795	3317
3-2x4	26229	2309	28538	3381
4-2x4	34972	2309	37281	3418
2-2x6	24358	2309	26667	3189
3-2x6	36537	2309	38846	3226
4-2x6	48716	2309	51025	3246
2-2x8	28417	2309	30726	3051
3-2x8	42626	2309	44935	3074
4-2x8	56835	2309	59144	3086
2-2x10	31270	2309	33579	2898
3-2x10	46904	2309	49213	2910
4-2x10	62539	2309	64848	2917
2-2x12	32693	2309	35001	2768
3-2x12	49039	2309	51348	2773
4-2x12	65385	2309	67694	2776

Depth, Flange	Max. Moment,[1][2] M (ft-lb)			Max. Shear,[1] V (lb)
	M_{flange}	M_{web}[3][4]	M_{total}	$V_{horizontal}$[5][6]
36″ 2-2x4	21894	3343	25237	4014
3-2x4	32842	3343	36185	4104
4-2x4	43789	3343	47132	4156
2-2x6	31324	3343	34667	3915
3-2x6	46985	3343	50328	3971
4-2x6	62647	3343	65990	4003
2-2x8	37442	3343	40785	3785
3-2x8	56163	3343	59506	3823
4-2x8	74884	3343	78227	3844
2-2x10	42368	3343	45711	3626
3-2x10	63553	3343	66896	3650
4-2x10	84737	3343	88080	3663
2-2x12	45487	3343	48830	3475
3-2x12	68231	3343	71574	3489
4-2x12	90975	3343	94318	3497
42″ 2-2x6	38362	4569	42931	4632
3-2x6	57543	4569	62112	4711
4-2x6	76725	4569	81294	4755
2-2x8	46640	4569	51209	4515
3-2x8	69960	4569	74529	4571
4-2x8	93280	4569	97849	4602
2-2x10	53836	4569	58405	4360
3-2x10	80754	4569	85323	4398
4-2x10	107672	4569	112241	4419
2-2x12	58956	4569	63525	4202
3-2x12	88434	4569	93003	4227
4-2x12	117912	4569	122481	4241
48″ 2-2x6	45446	5985	51431	5340
3-2x6	68170	5985	74155	5443
4-2x6	90893	5985	96878	5502
2-2x8	55946	5985	61931	5240
3-2x8	83919	5985	89904	5316
4-2x8	111892	5985	117877	5358
2-2x10	65533	5985	71518	5093
3-2x10	98300	5985	104285	5147
4-2x10	131066	5985	137051	5177
2-2x12	72843	5985	78828	4935
3-2x12	109265	5985	115250	4973
4-2x12	145686	5985	151671	4994

Used with permission of the American Plywood Association, Tacoma, WA.

Table 9.7 (cont'd)
Preliminary Capacities of Plywood-Lumber Beam Cross Sections

Bases and Adjustments:

(1) Basis: Normal duration of load.
Adjustments: 0.90 for permanent load (over 50 years)
1.15 for 2 months, as for snow
1.25 for 7 days
1.33 for wind or earthquake
2.00 for impact

(2) Basis: F_t of flange = 1000 psi
Adjustment: $F_t/1000$ for other allowable tension stresses. Also see PDS Section 5.7.3 for adjustments due to butt joints.

(3) Basis: One web effective in bending
Adjustment: 2.0 for web splices per PDS 5.6.1

(4) Basis: 15/32″ or 1/2″ APA RATED SHEATHING EXP 1 (CDX)
Adjustments: 0.81 for 3/8″
0.97 for 3/8″ STRUCTURAL I
1.19 for 15/32″ or 1/2″ STRUCTURAL I
1.02 for 19/32″ or 5/8″
1.51 for 19/32″ or 5/8″ STRUCTURAL I
1.42 for 23/32″ or 3/4″
1.84 for 23/32″ or 3/4″ STRUCTURAL I

(5) Basis: 15/32″ or 1/2″ APA RATED SHEATHING EXP 1 (CDX)
Note: Adjustments below may in some cases cause rolling shear to control final design.
Adjustments: 0.93 for 3/8″
1.24 for 3/8″ STRUCTURAL I
1.80 for 15/32″ or 1/2″ STRUCTURAL I
1.07 for 19/32″ or 5/8″
2.37 for 19/32″ or 5/8″ STRUCTURAL I
1.49 for 23/32″ or 3/4″
2.48 for 23/32″ or 3/4″ STRUCTURAL I

(6) Basis: Plywood edges parallel to face grain glued to continuous framing per PDS 3.8.1
Adjustments: 1.12 for all plywood edges glued to framing per PDS 3.8.1
0.84 for all other conditions

Used with permission of the American Plywood Association, Tacoma, WA.

Table 9.8
Effective Area of Unspliced Flange Members

butt-joint spacing (t = lamination thickness)	effective laminae area
30t	90%
20t	80%
10t	60%

Used with permission of the American Plywood Association, Tacoma, WA.

D. Plywood Webs

The major stress in the plywood web is through-the-panel shear stress. When calculating the maximum value of the shear stress (at the neutral axis), Eq. 6.6 is used. In this calculation, however, the Q and I section properties are calculated including all longitudinal fibers, regardless of butt splicing. The thickness in Eq. 6.6 is the sum of all shear thicknesses of plywood present at the section.

E. Flange to Web Connection

The shear connection between the web(s) and flange(s) causes rolling shear in the plywood. The shear stress is evaluated at the glue line with Eq. 6.6. This stress is compared with an allowable rolling shear from Table 9.4. The table value should be reduced by 50 percent to account for the stress concentrations that arise at the connection.

F. Deflections

The APA Supplement 2 contains a refined way to calculate the separate bending and shear components of deflection in plywood-lumber beams. An approximate method is to calculate the bending component with standard deflection equations, and increase it to account for shear deflection. The magnitude of the increase is a function of the span-to-depth ratio, as indicated in Table 9.9. The values of Table 9.9 may be linearly interpolated for actual span-to-depth ratios.

Table 9.9
Bending Deflection Increase to Account for Shear

span/depth	increase
10	50%
15	20%
20	0%

Used with permission of the American Plywood Association, Tacoma, WA.

G. Details

Any splices must be detailed to transmit the result-ant design forces. In addition, stiffeners are added wher-ever a point load or support reaction is applied to the beam. These stiffeners fit vertically between the flanges to reinforce the web and distribute the point load. They are sized to not crush the flanges at the bearing points, and to not induce rolling shear failure in the web, as the load is transferred from flange to web.

H. Lateral Stability

Plywood-lumber beams can be long and subject to lateral buckling. The American Plywood Association suggests considering the ratio of cross-sectional stiff-nesses about the vertical and horizontal axes as a mea-sure of the beam's tendency to buckle laterally. The moments of inertia include all longitudinal fibers, re-gardless of splicing. The bracing recommendations, as a function of that ratio, are found in Table 9.10.

Table 9.10
Lateral Bracing Required for
Plywood-Lumber Beams

I_x/I_y	lateral bracing required
≤ 5	none
5–10	ends held at bottom at supports
10–20	top and bottom held at ends
20–30	top (or bottom) edge held
30–40	bridging or equivalent on 8 foot centers, or less
≥ 40	compression flange held by well-fastened sheathing, or equal

Used with permission of the American Plywood Association, Tacoma, WA.

Example 9.2

A plywood-lumber beam is 24″ deep (nominally) with a 25 ft clear span. The webs are $\frac{5}{8}$″ 32/16 APA rated sheathing with exterior glue. The webs are not spliced at the butt joints. The flanges are 3 DF-L, dense no. 1 2×6's, that are butt jointed on staggered 48″ centers. The standard resurfacing has been done. The beam is subjected to normal duration and dry loading. Deflec-tion is limited to span/360. What is the beam's uniform load capacity as limited by (a) flange stresses, (b) web stresses, (c) web/flange connection stresses, and (d) de-flection?

The first step is to evaluate the section properties. Butt-jointed members are considered as intermittently effec-tive in the net section properties. Once the section properties are known, the design equations are solved for the allowable uniform load.

The members are resurfaced during beam fabrication. The flange members are sanded $\frac{1}{8}$″ thinner for better

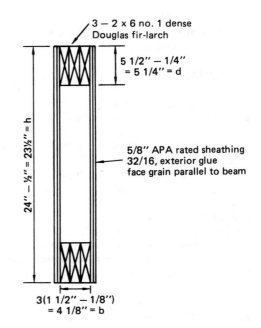

3 – 2 x 6 no. 1 dense
Douglas fir-larch

$5 \frac{1}{2}″ - \frac{1}{4}″ = 5 \frac{1}{4}″ = d$

$24″ - \frac{1}{2}″ = 23 \frac{1}{2}″ = h$

5/8″ APA rated sheathing 32/16, exterior glue face grain parallel to beam

$3(1 \frac{1}{2}″ - \frac{1}{8}″) = 4 \frac{1}{8}″ = b$

gluing. After assembly, the beam's depth is resurfaced and reduced by $\frac{1}{2}″$. This depth reduction is assumed to reduce the depth of each flange by $\frac{1}{4}″$.

I. Section Properties

Moments of Inertia, I (total and net)

$$I_{\text{flanges}} =$$

$$\frac{b[h^3 - (h - 2d)^3]}{12}$$

$$= \frac{(2)(0.90)(1.5 - 0.125)[(23.5)^3 - (23.5 - (2)(5.25))^3]}{12}$$

$$= 2224 \text{ in}^4$$

This is the net moment of inertia for the flanges, where one of the laminae is neglected (leaving two pieces), and the remaining members are only 90 percent effective. The butt-joint spacing, 48 inches, is 48 in/1.5 in $\approx 30\,t$ and Table 9.8 yields the 90 percent. The total moment of inertia includes all parallel fibers, regardless of butt splicing.

$$I_{\text{flanges}} = \frac{(2224 \text{ in}^4)\left(\dfrac{3 \text{ pieces}}{2 \text{ pieces}}\right)}{0.9}$$

$$= 3707 \text{ in}^4$$

$$I_{\text{webs}} = t_{\parallel} \frac{h^3}{12}$$

$$= \frac{\left(2.951 \dfrac{\text{in}^2}{\text{ft}}\right)(23.5 \text{ in})^3}{\left(12 \dfrac{\text{in}}{\text{ft}}\right)(12)}$$

$$= 266 \text{ in}^4 \text{ (per web)}$$

Only the plywood fibers that are parallel to the beam axis contribute to section properties. The effective thickness, $t_\parallel$, is derived from the area of parallel fibers per foot of width, 2.951 in^2/ft. Figure 9.2 gives the group III species, and Table 9.2 gives the unsanded finish and S-1 stress rating.

The composite section properties are a combination of the plywood webs and the lumber flanges.

$$I_{net} = 2224 + 266 = 2490 \text{ in}^4$$

(only one web is considered)

$$I_{total} = 3706 + (2)(266) = 4238 \text{ in}^4$$

(all parallel fibers count)

$$Q_{flanges} = bd\left(\frac{h}{2} - \frac{d}{2}\right)$$

$$= (4.125 \text{ in})(5.25 \text{ in})\left(\frac{23.5 \text{ in}}{2} - \frac{5.25 \text{ in}}{2}\right)$$

$$= 197.6 \text{ in}^3$$

$$Q_{webs} = (t_\parallel)\left(\frac{h}{2}\right)\left(\frac{h}{4}\right) \text{ (no. of webs)}$$

$$= \left(2.951 \frac{in^2}{ft}\right)\left(\frac{1 \text{ ft}}{12 \text{ in}}\right)$$

$$\times \left(\frac{23.5 \text{ in}}{2}\right)\left(\frac{23.5 \text{ in}}{4}\right)(2)$$

$$= 34.0 \text{ in}^3$$

$$Q_{total} = Q_{webs} + Q_{flanges}$$
$$= 197.6 + 34.0$$
$$= 231.6 \text{ in}^3$$

Note that the only Q used is the total value. Therefore, a net value of Q is not calculated. In both I and Q calculations, the web contribution is much smaller than that of the flanges. This is one justification for not correcting for the different stiffnesses of the lumber flanges and plywood webs before combining them in their composite section.

Allowable Loads

Allowable load, limited by bending stresses in the flanges: The allowable tensile stress for the lumber flanges is 1200 psi, found in Appendix B. This controls over the allowable stress in the compression flange, F_c, 1400 psi. F_t is further reduced by 20 percent at the butt-jointed sections.

$$\text{allowable moment} = \frac{(F_t)(I_n)}{(0.5)(h)}$$

$$= \frac{(0.8)(1200 \text{ psi})(2492 \text{ in}^4)}{(0.5)(23.5 \text{ in})}$$

$$= 203{,}602 \text{ in-lb}$$

$$= 16{,}967 \text{ ft-lb}$$

$$\text{allowable load} = \frac{(M_{all})(8)}{(\text{span})^2}$$

$$= \frac{(16{,}967 \text{ ft-lb})(8)}{(25 \text{ ft})^2}$$

$$= 217 \text{ plf}$$

Allowable load, limited by shear stress in web: The Plywood Design Specification allows a 33 percent increase in allowable shear through the thickness of plywood if the plywood panel is rigidly glued to continuous framing around its edges. Table 9.4 gives F_v as 140 psi, for S-1, species III, dry use. For this application,

$$F_v = (1.33)(140) = 186.7 \text{ psi}$$

The allowable horizontal shear is

$$V_h = \frac{F_v I_t t_s}{Q}$$

$$= \frac{(186.7 \text{ psi})(4238 \text{ in}^4)(2 \text{ webs})\left(0.336 \frac{in}{web}\right)}{231.6 \text{ in}^3}$$

$$= 2296 \text{ lb}$$

Neglecting the uniform load within a beam depth of the supports, the allowable uniform load for this allowable horizontal shear is

$$w_{all} = \frac{2V}{L - 2h}$$

$$= \frac{(2)(2295 \text{ lb})}{25 \text{ ft} - \dfrac{(2)(23.5 \text{ in})}{12 \frac{in}{ft}}}$$

$$= 218 \text{ plf}$$

Allowable load, limited by rolling shear at the web/flange connection: The rolling shear at the glue line between web and flange, V_s, is

$$V_s = \frac{2F_s d I_t}{Q_{flanges}}$$

$$= \frac{(2)\left(\dfrac{53 \text{ psi}}{2}\right)(5.25 \text{ in})(4238 \text{ in}^4)}{197.6 \text{ in}^3}$$

$$= 5968 \text{ lb}$$

Note that the allowable rolling shear stress was halved because of the shear stress concentrations at the edge of the panel. This allowable shear translates into the following allowable uniform load.

$$w_{\text{all}} = (218 \text{ plf}) \left(\frac{5968 \text{ lb}}{2296 \text{ lb}} \right)$$

$$= 567 \text{ plf}$$

Allowable load, limited by deflection: A simple method of calculating deflections in plywood-lumber beams is to increase calculated bending deflections by a factor to account for the neglected, but significant, shear deflections. Table 9.9 gives this factor as a function of the span-to-depth ratio.

$$\frac{\text{span}}{\text{depth}} = \frac{25 \text{ ft}}{\left(\dfrac{23.5 \text{ in}}{12 \frac{\text{in}}{\text{ft}}} \right)}$$

$$= 12.8$$

Interpolating between ratios of 10 and 15 yields a factor of 1.33.

The allowable deflection, span/360, is equal to $(25)(12)/360 = 0.83$ inch. Use the maximum bending deflection equation for uniform load on simple spans to calculate the allowable uniform load.

$$w_{\text{all}} = \frac{(0.83 \text{ in})(384)(1.03)(1,900,000 \text{ psi})(4238 \text{ in}^4)}{(1.33)(5)(25 \text{ ft})^4 \left(1728 \frac{\text{in}^3}{\text{ft}^3} \right)}$$

$$= 589 \text{ plf}$$

Note that a three percent increase in the lumber flange E was included, because the extra deflection due to shear is accounted for with the 33 percent increase. The built-in shear deflection allowance in the tabled E value of Appendix B is overly conservative and redundant in this calculation and is therefore eliminated.

The uniform load capacity of the plywood-lumber beam is limited by bending stresses to 217 plf, and by shear in the plywood webs to 218 plf. There are several ways to increase the capacity: use thicker plywood; use a higher grade plywood—such as structural 1, with its species group I allowable stresses; or simply use more webs of the same plywood at the beam ends where shear stresses are maximum. The flanges could also be increased in number or size, or a higher stress species or grade could be specified.

Practice Problems

The first five practice problems are very similar to problems from past professional engineering exams. They represent, therefore, the level of complexity that could be expected on future exams. The proposed solutions are the author's own, and they are not necessarily the answers used by the grader for the problem in the year it was given. The other problems approximate the same level of complexity.

1. A beam supported by non-yielding supports at each end and a steel rod at midspan has the dimensions and loads shown.

The beam is timber, 4 inches wide by 6 inches deep, with a modulus of elasticity of 1.5×10^6 psi.

The rod is $\frac{3}{8}$ inch in diameter and $E = 30 \times 10^6$ psi. Assume the rod passes through a $\frac{1}{2}$ inch diameter hole in the beam.

Find the (a) reactions at A, B, and C, (b) bending moment at B, (c) maximum positive moment in the beam, and (d) maximum flexure stress in the beam.

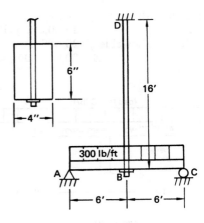

This beam is indeterminate to the first degree. A compatibility equation for the beam deflection at the centerline will provide the information required to analyze the entire beam.

The compatibility equation, with downward deflection defined as positive, is

$$Y_{\text{beam due to loads, without rod}} - Y_{\text{beam; rod force}}$$
$$= \text{rod elongation}$$

Solve for the three terms of this equation, in terms of the unknown rod force.

$Y_{\text{beam due to loads, without rod}}$
(beam will deflect downward)

$$= \frac{5WL^4}{384 EI}$$

$$= \frac{(5)\left(300\,\frac{\text{lb}}{\text{ft}}\right)(12\,\text{ft})^4\left(1728\,\frac{\text{in}^3}{\text{ft}^3}\right)}{(384)\left(1.5\times10^6\,\frac{\text{lb}}{\text{in}^2}\right)(72\,\text{in}^4)}$$

$$= 1.30\ \text{in}$$

This equation is found in any structural handbook or text. The 72 in^4 is the moment of inertia, $bd^3/12$, of the full-size $4'' \times 6''$ cross section.

$Y_{\text{beam; rod force}}$
(tension in rod will deflect beam upward)

$$= \frac{PL^3}{48 EI}$$

$$= \frac{P_{\text{rod}}(12\,\text{ft})^3\left(1728\,\frac{\text{in}^3}{\text{ft}^3}\right)}{(48)\left(1.5\times10^6\,\frac{\text{lb}}{\text{in}^2}\right)(72\,\text{in}^4)}$$

$$= 5.76\times10^{-4}(P_{\text{rod}})\ \text{in}$$

Rod elongation (tension in rod corresponds to downward deflection)

$$= \frac{PL}{AE}$$

$$= \frac{P_{\text{rod}}(16\,\text{ft})\left(12\,\frac{\text{in}}{\text{ft}}\right)}{\pi\left[\dfrac{\left(\frac{3}{8}\right)}{2}\,\text{in}\right]^2\left(30\times10^6\,\frac{\text{lb}}{\text{in}^2}\right)}$$

$$= 5.79\times10^{-5}(P_{\text{rod}})$$

Inserting these values into the compatibility equation:

$$1.30\ \text{in} - (5.76\times10^{-4})(P_{\text{rod}}) = (5.79\times10^{-5})(P_{\text{rod}})$$

Solving this equation for P_{rod},

$$P_{\text{rod}} = \frac{1.30}{5.79\times10^{-5}+5.76\times10^{-4}} = 2050\ \text{lb}$$

Before going any further, it is wise to check the reasonableness of this answer. One easy way to check it is to compare it with statically determinate limits on the rod force. If the rod were infinitely stiff, the problem would be a simple two-span, continuous beam. The rod force under those conditions would be

$$\left(\frac{5}{8}\right)(12 \text{ ft})\left(300\frac{\text{lb}}{\text{ft}}\right) = 2250 \text{ lb}$$

Since the rod is flexible, the load should be, and is, less than this upper bound. The lower limit on the rod force is zero, with no stiffness at all, but a more meaningful lower bound is determined by assuming the beam is very flexible compared to the rod. This is an assumption of two simple spans, giving a rod force of

$$\left(\frac{1}{2}\right)(12 \text{ ft})\left(300\frac{\text{lb}}{\text{ft}}\right) = 1800 \text{ lb}$$

The indeterminate solution for the rod force falls between these two bounds, and therefore seems reasonable.

The elongation of the rod, equal to the beam settlement, is

$$(2050 \text{ lb})\left(5.76 \times 10^{-5}\frac{\text{in}}{\text{lb}}\right) = 0.12 \text{ in}$$

Now that the indeterminate beam has been solved, use statics to find the rest of the quantities.

(a) Symmetry shows

$$R_A = R_C = \frac{\left(300\frac{\text{lb}}{\text{ft}}\right)(12 \text{ ft}) - (2050 \text{ lb})}{2}$$

$$= 775 \text{ lb}$$

(b) Bending moment at B

$$M_B = \left[(775 \text{ lb})(6 \text{ ft}) - \left(300\frac{\text{lb}}{\text{ft}}\right)(6 \text{ ft})\left(\frac{6 \text{ ft}}{2}\right)\right]$$

$$\times \left(12\frac{\text{in}}{\text{ft}}\right)$$

$$= -9000 \text{ in-lb, compression on bottom}$$

(c) The maximum positive bending moment occurs where the shear is zero.

$$V = 0 \text{ at}: \frac{775 \text{ lb}}{300\frac{\text{lb}}{\text{ft}}}$$

$$= 2.58 \text{ ft from either end of the beam}$$

$$M_{2.58\,\text{ft}} = \left[(775 \text{ lb})(2.58 \text{ ft}) - \left(300\frac{\text{lb}}{\text{ft}}\right)\left(\frac{(2.58 \text{ ft})^2}{2}\right)\right]$$

$$\times 12\frac{\text{in}}{\text{ft}}$$

$$= 12,000 \text{ in-lb}$$

(d) The maximum bending stress will either be at 2.58 ft from the end, or at the center—when the net section at the hole is considered.

At the maximum positive moment,

$$S = \frac{bd^2}{6} = \frac{(4)(6)^2}{6} = 24 \text{ in}^3$$

$$f_b = \frac{M}{S} = \frac{12,000 \text{ in-lb}}{24 \text{ in}^3} = 500 \text{ psi}$$

At the centerline the hole is removed in the section modulus calculation.

$$S = \left(4 \text{ in} - \frac{1}{2} \text{ in}\right)\left(\frac{(6 \text{ in})^2}{6}\right) = 21.0 \text{ in}^3$$

$$f_b = \frac{9000 \text{ in-lb}}{21 \text{ in}^3} = 429 \text{ psi}$$

The maximum bending stress occurs 2.58 feet from either end, and is equal to 500 psi.

2. In order to gain additional clear floor area for use in a building, plan to remove the center post under the 4″ × 8″ (nominal dimensions) beam. A king post truss is formed, as indicated in the second figure, making the beam continuous over the strut.

Calculate the stresses in the members of the trussed beam, and determine if they are within the allowable stresses indicated.

<u>Data</u>

timber: allowable f 1400 psi
         E   1,600,000 psi
steel: allowable f 20,000 psi
         E   30,000,000 psi

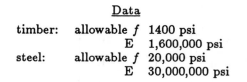

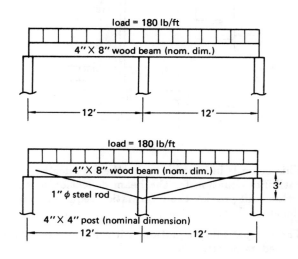

The trussed beam is indeterminate to the first degree. The king post truss layout was very popular in mill buildings in the 19th century. Handbook solutions of that era do exist, but will probably be more trouble to find than simply solving the problem.

This problem is similar to practice problem 1. A single compatibility equation for the beam deflection at the centerline will provide the information required to analyze the entire beam. The only difference is determining the elasticity of the support provided by the king post. Solve for the deflection terms, again with downward deflection taken as positive.

$$Y_{\text{beam; loaded, without the king post}} (\text{downward})$$
$$= \frac{5WL^4}{384EI}$$
$$= \frac{(5)\left(180\,\frac{\text{lb}}{\text{ft}}\right)(24\,\text{ft})^4\left(1728\,\frac{\text{in}^3}{\text{ft}^3}\right)}{(384)\left(1.6\times10^6\,\frac{\text{lb}}{\text{in}^2}\right)(111.148\,\text{in}^4)}$$
$$= 7.56\,\text{in}$$

The 111.148 in^4 moment of inertia is found in Appendix E.

$$Y_{\text{beam; due to an upward point load at center}} (\text{upward})$$
$$= \frac{PL^3}{48EI}$$
$$= \frac{P_{\text{(king post)}}(24\,\text{ft})^3\left(1728\,\frac{\text{in}^3}{\text{ft}^3}\right)}{(48)\left(1.6\times10^6\,\frac{\text{lb}}{\text{in}^2}\right)(111.148\,\text{in}^3)}$$
$$= -2.80\times10^{-3}(P_{\text{king post}})$$

To establish the flexibility of the king post, place an imaginary one pound load on top of the post and determine the displacement with the virtual work method.

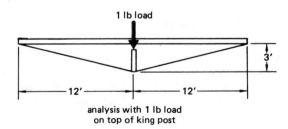

analysis with 1 lb load
on top of king post

A truss analysis (starting with a freebody diagram of point A) gives the following results:

member	length (ft)	area (in^2)	E (psi)	p (lb)	P (lb)
beam	24.0	25.375	1.6×10^6	-2.0	$-2.0\,P_{\text{kp}}$
rod 1	12.37	0.785	30×10^6	2.06	$2.06\,P_{\text{kp}}$
rod 2	12.37	0.785	30×10^6	2.06	$2.06\,P_{\text{kp}}$
king post	3.0	12.25	1.6×10^6	-1.0	$-1.0\,P_{\text{kp}}$

The deflection due to a unit load in the king post is equal to the sum of the PpL/AE terms:

beam
$$\frac{(-2P_{\text{kp}})(-2\,\text{lb}^2)(24\,\text{ft})\left(12\,\frac{\text{in}}{\text{ft}}\right)}{(25.375\,\text{in}^2)\left(1.6\times10^6\,\frac{\text{lb}}{\text{in}^2}\right)}$$
$$= 2.837\times10^{-5}(P_{\text{kp}})$$

rods
$$\frac{(2)(2.06P_{\text{kp}})(2.06)(12.37)(12)}{(0.785)(30\times10^6)}$$
$$= 5.35\times10^{-5}(P_{\text{kp}})$$

king post
$$\frac{(-1)(-1P_{\text{kp}})(3)(12)}{(12.25)(1.6\times10^6)}$$
$$= 1.837\times10^{-6}(P_{\text{kp}})$$

total $= 8.371\times10^{-5}(P_{\text{kp}})$

The compatibility equation is, therefore,

$$7.56\,\text{in} - (2.80\times10^{-3})(P_{\text{kp}})$$
$$= (8.371\times10^{-5})(P_{\text{kp}})$$

Solving for the force in the king post,

$$P_{\text{kp}} = \frac{7.56}{(8.371\times10^{-5}) + (2.80\times10^{-3})}$$
$$= 2622\,\text{lb}$$

As with the previous problem, a quick check on the upper and lower bounds for this indeterminate solution is worth the effort. If the post were rigid, the force would be $\frac{5}{8}$ of the applied load, or 2700 pounds. If the beam were very flexible, the force would be $\frac{1}{2}$ the applied load, or 2160 pounds. Since the solution to the compatibility equation falls between these bounds, it seems reasonable.

While the problem does not require establishing deflections, it is readily done with superposition.

- 7.56 inches down; how much it would have settled, without the king post
- $(2.80\times10^{-3})(2622) = 7.34$ inches up, because of king post support
- $(8.371\times10^{-5})(2622) = 0.22$ inches down, because of axial deformation

The net deflection is $7.56 - 7.34 + 0.22 = 0.44$ inches.

The deflection-to-span length ratio is $(24)(12)/(0.44) = 655$, an acceptable amount of deflection (i.e., less than $L/180$).

In order to evaluate the stresses in the beam, first solve for the reactions. Then find the maximum bending and shear stresses. The beam is loaded in axial compression, as well as bending, so the two longitudinal stresses must be superimposed.

$$\text{end reactions} = \frac{\left(180 \frac{\text{lb}}{\text{ft}}\right)(24 \text{ ft}) - 2622 \text{ lb}}{2}$$
$$= 849 \text{ lb}$$

Moment at the king post is

$$\left[(849 \text{ lb})(12 \text{ ft}) - \left(180 \frac{\text{lb}}{\text{ft}}\right)(12 \text{ ft})\left(\frac{12 \text{ ft}}{2}\right)\right]\left(12 \frac{\text{in}}{\text{ft}}\right)$$
$$= 33,264 \text{ in-lb}$$

Maximum positive moment occurs at the point where the shear is zero.

$$V = 0 \text{ at } \frac{849 \text{ lb}}{180 \frac{\text{lb}}{\text{ft}}} = 4.72 \text{ ft}$$

$$M_{4.72 \text{ ft}} = \left[(849)(4.72) - \left(\frac{(180)(4.72)^2}{2}\right)\right](12)$$
$$= 24,027 \text{ in-lb}$$

The section modulus, 30.661 in^3, is found in Appendix E.

The maximum bending stress is

$$\frac{M_{\max}}{S} = \frac{33,264}{30.661} = 1085 \text{ psi}$$

The axial forces have to be determined in order to find the axial stresses in the rods, beam, and king post. Look first at the equilibrium of the bottom of the king post.

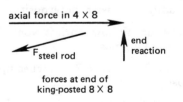

forces at end of
king-posted 8 × 8

The force in a rod is

$$P_{\text{rod}} = \frac{2622 \text{ lb}}{2} \times \frac{12.37 \text{ ft}}{3 \text{ ft}} = 5406 \text{ lb}$$

The king post force was divided in half because there are two rods, and hence, two vertical rod components.

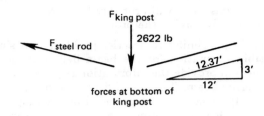

forces at bottom of
king post

The axial force in the beam is

$$P_{\text{beam}} = \frac{(5406 \text{ lb})(12 \text{ ft})}{12.37 \text{ ft}} = 5244 \text{ lb}$$

The axial compressive stress in the beam caused by this axial load is

$$f_a = \frac{5244 \text{ lb}}{25.375 \text{ in}^2} = 207 \text{ psi}$$

The maximum combined compressive stress, therefore, occurs at the top of the beam, 4.72 feet from either end, and is equal to

$$207 \text{ psi} + 1085 \text{ psi} = 1292 \text{ psi}$$

This is less than the allowable bending stress of 1400 psi. Using the interaction equation for combined bending and axial compression would be preferred in this problem. However, since only the allowable bending stress is given, a simple superposition is the only solution method possible.

The axial stress in the steel rods is

$$f_a = \frac{5406 \text{ lb}}{0.785 \text{ in}^2}$$
$$= 6887 \text{ psi} < 20,000 \text{ psi allowable}$$

The stress in the king post is 2622 lb/12.25 in^2 = 214 psi, very low.

The king posted beam meets allowable stress requirements in the steel rods and the 4×8 beam. The maximum deflection is less than the span divided by 665, which meets the most limiting deflection criteria.

3. Investigate the bending and shear stresses in the glue-laminated timber shown. Use the National Design Specification of the National Forest Products Association. Specify the edition used in your solution. Neglect the self-weight of the beam.

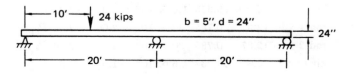

Given: Douglas fir, 24F-V5, normal duration of load, dry conditions, $b = 5$ inches, $d = 24$ inches (actual dimensions)

The beam is bent about the strong axis. The beam is supported laterally only at the supports. For the purposes of this problem, use L_u as that of a simple span.

Using handbook solutions, evaluate the maximum bending and shear stresses in the beam. Compare these with the allowable stresses. The allowable bending stress will be determined either by lateral buckling or extreme fiber stress.

The maximum shear occurs between the load and the central support, and is equal to $(19/32)P$ (as determined from beam tables for 2-span continuous beams).

$$V_{max} = \left(\frac{19}{32}\right)P = \left(\frac{19}{32}\right)(24,000 \text{ lb}) = 14,250 \text{ lb}$$

The maximum shear stress is

$$f_v = \frac{(14,250 \text{ lb})(1.5)}{(5)(24 \text{ in}^2)} = 178 \text{ psi}$$

Appendix B gives an allowable shear stress, F_v, of 155 psi for V5 lay-up. The beam is 15% overstressed in shear.

The maximum positive bending moment occurs under the load, and is equal to $(13/64)\,PL$, again as determined from beam tables for two-span continuous beams.

$$(M_{positive})_{max} = \left(\frac{13}{64}\right)PL$$

$$= \left(\frac{13}{64}\right)(24,000 \text{ lb})(20 \text{ ft})\left(12 \frac{\text{in}}{\text{ft}}\right)$$

$$= 1,170,000 \text{ in-lb}$$

Since the laminate layout used in this particular design was not intended to be used in continuous spans, the maximum negative moment should also be checked. This maximum negative moment occurs at the support and is equal to $(3/32)PL$.

$$(M_{negative})_{max} = \left(\frac{3}{32}\right)(24,000 \text{ lb})(20 \text{ ft})\left(12 \frac{\text{in}}{\text{ft}}\right)$$

$$= 540,000 \text{ in-lb}$$

Since the given dimensions are actual sizes, the section modulus is calculated as

$$S = \frac{bd^2}{6} = \frac{(5)(24)^2}{6} = 480 \text{ in}^3$$

$$(f_b)_{positive} = \frac{M}{S} = \frac{1,170,000}{480} = 2440 \text{ psi}$$

$$(f_b)_{negative} = \frac{540,000 \text{ in-lb}}{480} = 1125 \text{ psi}$$

In order to find the allowable bending stress, both lateral buckling and extreme fiber stresses must be considered.

lateral buckling:

$$\frac{\ell_u}{d} = \frac{(20 \text{ ft})\left(12 \frac{\text{in}}{\text{ft}}\right)}{(24 \text{ in})} = 10.0$$

The effective length, ℓ_e, is equal to

$$\ell_e = 1.63\ell_u + 3d$$

$$= (1.63)(20 \text{ ft})\left(12 \frac{\text{in}}{\text{ft}}\right) + (3)(24 \text{ in})$$

$$= 463.2 \text{ in}$$

The equation comes from Fig. 8.2. The slenderness ratio, C_s, is calculated from Eq. 8.2.

$$C_s = \sqrt{\frac{(463.2 \text{ in})(24 \text{ in})}{(5 \text{ in})^2}} = 21.29$$

This is larger than 10, so the beam is not short. In order to evaluate C_k, E and F_b from Appendix B are needed.

For the positive moment zones,

$$F_b = 2400 \text{ psi}; \quad E = 1,700,000 \text{ psi}$$

For the negative moment zone,

$$F_b = 1200 \text{ psi}; \quad E = 1,700,000 \text{ psi}$$

The value, C_k, which separates long and intermediate beams, is:

in the positive moment zones,

$$C_k = (0.956)\sqrt{\frac{1,700,000 \text{ psi}}{2400 \text{ psi}}} = 25.44$$

in the negative moment zone,

$$C_k = (0.956)\sqrt{\frac{1,700,000 \text{ psi}}{1200 \text{ psi}}} = 35.98$$

This beam is in the intermediate range. Considering lateral buckling, the allowable bending stress in the positive moment zone is

$$F_b' = (2400)\left[1 - \left(\frac{1}{3}\right)\left(\frac{21.29}{25.44}\right)^4\right] = 2008 \text{ psi}$$

In the negative zone, the allowable bending stress is

$$F_b' = (1200)\left[1 - \left(\frac{1}{3}\right)\left(\frac{21.29}{35.98}\right)^4\right] = 1151 \text{ psi}$$

This beam is overstressed in bending in the positive bending zone only, but check the extreme fiber stress for completeness. The only factor which applies to this case is the size factor, C_F. Table 8.1 gives this as 1.01, so the beam nearly exceeds the allowable stress at the extreme fibers, but it is overstressed when lateral stability is considered.

4. Investigate only the bending and radial stresses in the glued-laminated timber beam shown, according to the 1986 National Design Specification of the National Forest Association.

Given: total dead plus live load of 1000 lb per foot
normal load duration, dry use
Douglas fir 24F, $b = 7$ inches, $d = 30$ inches
laminations one-half inch thick
beam supported laterally at ends and midspan

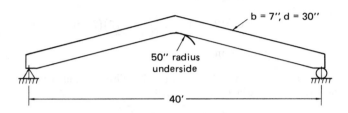

The actual bending and radial stresses must be compared with allowable stresses that are not easily determined. The allowable bending stress is either limited by lateral stability or extreme fiber stresses. Both cases will be investigated, with the lower value controlling. The allowable radial stress depends on whether the radial stress is tension or compression.

The maximum bending stresses occur at the centerline, where the moment is equal to $wL^2/8$.

$$M_{\max} = \left(1000 \frac{\text{lb}}{\text{ft}}\right)(40\,\text{ft})^2\left(\frac{12 \frac{\text{in}}{\text{ft}}}{8}\right)$$

$$= 2,400,000 \text{ in-lb}$$

$$S = \frac{bd^2}{6} = \frac{(7)(30)^2}{6} = 1050\,\text{in}^3$$

$$f_b = \frac{M}{S} = \frac{2,400,000}{1050} = 2286\,\text{psi}$$

Now, evaluate the two different allowable bending stresses. First, consider lateral stability.

$$\ell_u = \frac{40\,\text{ft}}{2} = 20\,\text{ft}$$

$$\frac{\ell_u}{d} = \frac{(20)(12)}{30} = 8.0$$

Figure 8.2, case 2 gives an effective unbraced length of

$$\ell_e = 1.63\,\ell_u + 3d$$

$$= (1.63)(20\,\text{ft})\left(12 \frac{\text{in}}{\text{ft}}\right) + (3)(30\,\text{in})$$

$$= 481.2\,\text{in}$$

The slenderness factor, C_s, is

$$C_s = \sqrt{(481.2\,\text{in})\left(\frac{30\,\text{in}}{(7\,\text{in})^2}\right)}$$

$$= 17.16\,(> 10)$$

In order to find C_k, the dividing line between long and intermediate beams, F_b and E are required. Appendix B gives several possible values for 24 F Douglas fir. The $\frac{1}{2}''$ laminae imply that this is a fairly high quality member, so it is not out of line to assume the stiffest E of 1,800,000 psi. This yields a C_k of

$$C_k = (0.956)\sqrt{\frac{1,800,000}{2400}} = 26.18$$

Since $10 < C_s < C_k$, this is an intermediate beam and F_b' is

$$F_b' = (2400)\left[1 - \left(\frac{1}{3}\right)\left(\frac{17.16}{26.18}\right)^4\right] = 2252\,\text{psi}$$

The beam is barely overstressed considering lateral stability, but check the extreme fiber allowable stress, for completeness.

The size factor, C_F, from Table 8.1, is 0.90. The curvature factor, C_c, for the region of curved laminae—which is also the region of highest bending stress—is calculated with Eq. 8.6.

$$C_c = 1 - (2000)\left(\frac{0.5}{50}\right)^2 = 0.80$$

The use is dry, so the CUF is 1.0, resulting in an allowable extreme fiber bending stress of

$$F_b = (2400\,\text{psi})(0.90)(0.80)(1.0) = 1728\,\text{psi}$$

This is smaller than the allowable stress controlled by lateral stability. This beam is significantly overstressed, according to the 1986 National Design Specification recommendations.

The radial stress is evaluated using Eq. 8.7, and is equal to

$$f_r = \frac{3M}{2Rbd} = \frac{(3)(2,400,000\,\text{in-lb})}{(2)(65\,\text{in})(30\,\text{in})(7\,\text{in})}$$

$$= 264\,\text{psi (tension)}$$

The applied bending moment decreases the curvature (increases the radius of curvature), or straightens the member. This makes the radial stress tension. In Douglas fir the allowable radial stress in tension is only 15 psi, so the beam is highly overstressed in radial tension at midspan. If it is essential to use this species and configuration, mechanical radial reinforcement must be added. This reinforcement could either be through-bolts or lag screws, sized to have sufficient capacity to handle all the radial forces.

5. Design a timber beam to carry two concentrated loads of 800 lb each, spaced 5 ft from each other, acting anywhere on a simply supported span of 20 ft. Allowable extreme fiber stress parallel to grain is 1500 psi, and allowable horizontal shear is 40 psi. Only 2×6, 2×8, 2×10, 2×12, and 2×14 nominal size boards are available. Any size beam may be built up using the available boards. Neglect the dead weight of the beam.

The basic design procedure is to evaluate the maximum bending moment and shear by moving the applied load. Dividing by the allowable stresses yields the required area and section modulus. Various combinations of boards are investigated, with the minimum area solution being the most economical.

The practicality of combining different size boards in one beam is somewhat suspect, and should only be done with caution. If the required number of boards turns out to be large, then the engineer should consider assembling them in more efficient configurations than stacked. An I beam or box beam, for instance, might be worth the effort in certain situations.

Since loads within a beam depth of a support are neglected when calculating shears, the maximum shear will occur when one of the loads is one beam depth from an end. The beam depth is an unknown at this point, but an assumption of 1 ft should not be too far from the eventual design.

The maximum shear, therefore, is

$$V_{max} = \frac{(800 \text{ lb})(19 \text{ ft}) + (800 \text{ lb})(14 \text{ ft})}{(20 \text{ ft})}$$
$$= 1320 \text{ lb}$$

Most structural handbooks include maximum moment formulas for two moving loads. The formula used depends on the load spacing relative to the beam length. The load spacing, a, is 5 ft. This is compared with a load spacing which separates beam behaviors.

$$(20 \text{ ft})(2 - \sqrt{2}) = 11.72 \text{ ft}$$

Since the actual spacing is less than the separating value, the following formula applies:

$$M_{max} = \left(\frac{P}{2L}\right)\left(L - \frac{a}{2}\right)^2$$
$$= \left[\frac{800 \text{ lb}}{(2)(20 \text{ ft})}\right]\left[20 \text{ ft} - \frac{5 \text{ ft}}{2}\right]^2 \left(12 \frac{\text{in}}{\text{ft}}\right)$$
$$= 73,500 \text{ in-lb}$$

To calculate the required area and section modulus, modify the allowable stresses first for actual conditions. Assume that the use conditions are dry and load duration is normal, since the problem statement mentions nothing to the contrary. The National Design Specification allows a 50% increase in allowable shear stress if the maximum shear force is evaluated in a systematic way. Given the very low allowable shear stress in this problem and the care spent in finding the maximum shear, this 50% increase is justifiable. The required section properties, therefore, are

$$A_{req'd} \geq \frac{(1.5)(1320 \text{ lb})}{(1.5)(40 \text{ psi})} = 33.0 \text{ in}^2$$
$$= bd$$

The upper 1.5 comes from Eq. 8.8, the lower is the 50% increase in allowable shear stress.

$$S_{req'd} \geq \frac{(73,500 \text{ in-lb})}{(1500 \text{ psi})} = 49.0 \text{ in}^3$$
$$= \frac{bd^2}{6}$$

Since a simple built-up beam will have a width that is a multiple of 1.5 inches, solve for the required depths for bending and shear at a range of potential widths.

b	3 in	4.5 in	6 in	7.5 in
d_V	11.0 in	7.33 in	5.5 in	4.4 in
d_M	9.9 in	8.08 in	7.0 in	6.26 in

Avoiding 2×14's as being too rare and expensive, the following combinations will provide the depths required:

two 2×12's   area = (2)(16.875) = 33.75 in²
three 2×10's   area = (3)(13.875) = 41.63 in²
four 2×8's   area = (4)(10.875) = 43.50 in²

Since lumber cost is largely a function of material volume, minimizing the cross-sectional area is a valid selection criterion. Therefore, use two 2×12's.

The problem statement does not include any mention of deflections, so they will be neglected. The beam designed is simple enough that more complicated, but efficient, configurations are not justifiable.

6. A 40 ft simple span, $6.75'' \times 30''$, 24F-V5 glulam beam (western species wood used in fabrication), braced laterally on 10 ft centers, normal load duration, dry use conditions, carries a dead load of 100 plf and a live load of 700 plf.

Determine: (a) section properties (include any size or form factors), (b) relevant tabulated allowable stresses, (c) design moment, shear, and reactions, (d) deflections under dead and total loads, with suggested camber, and (e) allowable moment, shear, and minimum support length.

(a) The member dimensions are actual. The section properties are, therefore,

$$A = (6.75)(30) = 202.5 \text{ in}^2$$

$$S = \frac{(6.75)(30)^2}{6} = 1012.5 \text{ in}^3$$

$$I = \frac{(6.75)(30)^3}{12} = 15,187.5 \text{ in}^4$$

$$C_F = 0.90 \text{ (see Table 8.1)}$$

(b) The member is loaded principally in bending about the X-X axis, so Appendix B gives the following allowable stresses:

$F_b = 2400$ psi (assume beam installed right-side up)

$F_{c\perp} = 650$ psi (support load is on lower, tension face)

$F_v = 155$ psi

$E = 1,700,000$ psi

(c)
$$M = \frac{wL^2}{8} = \frac{(800 \text{ plf})(40 \text{ ft})^2 \left(12 \frac{\text{in}}{\text{ft}}\right)}{8}$$
$$= 1,920,000 \text{ in-lb}$$

$$V = (800 \text{ plf}) \left(\frac{40 \text{ ft}}{2} - \frac{30 \text{ in}}{12 \frac{\text{in}}{\text{ft}}} \right)$$
$$= 14,000 \text{ lb}$$

Note that the load within a beam depth of a support was neglected when calculating the maximum shear.

$$R = \frac{(800 \text{ plf})(40 \text{ ft})}{2} = 16,000 \text{ lb}$$

(d)
$$D_{\max} = \frac{5wL^4}{384 EI}$$

$$D_{\text{dead}} = \frac{(5)(100 \text{ plf})(40 \text{ ft})^4 \left(1728 \frac{\text{in}^3}{\text{ft}^3}\right)}{(384)(15,187.5 \text{ in}^4)(1,700,000 \text{ psi})}$$
$$= 0.22 \text{ in}$$

$$D_{\text{live}} = (0.22 \text{ in}) \left(\frac{700 \text{ plf}}{100 \text{ plf}} \right) = 1.56 \text{ in}$$

For roof beam glulams, suggested camber is 150% of the dead load camber (AITC Table 4-25) or, $(1.5)(0.22) = 0.33$ in, say $\frac{3}{8}''$ at the centerline.

(e) The allowable bending stress will be governed by stability or fiber stress. First check stability.

$$\ell_e = 1.63\ell_u + 3d$$
$$= (1.63)(10 \text{ ft}) \left(12 \frac{\text{in}}{\text{ft}}\right) + (3)(30 \text{ in})$$
$$= 285.6 \text{ in, (case 2, Fig. 8.1)}$$

$$C_s = \sqrt{(285.6 \text{ in}) \left(\frac{30 \text{ in}}{(6.75 \text{ in})^2} \right)}$$
$$= 13.71$$

Since C_s is > 10, the beam is not short.

$$C_K = (0.956)\sqrt{\frac{1,700,000}{2400}}$$
$$= 25.44$$

C_s is less than C_K and greater than 10, so the beam is an intermediate one.

$$F_b' = (2400) \left[1 - \left(\frac{1}{3} \right) \left(\frac{13.71}{25.44} \right)^4 \right] = 2332 \text{ psi}$$

Now check fiber stress.

$$F_b = (0.90)(2400)$$
$$= 2160 \text{ psi}$$

Stress in the extreme fibers controls allowable bending stresses.

$$M_{\text{all}} = F_b S$$
$$= (2400 \text{ psi})(0.90)(1012.5 \text{ in}^3)$$
$$= 2,187,000 \text{ in-lb}$$

$$V_{\text{all}} = \frac{F_v A}{1.5} = (155 \text{ psi}) \left(\frac{202.5 \text{ in}^2}{1.5} \right)$$
$$= 20.925 \text{ lb} > 14,000 \text{ lb}$$

The beam is adequate in bending and shear stress considerations.

The required bearing length may be determined by trial and error or by solving explicitly for the minimum required length. This is done by equating the allowable and actual bearing stresses, both as functions of the bearing length, ℓ_b.

$$(650)\left(\frac{\ell_b + 0.375}{\ell_b}\right) = \frac{(16,000)}{6.75\,\ell_b}$$

The solution to this equation is $\ell_b = 3.27$ in.

Use a 3.5 inch bearing length.

7. Determine two acceptable S4S (surfaced 4 sides) sections for a sheltered 19 ft long column. The imposed design loads are a 4,000 pound axial snow load with a 3 inch eccentricity, and a 150 lb/ft uniform, transverse wind load. Assume a lateral support is provided at midspan, in a direction perpendicular to the transverse load only. The species and grade available provides these design properties:

$$F_c = 1300 \text{ psi}$$
$$F_b = 1600 \text{ psi (single use)}$$
$$E = 1,800,000 \text{ psi}$$

This beam-column is subjected to eccentric axial and transverse loads. Equation 6.12 is the interaction formula used to evaluate combined stress levels in this general case.

Both actual and allowable stresses will vary with member size. The design method, therefore, is an iterative process, with a minimum-size member as the goal. With snow and wind loadings, there are two load duration factors to consider. Design the column for the combined loading and check its capacity against the individual cases.

Making a good first size estimate can save time. Given the lateral bracing, look for sections roughly twice as deep as they are wide.

The maximum bending moment is

$$\left[(150 \text{ plf})\left(\frac{(19 \text{ ft})^2}{8}\right)\right]\left(12\,\frac{\text{in}}{\text{ft}}\right) + (4,000 \text{ lb})(3 \text{ in})$$
$$= 93,225 \text{ in-lb}$$

Note that the eccentricity has been conservatively assumed to create bending about the same axis as does the transverse loading.

Try a 6×10; 5.5″ × 9.5″, $A = 52.25$ in^2, $S = 82.729$ in^3 (Appendix E)

First, evaluate the actual stresses.

$$f_c = \frac{4000 \text{ lb}}{52.25 \text{ in}^2} = 76.6 \text{ psi}$$

$$f_b = \frac{93,225 \text{ in-lb}}{82.729 \text{ in}^3} = 1126.9 \text{ psi}$$

Assume the lateral support will brace the weak axis of buckling.

Next, establish the allowable stresses.

F_b: First consider lateral buckling.

$$\ell_e = 1.63\,\ell_u + 3d$$
$$= (1.63)\left(\frac{19 \text{ ft}}{2}\right)\left(12\,\frac{\text{in}}{\text{ft}}\right) + (3)(9.5 \text{ in})$$
$$= 214.3 \text{ in (see Fig. 8.1)}$$

The slenderness factor, C_s is

$$= \sqrt{\frac{(214.3 \text{ in})(9.5 \text{ in})}{(5.5 \text{ in})^2}}$$
$$= 8.20 < 10$$

Since C_s is less than 10, the beam-column acts as a short beam. This is often true for the beam action in a beam-column.

$$F_b' = (1.33)(1,600 \text{ psi}) = 2128 \text{ psi}$$

The 1.33 wind load duration factor comes from Table 3.1. Since the member is less than 12 inches deep, there is no size effect to consider.

F_c: Determine which axis controls in buckling.

strong axis: $\dfrac{\ell_e}{d} = (1.0)(19 \text{ ft})\left(\dfrac{12\,\frac{\text{in}}{\text{ft}}}{9.5 \text{ in}}\right) = 24.00$

weak axis: $\dfrac{\ell_e}{d} = (1.0)\left(\dfrac{19 \text{ ft}}{2}\right)\left(\dfrac{12\,\frac{\text{in}}{\text{ft}}}{5.5 \text{ in}}\right) = 20.74$

The 1.0 effective length factor is found in Table 6.1. Strong axis buckling controls in this member size. C_s is 24.00 in this case.

$$K = (0.671)\sqrt{\frac{1,800,000 \text{ psi}}{(1300 \text{ psi})(1.33)}}$$
$$= 21.65$$

Note that the 1.33 load duration factor applies only to the compression stress, not to the modulus of elasticity, in this equation. The K factor is a material property, so it need not be recalculated for any subsequent member sizes.

Since C_s is greater than K, the beam-column acts as a long column.

$$F_c' = \frac{(0.3)(1,800,000 \text{ psi})}{(24.00)^2}$$
$$= 937.5 \text{ psi}$$

$$J = 1.0$$

Substitute these values into the interaction equation (Eq. 6.12).

$$\frac{76.6 \text{ psi}}{937.5 \text{ psi}} \pm$$

$$\frac{1126.9 \text{ psi} + (76.6 \text{ psi})[6 + (1.5)(1.0)]\left(\dfrac{3 \text{ in}}{9.5 \text{ in}}\right)}{2128 \text{ psi} - (1.0)(76.6 \text{ psi})}$$

$$= 0.08 + 0.62 = 0.70 \ < \ 1.0$$

The 6×10 is adequate. As a check, the reader should perform a similar calculation for a 6×8. The interaction formula shows that that member would be 20% overloaded.

The second trial should be a 4 inch wide member. A 4×14 has a smaller area than the 6×10, but will be difficult to find in many places.

Try a 4×12; 3.5″×11.25″,

$$A = 39.375 \text{ in}^2 \quad S = 73.828 \text{ in}^3$$

Evaluate the actual stresses.

$$f_c = \frac{4000 \text{ lb}}{39.375 \text{ in}^2} = 101.6 \text{ psi}$$

$$f_b = \frac{93,225 \text{ in-lb}}{73.828 \text{ in}^3} = 1262.7 \text{ psi}$$

Establish the allowable stresses.

F_b: First consider lateral buckling.

The slenderness factor, C_s is

$$= \sqrt{\frac{(218.9 \text{ in})(11.25 \text{ in})}{(3.5 \text{ in})^2}} = 14.18 < 10$$

Since C_s is greater than 10, the beam-column is not a short beam.

$$C_k = (0.811)\sqrt{\frac{1,800,00}{(1.33)(1600)}} = 23.59$$

The beam-column acts as an intermediate beam.

$$F_b' = (1.33)(1,600 \text{ psi})\left[1 - \left(\frac{1}{3}\right)\left(\frac{14.18}{23.59}\right)^4\right]$$

$$= 2035.4 \text{ psi}$$

The 1.33 wind load duration factor comes from Table 3.1. Since the member is less than 12 inches deep, there is no size effect to consider.

F_c: Determine which axis controls in buckling.

strong axis: $\dfrac{\ell_e}{d} = (1.0)(19 \text{ ft})\left(\dfrac{\left(12 \frac{\text{in}}{\text{ft}}\right)}{11.25 \text{ in}}\right) = 20.27$

weak axis: $\dfrac{\ell_e}{d} = (1.0)\left(\dfrac{19 \text{ ft}}{2}\right)\left(\dfrac{\left(12 \frac{\text{in}}{\text{ft}}\right)}{3.5 \text{ in}}\right) = 32.57$

Weak axis buckling controls in this member size, and ℓ_e/d is 32.57. Since ℓ_e/d is greater than K, the beam-column acts as a long column.

$$F_c' = \frac{(0.3)(1,800,000 \text{ psi})}{(32.57)^2}$$

$$= 509.0 \text{ psi}$$

$$J = 1.0$$

Substitute these values into the interaction equation (Eq. 6.9).

$$\frac{101.6 \text{ psi}}{509.0 \text{ psi}} \pm$$

$$\frac{1262.7 \text{ psi} + (101.6 \text{ psi})[6 + (1.5)(1.0)]\left(\dfrac{3 \text{ in}}{11.25 \text{ in}}\right)}{2035.4 \text{ psi} - (1.0)(101.6 \text{ psi})}$$

$$= 0.20 + 0.76 = 0.96 < 1.0$$

The 4×12 is adequate, but a 4×8 would clearly be overloaded and is not worth checking.

Now consider the loads acting individually. Wind load alone would not control because the LDF would not change, but the moment and axial stresses would decrease. Nor will snow load alone control, because both sections behave as long columns, on which the LDF has no influence. Therefore, F_c' will be unchanged and only the moment will be decreased because the wind load is omitted.

Either a 4×12 or a 6×10 will satisfy the design requirements.

8. What is the reversible wind load capacity of the $\frac{1}{2}''$ diameter bolts in the brace shown?

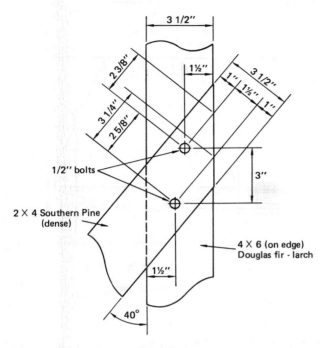

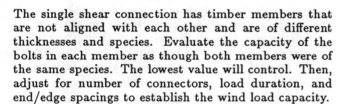

The single shear connection has timber members that are not aligned with each other and are of different thicknesses and species. Evaluate the capacity of the bolts in each member as though both members were of the same species. The lowest value will control. Then, adjust for number of connectors, load duration, and end/edge spacings to establish the wind load capacity.

First, check capacities as though both members were dense southern pine.

In the 4×6, the capacity is

$$\frac{\left(\frac{1}{2}\right)(1490 \text{ lb})(1010 \text{ lb})}{(1490 \text{ lb})[\sin^2(40°)] + (1010 \text{ lb})[\cos^2(40°)]} = 623 \text{ lb}$$

The $\frac{1}{2}$ accounts for single shear. Hankinson's formula was used with the values of Table 5.11 because the load is applied at 40° to the grain of the 4×6. The bolt actually has 5.5'' in the main member, but Table 5.11 has no value for a $\frac{1}{2}''$ bolt that long. The longest length included for a $\frac{1}{2}''$ bolt is 4'', which yields the values used above.

In the 2×4, the capacity is

$$\frac{1}{2}(1490 \text{ lb}) = 745 \text{ lb}$$

This value is for a length of $(2)(1.5 \text{ in}) = 3 \text{ in}$. The doubled thickness is used because this is the thinner member of the two.

Now check the capacities as though both members were Douglas fir-larch.

In the 4×6, the capacity is

$$\frac{\left(\frac{1}{2}\right)(1270 \text{ lb})(1010 \text{ lb})}{(1270 \text{ lb})[\sin^2(40°)] + (1010 \text{ lb})[\cos^2(40°)]} = 574 \text{ lb}$$

In the 2×4, the capacity is

$$\frac{1}{2}(1270 \text{ lb}) = 763 \text{ lb}$$

So far, the 574 lb capacity of the bolt in the 4×6 appears to control.

Check reductions for number of bolts. Table 5.6.A shows that there is no reduction in capacity for two bolts, no matter how they are arranged. The wind load duration factor of 1.33, from Table 3.1, will apply.

Now, check the spacings for any possible reduction of the connection capacity.

First check spacings in the 4×6. Establish whether the two bolts are considered as one two-bolt row or two one-bolt rows.

$$\begin{aligned} d &= 3\frac{1}{2} \text{ in} - 1\frac{1}{2} \text{ in} - 1\frac{1}{2} \text{ in} \\ &= \frac{1}{2} \text{ in} < \frac{3}{4} \text{ in} \\ &= \frac{3}{4} \text{ in} \\ &= \frac{s}{4} \end{aligned}$$

Therefore, the bolts are considered a single vertical row of two bolts in the 4×6. The bolt spacing in that row is 3 inches, which is equal to six bolt diameters—two more than the required four diameters.

The end distance is meaningless in the long 4×6. The edge distance is complicated by the 40° load angle. If the load were parallel with the grain, $1\frac{1}{2}$ diameters would be the required edge distance. If the load were perpendicular to the grain, four diameters would be required. One way to deal with a load angle between parallel and perpendicular is to apply the Hankinson formula to the edge distance.

$$\begin{aligned} \text{edge distance} &= \frac{(4 \text{ diameters})(1.5 \text{ diameters})}{(4)[\sin^2(40°)] + (1.5)[\cos^2(40°)]} \\ &= 2.37 \text{ diameters} \end{aligned}$$

The required edge distance is $(2.37)(0.5)$ inches = 1.18 inches, less than the 1.5 inches provided. Note that this edge distance is the loaded edge distance. It should be provided at both edges of the 4×6 with a wind load which can be expected to act in both directions.

Now, look at the spacings in the 2×4. First check whether the two bolts are two one-bolt rows, or one two-bolt row.

$$d = 1.5 \text{ in} > \frac{21}{32} \text{ in}$$
$$= \frac{2\frac{5}{8} \text{ in}}{4}$$
$$= \frac{s}{4}$$

The two bolts can be viewed as two rows of one bolt each. The required spacing between rows of bolts, with load parallel with the grain, is $1\frac{1}{2}$ diameters, or $\frac{3}{4}$ inch. The spacing provided is 1.5 inches, which is adequate.

With the load parallel with the grain, the edge distance should be 1.5 diameters, or 0.75 inch. The 1.0 inch provided is adequate.

The end distance required for full design capacity in tension is seven diameters, or 3.5 inches. Although the load is shown in tension, wind-induced forces can reverse direction. Neither bolt has this required end distance, but a linear reduction in capacity is allowed for less than the full end distance—so long as at least one-half the required distance is provided. Calculate the reduced capacity of the two bolts, considering their individual end distances.

$$(574 \text{ lb}) \left(\frac{3.25 \text{ in}}{3.5 \text{ in}} + \frac{2.375 \text{ in}}{3.5} \right) = 923 \text{ lb}$$

A case could be made for using the 745 lb capacity of the southern pine 2×4 as the basic capacity in the above equation. It is conservative to use the 574 lb, and it better accounts for the complex interaction between bolted members.

Finally, use the 1.33 load duration factor of Table 3.1 to find the wind load capacity for this connection.

$$(1.33)(922 \text{ lb}) = 1,230 \text{ lb}$$

9. An assembled lumber box beam is shown. What is the shear capacity of the section, considering load in the nails and stress in the lumber?

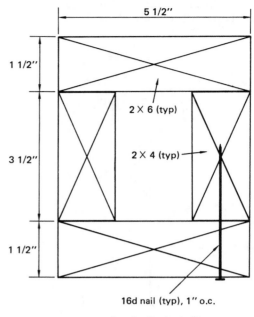

16d nail (typ), 1″ o.c.

Douglas fir - larch #1

A distinction will be drawn between shear stress and shear flow in the analysis of this section. Shear flow is the shear carried across a given plane anywhere in the section, irrespective of the width of that plane. The maximum shear stress in the lumber is almost always at the neutral axis, which means that two Q's will be calculated.

Both shear calculations require the section moment of inertia.

$$I = (2)(177.979 \text{ in}^4)$$
$$+ (2)(8.25 \text{ in}^2) \left(\frac{11\frac{1}{4} \text{ in}}{2} - \frac{1\frac{1}{2} \text{ in}}{2} \right)^2$$
$$+ (2)(1.547 \text{ in}^4)$$
$$= 751.18 \text{ in}^4$$

Appendix E gives the areas and moments of inertia used above. Note that the 2×6 used flat is the same as a 6×2 in Appendix E. The parallel axis theorem was used to account for the displacement of the 2×6 flanges from the beam's neutral axis. Symmetry dictates that the neutral axis is at the cross-sectional centerline.

The shear flow, q, is found with a form of the standard shear stress equation.

$$q = \frac{VQ}{I} = f_\text{v} t$$

Rearranging, $V_\text{all} = \dfrac{q_\text{all} I}{Q}$

The allowable shear flow is the product of the nail spacing and capacity.

$$q_{all} = \left[\dfrac{\left(\dfrac{1 \text{ nail}}{1\frac{1}{2} \text{ in}} \right)}{\text{side}} \right] (2 \text{ sides}) \left(108 \dfrac{\text{lb}}{\text{nail}} \right) = 144 \dfrac{\text{lb}}{\text{in}}$$

Table 5.1 shows Douglas fir to be a group II species. Table 5.4 gives the capacity for the group II species. Note that both lines of nails are included in the connection capacity.

Next, calculate the Q at the nail lines.

$$Q_{\text{nail line}} = (8.25 \text{ in}^2) \left(\dfrac{11\frac{1}{4} \text{ in}}{2} - \dfrac{1\frac{1}{2} \text{ in}}{2} \right)$$
$$= 40.22 \text{ in}^3$$

This quantity is simply the moment of the area of a 2×6 about the neutral axis.

Calculate the shear capacity, as limited by the nails.

$$(V_{all})_{\text{nail}} = \left(\dfrac{144 \text{ lb}}{\text{in}} \right) \left(\dfrac{751.18 \text{ in}^4}{40.22 \text{ in}^3} \right)$$
$$= 2690 \text{ lb}$$

The lumber shear stress evaluation takes into account the width of the plane at which the stresses are being calculated. Rearranging the standard equation gives the allowable shear capacity.

$$V_{all} = \dfrac{F_v I t}{Q_{max}}$$

The maximum Q is at the neutral axis. It will be equal to the Q found earlier, plus the two upper halves of the webs.

$$Q_{max} = (40.22 \text{ in}^3) + (2) \left(1\frac{1}{2} \text{ in} \right) \left(\dfrac{11\frac{1}{4} \text{ in}}{2} \right) \left(\dfrac{11\frac{1}{4} \text{ in}}{4} \right)$$
$$= 87.68 \text{ in}^3$$

Appendix B gives a F_v of 95 psi for Douglas fir-larch.

$$(V_{all})_{\text{wood}} = \dfrac{(9.5 \text{ psi}) (751.68 \text{ in}^4)(2)(15 \text{ in})}{87.68 \text{ in}^3}$$
$$= 2422 \text{ lb}$$

The wood shear capacity controls and limits the shear capacity of the assembled section to 2422 lb. The nail spacing could be increased in regions of the beam where the shear is reduced. While the NDS is vague on nail

spacings, past experience has shown the following practices to be adequate:

no. of nail diameters	pre-boring holes	no. pre-boring
∥ to grain	10	20
⊥ to grain	3	10
edge distance	5	5
end distance	10	20

The prebored holes should be no larger than 90% of the nail diameter in group I species, and no larger than 70% of the nail diameter in all others. The spacing and preboring are (barely) acceptable in this case.

10. Find the maximum allowable combined snow and dead loads on the 2×12 rafter shown. Determine the maximum notch depth allowed at the ends of the rafter. The deflection is to be limited to $L/180$. Use kiln-dried no. 2 southern pine.

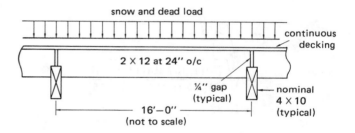

With a rafter this long, bending will most likely control the load capacity. Determine the capacity with bending stresses and check shear, bearing, and deflection.

Appendix B gives the following material properties:

$$F_b = 1500 \text{ psi (repetitive use)}$$
$$F_v = 95 \text{ psi}$$
$$E = 1,600,000 \text{ psi}$$
$$F_{c\perp} = 565 \text{ psi}$$

Table 3.1 yields a load duration factor of 1.15, which applies only to the bending and shear stresses, not to E or $F_{c\perp}$.

Appendix E gives the section properties for the 2×12.

The bending capacity is limited by the maximum moment.

$$w = \dfrac{F_b 8 S}{L^2}$$
$$= \dfrac{(1.15)(1,500 \text{ psi})(8)(31.641 \text{ in}^3) \left(\dfrac{\text{ft}}{12 \text{ in}} \right)}{(16 \text{ ft})^2}$$
$$= 142.1 \text{ lb/ft}$$

Check the bearing stress with an end reaction for this maximum load.

$$R = \left(142.1 \frac{\text{lb}}{\text{ft}}\right)\left(\frac{16 \text{ ft}}{2}\right)$$
$$= 1{,}137 \text{ lb}$$

Determine the bearing length provided.

$$\text{available } L_b = \frac{3.5 \text{ in} - 0.25 \text{ in}}{2}$$
$$= 1.625 \text{ in}$$
$$\text{actual } f_{c\perp} = \frac{1{,}315 \text{ lb}}{(1.625 \text{ in})(1.5 \text{ in})}$$
$$= 540 \text{ psi} < 565 \text{ psi allowable}$$

Determine the minimum required effective depth required at the ends of the rafter. Solve Eq. 8.9 for d'.

$$d' = \sqrt{\frac{3Vd}{2b_v}}$$
$$= \sqrt{\frac{(3)(1{,}137 \text{ lb})(11.25 \text{ in})}{(2)(1.5 \text{ in})(95 \text{ psi})(1.15)}}$$
$$= 10.82 \text{ in}$$

This minimum required depth means the maximum allowable notch depth is $\frac{3}{8}''$.

Check the deflection.

$$Y_{\max} = \frac{5wL^4}{384EI}$$
$$= \frac{(5)\left(142.1 \frac{\text{lb}}{\text{ft}}\right)(16 \text{ ft})^4 \left(1728 \frac{\text{in}^3}{\text{ft}^3}\right)}{(384)(1{,}600{,}000 \text{ psi})(177.979 \text{ in}^4)}$$
$$= 0.74 \text{ in}$$

This deflection is converted into a fraction of the span.

$$\frac{(16 \text{ ft})\left(12 \frac{\text{in}}{\text{ft}}\right)}{0.74 \text{ in}} = 256$$

The deflection is equal to $L/259 < L/180 =$ maximum allowable total deflection.

Bending limits the snow and dead load to 142.1 lb/ft. This load per length of beam is converted to an equivalent distributed load.

$$\frac{142.1 \frac{\text{lb}}{\text{ft}}}{2 \text{ ft on center}} = 71 \text{ psf}$$

There are at least two further refinements possible in this problem. The span could be decreased from the assumed center-to center of the 4×12 beams. The span could be justified as the face-to-face clear distance between the 4×12's, plus the distance to the centers of bearing area required to handle the actual reactions. The shear could be further reduced by neglecting the distributed load within a 2×12 beam depth of the supporting 4×12's. Neither of these refinements would have much effect. Given the unpredictable behavior of notched beams, conservatively neglecting these effects is reasonable.

11. For the illustration shown, design timber formwork and shoring to support the 9 inch concrete slab. Establish (a) reasonable joist spacing (check plywood), (b) reasonable stringer spacing (check joists), (c) reasonable shore spacing (check stringers), and check (d) shore capacity, and (e) bearing stresses, and make any required recommendations.

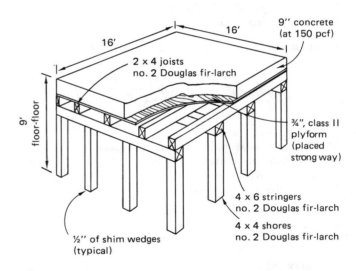

The live load (in addition to concrete) = 50 psf (no motorized buggies). Limit all deflections to $\ell/360$. Assume standard concrete (150 pcf).

Calculate the applied loads.

$$\text{concrete}: \left(150\frac{\text{lb}}{\text{ft}^3}\right)(9 \text{ in})\left(\frac{\text{ft}}{12 \text{ in}}\right) = 113 \text{ psf}$$
$$\text{live load} = 50 \text{ psf}$$
$$\text{(estimated) dead load} = 4 \text{ psf}$$
$$\text{total} = 167 \text{ psf}$$

(a) In order to establish joist spacing, check plywood for shear, bending, and deflection.

From Table 9.2, class II plyform is group III species. From Table 9.1 (sanded), S-2 stress level.

Assume that the plyform is supported the strong way (8 ft side crosses joists) and the plyform will be continuous over (at least) three spans (four joists).

The rolling shear stress is

$$F_s = (44 \text{ psi})(1.25)(1.3) = 71.5 \text{ psi}$$

The 44 psi comes from Table 9.4, assuming wet conditions. The 1.25 is the 7-day load duration factor, from Table 3.1. The 1.3 is an *experience factor*, recommended by the APA, used to adjust allowable stresses in plywood used in concrete forms.

$$f_s = V\left(\frac{Q}{Ib}\right)$$

and

$$V_{max} = 0.60\,W\ell \quad \text{(3-span case)}$$

Rearranging,

$$\ell_{\text{rolling shear}} = \frac{F_s\left(\dfrac{Ib}{Q}\right)}{W(0.60)}$$

$$= \frac{\left(71.5\,\dfrac{\text{lb}}{\text{in}^2}\right)\left(6.762\,\dfrac{\text{in}^2}{\text{ft}}\right)}{\left(\dfrac{167\,\dfrac{\text{lb}}{\text{ft}}}{\text{ft}}\right)(0.60)}$$

$$= 4.83 \text{ ft } (57.9 \text{ in})$$

The (Ib/Q) is found in Table 9.1.

Calculate the allowable bending stress in the plyform.

$$F_b = (820 \text{ psi})(1.25)(1.30) = 1332 \text{ psi}$$

The 820 psi is the wet conditions value from Table 9.4. The 1.25 load duration factor is from Table 3.1. The 1.3 is the APA experience factor for plywood in concrete forms.

$$f_b = \frac{M}{S} = \frac{0.10\,W\ell^2}{S}$$

(at internal supports, 3-span case)

Rearranging,

$$\ell_{\text{bending}} = \sqrt{\frac{F_b S}{0.10\,W}}$$

$$= \sqrt{\frac{\left(1332\,\dfrac{\text{lb}}{\text{in}^2}\right)\left(0.412\,\dfrac{\text{in}^3}{\text{ft}}\right)}{(0.10)\left(\dfrac{167\,\dfrac{\text{lb}}{\text{ft}}}{\text{ft}}\right)\left(\dfrac{\text{ft}}{12 \text{ in}}\right)}}$$

$$= 19.86 \text{ in}$$

The 0.412 in³/ft is found in Table 9.1.

Calculate plyform deflection.

$E = 1,100,000$ psi (from Table 9.4, wet conditions, no experience nor load duration factors)

$$\text{deflection}_{max} = \frac{W\ell^4}{145EI} \quad \text{(at } 0.446\,\ell \text{ from ends of 3-span case)}$$

Setting $\text{deflection}_{max} = \ell/360$ and rearranging,

$$\ell_{\text{deflection}} = \sqrt[3]{\frac{145EI}{360W}}$$

$$= \sqrt[3]{\frac{(145)\left(1,100,000\,\dfrac{\text{lb}}{\text{in}^2}\right)\left(0.197\,\dfrac{\text{in}^4}{\text{ft}}\right)}{(360)\left(\dfrac{167\,\dfrac{\text{lb}}{\text{ft}}}{\text{ft}}\right)\left(\dfrac{\text{ft}}{12 \text{ in}}\right)}}$$

$$= 18.44 \text{ in}$$

Note that the APA suggests calculating separate shear and bending deflection components, using an adjusted modulus of elasticity.

Plyform deflection controls, and limits joist spacing to 18.44 in.

For convenience, space 2×4 joists at 16″ o/c.

(b) To establish reasonable stringer spacing, check supported joist for F_v, F_b, and deflection.

$$\text{joist loading} = (167 \text{ psf})\left(\frac{16 \text{ in o/c}}{12\,\dfrac{\text{in}}{\text{ft}}}\right) = 223\,\frac{\text{lb}}{\text{ft}}$$

The allowable stress is from Appendix B and the 1.25 LDF is from Table 3.1.

$$F_v = (95 \text{ psi})(1.25) = 118.8 \text{ psi}$$

Note that Hurd recommends further increasing the allowable shear by 50%, when designing concrete forms. He calls this a *two-beam factor*, referencing a phenomenon (semi) described in Appendix E of the NDS. The author mentions this justifiable maneuver, but does not use it in this solution.

$$f_v = \frac{3V}{2A} \quad \text{and} \quad V_{max} = 0.6\,W\ell \quad \text{(3-span case)}$$

Rearranging,

$$\ell_{\text{shear}} = \frac{F_v 2A}{(3)(0.6W)}$$

$$= \frac{\left(118.8\,\dfrac{\text{lb}}{\text{in}^2}\right)(2)(5.25 \text{ in}^2)}{(3)(0.6)\left(223\,\dfrac{\text{lb}}{\text{ft}}\right)}$$

$$= 3.11 \text{ ft } (37.3 \text{ in})$$

The single member allowable bending stress is

$$F_b = (1450 \text{ psi})(1.15) = 1812 \text{ psi}$$

The single member allowable stress from Appendix B is justified in concrete forms because all the joists are loaded at once by a heavy fluid, so that load sharing really does not contribute so markedly to the system capacity. The 1.25 is the Table 3.1 LDF.

$$\ell_{\text{bending}} = \sqrt{\frac{F_b S}{(0.10)W}}$$
$$= \sqrt{\frac{\left(1812.5 \frac{\text{lb}}{\text{in}^2}\right)(3.063 \text{ in}^3)}{(0.10)\left(223 \frac{\text{lb}}{\text{ft}}\right)\left(\frac{\text{ft}}{12 \text{ in}}\right)}}$$
$$= 54.66 \text{ in}$$

The deflection limits the span as follows:

$$E = 1,700,000 \text{ psi}$$

$$\ell_{\text{deflection}} = \sqrt[3]{\frac{145EI}{360W}}$$
$$= \sqrt[3]{\frac{(145)\left(1,700,000 \frac{\text{lb}}{\text{in}^2}\right)(5.359 \text{ in}^4)}{(360)\left(223 \frac{\text{lb}}{\text{ft}}\right)\left(\frac{\text{ft}}{12 \text{ in}}\right)}}$$
$$= 58.23 \text{ in}$$

Shear controls the joist span and appears to limit it to 37″. The author, however, would space the stringers at 48″ o/c. Using the 48 inch spacing, in spite of the shear stress involved, is justifiable in view of the following:

The shear was calculated in c-c spacing; clear, face-face, span reduces the shear. Furthermore, loads within a beam depth of the supports may be neglected when calculating shear stresses.

The resultant, adjusted shear stress is

$$\left(\frac{3}{2}\right)\left[\frac{\left(223 \frac{\text{lb}}{\text{ft}}\right)\left(\frac{48 \text{ in} - 3\frac{1}{2} \text{ in} - (2)\left(3\frac{1}{2} \text{ in}\right)}{(2)\left(12 \frac{\text{in}}{\text{ft}}\right)}\right)}{5.25 \text{ in}^2}\right] = 99.6 \text{ psi}$$

Thus, the extra attention paid to calculating shear stresses permits using the 48″ stringer spacing, without involving Hurd's two-beam factor.

(c) To establish shore spacing, check the allowable stringer span.

$$\text{stringer loading} = (48 \text{ in})\left(\frac{\text{ft}}{12 \text{ in}}\right)(167 \text{ psf}) = 668 \frac{\text{lb}}{\text{ft}}$$

The allowable shear is

$$F_v = (95 \text{ psi})(1.25) = 118.8 \text{ psi}$$

(see Appendix B and Table 3.1)

$$\ell_{\text{shear}} = \frac{F_v 2A}{(3)(0.6)W}$$
$$= \frac{\left(118.8 \frac{\text{lb}}{\text{in}^2}\right)(2)(19.25 \text{ in}^2)}{(3)(0.6)\left(668 \frac{\text{lb}}{\text{ft}}\right)}$$
$$= 3.80 \text{ ft}$$

The allowable bending stress in the stringer is

$$F_b = (1250 \text{ psi})(1.25) = 1562 \text{ psi}$$

Again, the single use allowable stress is used from Appendix B with the LDF from Table 3.1.

$$\ell_{\text{bending}} = \sqrt{\frac{F_b s}{0.10W}}$$
$$= \sqrt{\frac{\left(1562 \frac{\text{lb}}{\text{in}^2}\right)(17.646 \text{ in}^3)}{(0.10)\left(668 \frac{\text{lb}}{\text{ft}}\right)\left(\frac{\text{ft}}{12 \text{ in}}\right)}}$$
$$= 70.37 \text{ in}$$

The deflection limits the span as follows:

$$E = 1,200,000 \text{ psi}$$

(Note: no LDF used on E)

$$\ell_{\text{deflection}} = \sqrt[3]{\frac{145EI}{360W}}$$
$$= \sqrt[3]{\frac{(145)\left(1,700,000 \frac{\text{lb}}{\text{in}^2}\right)(48.526 \text{ in}^4)}{(360)\left(668 \frac{\text{lb}}{\text{ft}}\right)\left(\frac{\text{ft}}{12 \text{ in}}\right)}}$$
$$= 84.20 \text{ in}$$

Again, shear controls and limits stringer span (or shore spacing) to 3.80′. Again, adjusted shear stress calculations would justify stretching to the recommended and convenient 48″ o/c.

(d) Check the shore capacity for the applied load.

$$\text{shore load} = (4 \text{ ft})(4 \text{ ft})(167 \text{ psf}) = 2672 \text{ lb}$$

The shore's capacity is established by evaluating it as a solid column.

$$
\begin{array}{rll}
\text{length} = & 9'\text{-}0'' & \text{floor-floor} \\
& 8'' & \text{slab} \\
& \frac{3}{4}'' & \text{plyform} \\
& 3\frac{1}{2}'' & 2\times4 \text{ joist} \\
& 5\frac{1}{2}'' & 4\times6 \text{ stringer} \\
& \frac{1}{2}'' & \text{shims and wedges} \\
\hline
& 89.75'' & \text{say } 90'' \text{ length}
\end{array}
$$

Therefore,

$$\frac{\ell_e}{d} = \frac{(1.0)(90 \text{ in})}{(3.5 \text{ in})}$$

$$= 25.71 \ (> 11; \text{ not short column})$$

$$K = 0.671\sqrt{\frac{E}{F_c}}$$

$$= 0.671\sqrt{\frac{1,700,000 \text{ psi}}{(1050 \text{ psi})(1.25)}}$$

$$= 24.15 > K; \text{ long column}$$

$$F'_c = \frac{0.3E}{\left(\frac{\ell_e}{d}\right)^2}$$

$$= \frac{(0.30)(1,700,000 \text{ psi})}{(25.71)^2}$$

$$= 771.3 \text{ psi}$$

The shore's capacity, then, is

$$F'_c \times A = 771.3 \text{ psi} \times 12.25 \text{ in}^2$$

$$= 9450 \text{ lb} \gg 2672 \text{ lb}$$

Therefore, the 4×4 shores are adequate on a 4 ft grid pattern.

(e) Check the bearing stresses at joints.

At shore-stringer,

$$f_B = \frac{2672 \text{ lb}}{12.25 \text{ in}^2}$$

$$= 213 < F_{c\perp}$$

$$= 625 \text{ psi}$$

Note that the duration of load factor is not applied to bearing, or compression perpendicular to the grain, stresses. This is a deflection-defined allowable stress, not capacity-restrained.

At stringer-joist,

$$f_B = \frac{(1.1)\left(223 \frac{\text{lb}}{\text{ft}}\right)(4 \text{ ft})}{(1.5 \text{ in})(3.5 \text{ in})}$$

$$= 186.9 \text{ psi} < 625 \text{ psi}$$

The 2×4 joists can be spaced at 16″ o/c, the 4×6 stringers at 4′ o/c, and the 4×4 shores at 4′ o/c. The bearing stresses involved are low enough that no special bearing pads are required.

Appendix A
End Grain In Bearing

Design values for end-grain bearing parallel to grain on a rigid surface F_g
in pounds per square inch

Species	Wet service conditions[1]	Dry service conditions[1]		Glued laminated timber
		Sawn lumber[2]		
		More than 4" thick	Not more than 4" thick[3]	
Ash, Commercial White	1370	1510	2060	2400
Aspen	740	820	1110	1300
Balsam Fir	1140	1250	1710	1990
Beech	1190	1310	1780	2080
Birch, Sweet and Yellow	1150	1260	1720	2010
Black Cottonwood	620	690	930	1090
California Redwood	1560	1720	2270	2620
California Redwood, Open grain	1150	1270	1670	1940
Coast Sitka Spruce	950	1040	1420	1660
Coast Species	950	1040	1420	1660
Cottonwood, Eastern	760	840	1150	1340
Douglas Fir - Larch (Dense)[4]	1570	1730	2360	2750
Douglas Fir - Larch[4]	1340	1480	2020	2350
Douglas Fir South	1220	1340	1820	2130
Eastern Hemlock - Tamarack[4]	1150	1270	1730	2020
Eastern Hemlock	1140	1260	1710	2000
Eastern Softwoods	890	980	1340	1560
Eastern Spruce	890	980	1340	1560
Eastern White Pine[4]	900	1000	1360	1580
Eastern Woods	740	820	1110	1300
Engelmann Spruce - Alpine Fir	810	890	1220	1420
Hem - Fir[4]	1110	1220	1670	1940
Hickory and Pecan	1370	1510	2050	2400
Idaho White Pine	930	1020	1390	1630
Lodgepole Pine	970	1060	1450	1690
Maple, Black and Sugar	1140	1260	1710	2000
Mountain Hemlock	1070	1170	1600	1870
Mountain Hemlock - Hem Fir	1070	1170	1600	1870
Northern Aspen	740	810	1110	1290
Northern Pine	1040	1150	1570	1830
Northern Species	880	970	1320	1540
Northern White Cedar	740	810	1110	1290
Oak, Red and White	1060	1160	1590	1850
Ponderosa Pine - Sugar Pine	910	1000	1370	1600
Red Pine	880	970	1320	1540
Sitka Spruce	990	1090	1480	1730
Southern Cypress	1330	1460	1990	2320
Southern Pine (Dense)	1540	1690	2310	2690
Southern Pine	1320	1450	1970	2300
Spruce - Pine - Fir	940	1040	1410	1650
Sweetgum and Tupelo	1020	1120	1530	1780
Virginia Pine - Pond Pine	1270	1390	1900	2220
Western Cedars[4]	1040	1140	1520	1750
Western Hemlock	1240	1360	1860	2170
Western White Pine	930	1030	1400	1630
White Woods (Western Woods)	810	890	1220	1420
West Coast Woods (Mixed Species)	810	890	1220	1420
Yellow Poplar	890	980	1340	1560

1. Wet and dry service conditions are defined in 4.1.4 for sawn lumber and 5.1.5 for glued laminated timber.

2. Applies to sawn lumber members which are at a moisture content of 19 percent or less when full design load is applied, regardless of moisture content at time of manufacture.

3. When 4 inch or thinner sawn lumber is surfaced at a moisture content of 15 percent or less and is used under dry service conditions, the values listed for glued laminated timber may be applied.

4. Values also apply when species name includes the designation "North."

Reproduced from National Design Specification for Wood Construction, 1986 Edition, with permission from National Forest Products Association, Washington, D.C.

Appendix B
Allowable Unit Stresses

SPECIES AND COMMERCIAL GRADE	SIZE CLASSIFI-CATION	ALLOWABLE UNIT STRESSES IN POUNDS PER SQUARE INCH							U.B.C. STDS UNDER WHICH GRADED
		EXTREME FIBER IN BENDING F_b		Tension Parallel to Grain F_t	Horizontal Shear F_v	Compression perpendicular to Grain $F_c\perp$ [21]	Compression Parallel to Grain F_c	MODULUS OF ELASTICITY E [21]	
		Single-member Uses	Repetitive-member Uses						
DOUGLAS FIR – LARCH (Surfaced dry or surfaced green. Used at 19% max. m.c.)									
DOUGLAS FIR – LARCH (North)									
Dense Select Structural		2450	2800	1400	95	730	1850	1,900,000	
Select Structural		2100	2400	1200	95	625	1600	1,800,000	
Dense No. 1		2050	2400	1200	95	730	1450	1,900,000	
No. 1	2″ to 4″	1750	2050	1050	95	625	1250	1,800,000	
Dense No. 2	thick	1700	1950	1000	95	730	1150	1,700,000	
No. 2	2″ to 4″	1450	1650	850	95	625	1000	1,700,000	
No. 3	wide	800	925	475	95	625	600	1,500,000	25-2
Appearance		1750	2050	1050	95	625	1500	1,800,000	25-3
Stud		800	925	475	95	625	600	1,500,000	and
Construction	2″ to 4″	1050	1200	625	95	625	1150	1,500,000	25-4
Standard	thick	600	675	350	95	625	925	1,500,000	(See footnotes
Utility	4″ wide	275	325	175	95	625	600	1,500,000	2 through 9, 11, 13,
Dense Select Structural		2100	2400	1400	95	730	1650	1,900,000	15 and 16)
Select Structural		1800	2050	1200	95	625	1400	1,800,000	
Dense No. 1	2″ to 4″	1800	2050	1200	95	730	1450	1,900,000	
No. 1	thick	1500	1750	1000	95	625	1250	1,800,000	
Dense No. 2	5″ and	1450	1700	775	95	730	1250	1,700,000	
No. 2	wider	1250	1450	650	95	625	1050	1,700,000	
No. 3 and Stud		725	850	375	95	625	675	1,500,000	
Appearance		1500	1750	1000	95	625	1500	1,800,000	

SPECIES AND COMMERCIAL GRADE	SIZE CLASSIFICATION	F_b Single	F_b Repetitive	F_t	F_v	$F_c\perp$	F_c	E	U.B.C. STDS
Dense Select Structural		1900	—	1100	85	730	1300	1,700,000	
Select Structural	Beams and	1600	—	950	85	625	1100	1,600,000	
Dense No. 1	Stringers [12]	1550	—	775	85	730	1100	1,700,000	
No. 1		1300	—	675	85	625	925	1,600,000	25-3
Dense Select Structural		1750	—	1150	85	730	1350	1,700,000	(See footnotes
Select Structural	Posts and	1500	—	1000	85	625	1150	1,600,000	2 through 9)
Dense No. 1	Timbers [12]	1400	—	950	85	730	1200	1,700,000	
No. 1		1200	—	825	85	625	1000	1,600,000	
Select Dex	Decking	1750	2000	—	—	625	—	1,800,000	
Commercial Dex		1450	1650	—	—	625	—	1,700,000	
Dense Select Structural		1850	—	1100	85	730	1300	1,700,000	
Select Structural	Beams and	1600	—	950	85	625	1100	1,600,000	
Dense No. 1	Stringers [12]	1550	—	775	85	730	1100	1,700,000	
No. 1		1350	—	675	85	625	925	1,600,000	
Dense No. 2		1000	—	500	85	730	700	1,400,000	
No. 2		875	—	425	85	625	600	1,300,000	25-4
Dense Select Structural		1750	—	1150	85	730	1350	1,700,000	(See footnotes
Select Structural	Posts and	1500	—	1000	85	625	1150	1,600,000	2 through 10)
Dense No. 1	Timbers [12]	1400	—	950	85	730	1200	1,700,000	
No. 1		1200	—	825	85	625	1000	1,600,000	
Dense No. 2		800	—	550	85	730	550	1,400,000	
No. 2		700	—	475	85	625	475	1,300,000	
Selected Decking	Decking	—	2000	—	—	—	—	1,800,000	
Commercial Decking		—	1650	—	—	—	—	1.700,000	
Selected Decking	Decking	—	2150	(Surfaced at 15% max. m.c. and				1,900,000	
Commercial Decking		—	1800	used at 15% max. m.c.)				1,700,000	

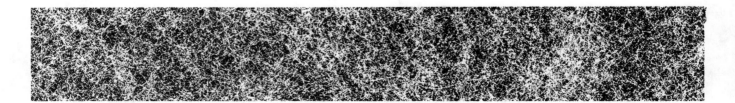

Appendix B (continued)
Allowable Unit Stresses

SPECIES AND COMMERCIAL GRADE	SIZE CLASSIFI-CATION	ALLOWABLE UNIT STRESSES IN POUNDS PER SQUARE INCH							U.B.C. STDS UNDER WHICH GRADED
		EXTREME FIBER IN BENDING F_b		Tension Parallel to Grain F_t	Horizontal Shear F_v	Compression perpendicular to Grain $F_c\perp$ 21	Compression Parallel to Grain F_c	MODULUS OF ELASTICITY E 21	
		Single-member Uses	Repetitive-member Uses						
Select Structural No. 1	Beams and Stringers	1600 1300	— —	950 675	85 85	625 625	1100 925	1,600,000 1,600,000	
Select Structural No. 1	Posts and Timbers	1500 1200	— —	1000 825	85 85	625 625	1150 1000	1,600,000 1,600,000	25-2 (See footnotes 2 through 9 and 11)
Select Commercial	Decking	1750 1450	2000 1650	— —	— —	625 625	— —	1,800,000 1,700,000	
DOUGLAS FIR SOUTH (Surfaced dry or surfaced green. Used at 19% max. m.c.)									
Select Structural No. 1 & Appearance No. 2 No. 3 Stud	2" to 4" thick 2" to 4" wide	2000 1700 1400 775 775	2300 1950 1600 875 875	1150 975 825 450 450	90 90 90 90 90	520 520 520 520 520	1400 1150 900 550 550	1,400,000 1,400,000 1,300,000 1,100,000 1,100,000	
Construction Standard Utility	2" to 4" thick 4" wide	1000 550 275	1150 650 300	600 325 150	90 90 90	520 520 520	1000 850 550	1,100,000 1,100,000 1,100,000	25-4 (See footnotes 2 through 10, 13, 15 and 16)
Select Structural No. 1 & Appearance No. 2 No. 3 and Stud	2" to 4" thick 5" and wider	1700 1450 1200 700	1950 1650 1350 800	1150 975 625 350	90 90 90 90	520 520 520 520	1250 1150 950 600	1,400,000 1,400,000 1,300,000 1,100,000	
Select Structural No. 1 No. 2	Beams and Stringers	1550 1300 825	— — —	900 625 425	85 85 85	520 520 520	1000 850 525	1,200,000 1,200,000 1,000,000	
Select Structural No. 1 No. 2	Posts and Timbers	1400 1150 650	— — —	950 775 400	85 85 85	520 520 520	1050 925 425	1,200,000 1,200,000 1,000,000	25-4 (See footnotes 2 through 10, 13, 15 and 16)
Selected Decking Commercial Decking	Decking	— —	1900 1600	— —	— —	— —	— —	1,400,000 1,300,000	
Selected Decking Commercial Decking	Decking	— —	2050 1750	(Stresses for Decking apply at 15% moisture content)				1,500,000 1,300,000	

Reproduced from the 1988 Edition of the Uniform Building Code, copyright © 1988, with the permission of the publishers, the International Conference of Building Officials.

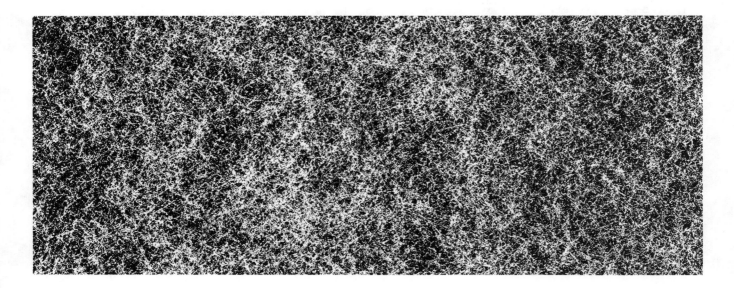

Appendix B (continued)
Allowable Unit Stresses

SPECIES AND COMMERCIAL GRADE	SIZE CLASSIFICATION	ALLOWABLE UNIT STRESSES IN POUNDS PER SQUARE INCH							
		EXTREME FIBER IN BENDING F_b		Tension Parallel to Grain F_t	Horizontal Shear F_v	Compression perpendicular to Grain $F_{c\perp}$ [21]	Compression Parallel to Grain F_c	MODULUS OF ELASTICITY E [21]	U.B.C. STDS UNDER WHICH GRADED
		Single-member Uses	Repetitive-member Uses						
SOUTHERN PINE (Surfaced at 15% moisture content, K.D. Used at 15% max. m.c.)									
Select Structural		2150	2500	1250	105	565	1800	1,800,000	
Dense Select Structural		2500	2900	1500	105	660	2100	1,900,000	
No. 1		1850	2100	1050	105	565	1450	1,800,000	
No. 1 Dense	2″ to 4″	2150	2450	1250	105	660	1700	1,900,000	
No. 2	thick	1550	1750	900	95	565	1150	1,600,000	
No. 2 Dense	2″ to 4″	1800	2050	1050	95	660	1350	1,700,000	
No. 3	wide	850	975	500	95	565	675	1,500,000	
No. 3 Dense		1000	1150	575	95	660	800	1,500,000	
Stud		850	975	500	95	565	675	1,500,000	25-6 (See footnotes 3, 4, 9, 13, 15, 16, 18 and 19)
Construction	2″ to 4″	1100	1250	650	105	565	1300	1,500,000	
Standard	thick	625	725	375	95	565	1050	1,500,000	
Utility	4″ wide	275	300	175	95	565	675	1,500,000	
Select Structural		1850	2150	1200	95	565	1600	1,800,000	
Dense Select Structural		2200	2500	1450	95	660	1850	1,900,000	
No. 1		1600	1850	1050	95	565	1450	1,800,000	
No. 1 Dense	2″ to 4″	1850	2150	1250	95	660	1700	1,900,000	
No. 2	thick	1300	1500	675	95	565	1200	1,600,000	
No. 2 Dense	5″ and	1550	1750	800	95	660	1400	1,700,000	
No. 3	wider	750	875	400	95	565	725	1,500,000	
No. 3 Dense		875	1000	450	95	660	850	1,500,000	
Stud		800	900	400	95	565	725	1,500,000	

SPECIES AND COMMERCIAL GRADE	SIZE CLASSIFICATION	Single-member Uses	Repetitive-member Uses	Tension Parallel F_t	Horizontal Shear F_v	Compression perp. $F_{c\perp}$	Compression Parallel F_c	MODULUS OF ELASTICITY E	U.B.C. STDS
Dense Standard Decking	2″ to 4″	2150	2450	1250	105	660	1700	1,900,000	
Select Decking	thick	1550	1750	900	95	565	1150	1,600,000	
Dense Select Decking	2″ and wider	1800	2050	1050	95	660	1350	1,700,000	
Commercial Decking	Decking	1550	1750	900	95	565	1150	1,600,000	25-6 (See footnotes 4 9, 15, 16, 18 and 19)
Dense Commercial Decking		1800	2050	1050	95	660	1350	1,700,000	
Dense Structural 86	2″ to 4″	2800	3250	1900	165	660	2300	1,900,000	
Dense Structural 72	thick	2400	2750	1600	135	660	1950	1,900,000	
Dense Structural 65		2150	2450	1450	125	660	1750	1,900,000	
KD-15 or MC-15									
Industrial 86 KD		2400	2750	1600	160	415	1950	1,800,000	
Dense Ind. 86 KD		2800	3250	1900	160	475	2300	1,900,000	
Industrial 72 KD	1″ to 4″ thick	2050	2350	1350	135	415	1650	1,800,000	
Dense Ind. 72 KD		2400	2750	1600	135	475	1950	1,900,000	
Industrial 65 KD		1850	2100	1200	125	415	1500	1,800,000	
Dense Ind. 65 KD		2150	2450	1400	125	475	1750	1,900,000	
SOUTHERN PINE (Surfaced dry. Used at 19% max. m.c.)									
Select Structural		2000	2300	1150	100	565	1550	1,700,000	
Dense Select Structural		2350	2700	1350	100	660	1800	1,800,000	
No. 1	2″ to 4″	1700	1950	1000	100	565	1250	1,700,000	
No. 1 Dense	thick	2000	2300	1150	100	660	1450	1,800,000	
No. 2	2″ to 4″	1400	1650	825	90	565	975	1,600,000	
No. 2 Dense	wide	1650	1900	975	90	660	1150	1,600,000	
No. 3		775	900	450	90	565	575	1,400,000	
No. 3 Dense		925	1050	525	90	660	675	1,500,000	
Stud		775	900	450	90	565	575	1,400,000	25-6 (See footnotes 2 4, 9, 13, 15, 16, 18 and 19)
Construction	2″ to 4″	1000	1150	600	100	565	1100	1,400,000	
Standard	thick	575	675	350	90	565	900	1,400,000	
Utility	4″ wide	275	300	150	90	565	575	1,400,000	
Select Structural		1750	2000	1150	90	565	1350	1,700,000	
Dense Select Structural		2050	2350	1300	90	660	1600	1,800,000	
No. 1	2″ to 4″	1450	1700	975	90	565	1250	1,700,000	
No. 1 Dense	thick	1700	2000	1150	90	660	1450	1,800,000	
No. 2	5″ and	1200	1400	625	90	565	1000	1,600,000	
No. 2 Dense	wider	1400	1650	725	90	660	1200	1,600,000	
No. 3		700	800	350	90	565	625	1,400,000	
No. 3 Dense		825	925	425	90	660	725	1,500,000	
Stud		725	850	350	90	565	625	1,400,000	

Appendix B (continued)
Allowable Unit Stresses

SPECIES AND COMMERCIAL GRADE	SIZE CLASSIFICATION	ALLOWABLE UNIT STRESSES IN POUNDS PER SQUARE INCH							U.B.C. STDS. UNDER WHICH GRADED
		EXTREME FIBER IN BENDING F_b		Tension Parallel to Grain F_t	Horizontal Shear F_v	Compression Perpendicular to Grain $F_c\perp$21	Compression Parallel to Grain F_c	MODULUS OF ELASTICITY E 21	
		Single-member Uses	Repetitive-member Uses						
Dense Standard Decking	2" to 4" thick	2000	2300	1150	100	660	1450	1,800,000	25-6 (See footnotes 3, 4, 9, 13, 15, 16, 17, 18 and 19)
Select Decking		1400	1650	825	90	565	975	1,600,000	
Dense Select Decking	2" and wider	1650	1900	975	90	660	1150	1,600,000	
Commercial Decking	Decking	1400	1650	825	90	565	975	1,600,000	
Dense Commercial Decking	Decking	1650	1900	975	90	660	1150	1,600,000	
Dense Structural 86	2" to 4" thick	2600	3000	1750	155	660	2000	1,800,000	
Dense Structural 72		2200	2550	1450	130	660	1650	1,800,000	
Dense Structural 65		2000	2800	1300	115	660	1500	1,800,000	
KD-19 or S-Dry									
Industrial 86		2250	2600	1500	155	415	1700	1,700,000	
Dense Ind. 86		2600	3000	1750	155	475	2000	1,800,000	
Industrial 72	1" to 4" thick	1900	2200	1250	130	415	1400	1,700,000	
Dense Ind. 72		2200	2550	1450	130	475	1650	1,800,000	
Industrial 65		1700	1950	1100	115	415	1250	1,700,000	
Dense Ind. 65		2000	2300	1300	115	475	1500	1,800,000	
SOUTHERN PINE (Surfaced green. Used any condition.)									
Select Structural		1600	1850	925	95	375	1050	1,500,000	
Dense Select Structural		1850	2150	1100	95	440	1200	1,600,000	
No. 1	2 1/2" to 4" thick	1350	1550	800	95	375	825	1,500,000	
No. 1 Dense		1600	1800	925	95	440	950	1,600,000	
No. 2	2 1/2" to 4" wide	1150	1300	675	85	375	650	1,400,000	
No. 2 Dense		1350	1500	775	85	440	750	1,400,000	
No. 3		625	725	375	85	375	400	1,200,000	
No. 3 Dense		725	850	425	85	440	450	1,300,000	
Stud		625	725	375	85	375	400	1,200,000	
Construction	2 1/2" to 4" thick	825	925	475	95	375	725	1,200,000	
Standard		475	525	275	85	375	600	1,200,000	
Utility	4" wide	200	259	125	85	375	400	1,200,000	

SPECIES AND COMMERCIAL GRADE	SIZE CLASSIFICATION	Single-member Uses	Repetitive-member Uses	Tension Parallel to Grain F_t	Horizontal Shear F_v	Compression Perpendicular to Grain $F_c\perp$21	Compression Parallel to Grain F_c	MODULUS OF ELASTICITY E 21	U.B.C. STDS. UNDER WHICH GRADED
Select Structural		1400	1600	900	85	375	900	1,500,000	25-6 (See footnotes 3, 4, 9, 13, 15, 16, 17, 18 and 19)
Dense Select Structural		1600	1850	1050	85	440	1050	1,600,000	
No. 1		1200	1350	775	85	375	825	1,500,000	
No. 1 Dense	2 1/2" to 4" thick	1400	1600	925	85	440	950	1,600,000	
No. 2		975	1100	500	85	375	675	1,400,000	
No. 2 Dense	5" and wider	1150	1300	600	85	440	800	1,400,000	
No. 3		550	650	300	85	375	425	1,200,000	
No. 3 Dense		650	750	350	85	440	475	1,300,000	
Stud		575	675	300	85	375	425	1,200,000	
Dense Standard Decking	2 1/2" to 4 thick	1600	1800	925	95	440	950	1,600,000	
Select Decking		1150	1300	675	85	375	650	1,400,000	
Dense Select Decking	2" and wider	1350	1500	775	85	440	750	1,400,000	
Commercial Decking	Decking	1150	1300	675	85	375	650	1,400,000	
Dense Commercial Decking		1350	1500	775	85	440	750	1,400,000	
No. 1 SR		1350	—	875	110	375	775	1,500,000	
No. 1 Dense SR	5" and thicker	1550	—	1050	110	440	925	1,600,000	
No. 2 SR		1100	—	725	95	375	625	1,400,000	
No. 2 Dense SR		1250	—	850	95	440	725	1,400,000	
Dense Structural 86	2 1/2" and thicker	2100	2400	1400	145	440	1300	1,600,000	
Dense Structural 72		1750	2050	1200	120	440	1100	1,600,000	
Dense Structural 65		1600	1800	1050	110	440	1000	1,600,000	
MC over 19%									
Industrial 86		1800	2050	1200	140	270	1150	1,500,000	
Dense Ind. 86		2100	2400	1400	140	315	1300	1,600,000	
Industrial 72	2 1/2" and thicker	1500	1750	1000	120	270	950	1,500,000	
Dense Ind. 72		1750	2050	1200	120	315	1100	1,600,000	
Industrial 65		1350	1500	900	110	270	850	1,500,000	
Dense Ind. 65		1600	1800	1050	110	315	1000	1,600,000	

Appendix B (continued)
Allowable Unit Stresses

[1]Where eastern spruce and balsam fir are shipped in a combination, the tabulated values for balsam fir shall apply.

[2]The design values shown in Table No. 25-A-1 are applicable to lumber that will be used under dry conditions such as in most covered structures. For 2-inch- to 4-inch-thick lumber the DRY surfaced size shall be used. In calculating design values, the natural gain in strength and stiffness that occurs as lumber dries has been taken into consideration as well as the reduction in size that occurs when unseasoned lumber shrinks. The gain in load-carrying capacity due to increased strength and stiffness resulting from drying more than offsets the design effect of size reductions due to shrinkage. For 5-inch and thicker lumber, the surfaced sizes also may be used because design values have been adjusted to compensate for any loss in size by shrinkage which may occur.

[3]Values for F_b, F_t and F_c for the grades of Construction, Standard and Utility apply only to 4-inch widths.

[4]The values in Table No. 25-A-1 for dimension 2 inches to 4 inches are based on edgewise use. Where such lumber is used flatwise, the recommended design values for extreme fiber stress in bending may be multiplied by the following factors:

WIDTH	THICKNESS		
	2"	3"	4"
2 inches to 4 inches	1.10	1.04	1.00
5 inches and wider	1.22	1.16	1.11

Values for decking may be increased by 10 percent for 2-inch decking and 4 percent for 3-inch decking.

[5]When 2-inch- to 4-inch-thick lumber is manufactured at a maximum moisture content of 15 percent and used in a condition where the moisture content does not exceed 15 percent, the design values shown in Table No. 25-A-1 for surfaced dry and surfaced green may be multiplied by the following factors:

EXTREME FIBER IN BENDING F_b	TENSION PARALLEL TO GRAIN F_t	HORIZONTAL SHEAR F_v	COMPRESSION PERPENDICULAR TO GRAIN $F_c\perp$	COMPRESSION PARALLEL TO GRAIN F_c	MODULUS OF ELASTICITY E
1.08	1.08	1.05	1.00	1.17*	1.05*

*For redwood use 1.15 for F_c and 1.04 for E.

[6]When 2-inch- to 4-inch-thick lumber is designed for use where the moisture content will exceed 19 percent for an extended period of time, the values shown in Table No. 25-A-1 shall be multiplied by the following factors:

EXTREME FIBER IN BENDING F_b	TENSION PARALLEL TO GRAIN F_t	HORIZONTAL SHEAR F_v	COMPRESSION PERPENDICULAR TO GRAIN $F_c\perp$	COMPRESSION PARALLEL TO GRAIN F_c	MODULUS OF ELASTICITY E
0.86	0.84	0.97	0.67	0.70	0.97

[7]When lumber 5 inches and thicker is designed for use where the moisture content will exceed 19 percent for an extended period of time, the values shown in Table No. 25-A-1 shall be multiplied by the following factors:

EXTREME FIBER IN BENDING F_b	TENSION PARALLEL TO GRAIN F_t	HORIZONTAL SHEAR F_v	COMPRESSION PERPENDICULAR TO GRAIN $F_c\perp$	COMPRESSION PARALLEL TO GRAIN F_c	MODULUS OF ELASTICITY E
1.00	1.00	1.00	0.67	0.91	1.00

[8]Specific horizontal shear values may be established by using the following tables when the length of split or check is known:

WHEN LENGTH OF SPLIT ON WIDE FACE IS:	MULTIPLY TABULATED F_v VALUE BY: (NOMINAL 2-INCH) LUMBER)
No split.	2.00
1/2 x wide face	1.67
3/4 x wide face	1.50
1 x wide face	1.33
1 1/2 x wide face or more	1.00

WHEN LENGTH OF SPLIT ON WIDE FACE IS:	MULTIPLY TABULATED F_v VALUE BY: (3-INCH AND THICKER LUMBER)
No split.	2.00
1/2 x narrow face.	1.67
1 x narrow face	1.33
1 1/2 x narrow face or more	1.00

[9]Stress-rated boards of nominal 1-inch, 1 1/4-inch and 1 1/2-inch thickness, 2 inches and wider, are permitted the recommended design values shown for Select Structural, No. 1, No. 2, No. 3, Construction, Standard, Utility, Appearance, Clear Heart Structural and Clear Structural grades as shown in the 2-inch- to 4-inch-thick categories herein, where graded in accordance with the stress-rated board provisions in the applicable grading rules.

Appendix B (continued)
Allowable Unit Stresses

[10]When decking is used where the moisture content will exceed 15 percent for an extended period of time, the tabulated design values shall be multiplied by the following factors: Extreme Fiber in Bending F_b – 0.79; Modulus of Elasticity E – 0.92.

[11]Where lumber is graded under U.B.C. Standard No. 25-2 values shown for Select Structural, No. 1, No. 2, No. 3, and Stud grades are not applicable to 3-inch x 4-inch and 4-inch x 4-inch sizes.

[12]Lumber in the beam and stringer or post and timber size classification may be assigned different working stresses for the same grade name and species based upon the grading rules of the specific agency involved. It is therefore necessary that the grading rule agency be identified to properly correlate permitted design stresses with the grade mark.

[13]Utility grades of all species may be used only under conditions specifically approved by the building official.

[14]A horizontal shear F_v of 70 may be used for eastern white pine graded under U.B.C. Standards No. 25-5 and No. 25-8 (grading rules of Northern Hardwood and Pine Manufacturers, Inc. and Northeastern Lumber Manufacturers Association, Inc.).

[15]Tabulated tension parallel to grain values for species 5 inches and wider, 2 inches to 4 inches thick (and 2½ inches to 4 inches thick) size classifications apply to 5-inch and 6-inch widths only, for grades of Select Structural, No. 1, No. 2, No. 3, Appearance and Stud (including dense grades). For lumber wider than 6 inches in these grades, the tabulated F_t values shall be multiplied by the following factors:

GRADE (2 inches to 4 inches thick, 5 inches and wider) (2½ inches to 4 inches thick, 5 inches and wider) (Includes "Dense" grades)	Multiply tabulated F_t values by		
	5 inches and 6 inches wide	8 inches wide	10 inches and wider
Select Structural	1.00	0.90	0.80
No. 1, No. 2, No. 3 and Appearance	1.00	0.80	0.60
Stud	1.00		

[16]Design values for all species of Stud grade in 5-inch and wider size classifications apply to 5-inch and 6-inch widths only.

[17]Repetitive member design values for extreme fiber in bending for southern pine grades of Dense Structural 86, 72 and 65 apply to 2-inch to 4-inch thicknesses only.

[18]When 2-inch- to 4-inch-thick southern pine lumber is surfaced dry or at 15 percent maximum moisture content (KD) and is designed for use where the moisture content will exceed 19 percent for an extended period of time, the design values in Table No. 25-A-1 for the corresponding grades of 2½-inch- to 4-inch-thick surfaced green southern pine lumber shall be used. The net green size may be used in such designs.

[19]When 2-inch- to 4-inch-thick southern pine lumber is surfaced dry or at 15 percent maximum moisture content (KD) and is designed for use under dry conditions, such as in most covered structures, the net DRY size shall be used in design. For other sizes and conditions of use, the net green size may be used in design.

[20]Values apply only to ponderosa pine graded under U.B.C. Standard No. 25-2.

[21]The duration of load modification factors given in Section 2504 (c) 4 shall not apply.

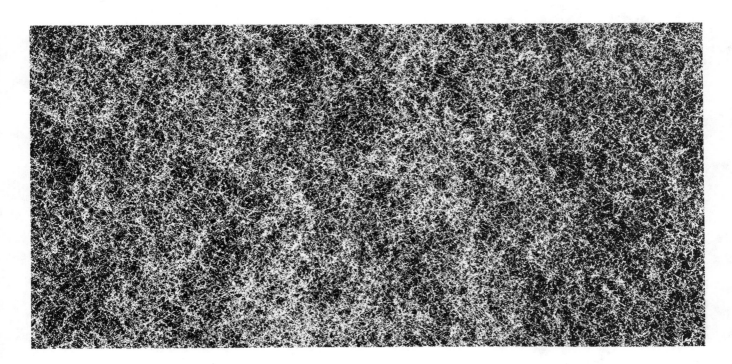

Appendix B (continued)
Allowable Unit Stresses

Members stressed principally in bending with load applied perpendicular to the wide faces of the laminations

COMBINATION SYMBOL[19]	SPECIES OUTER LAMINATIONS/CORE LAMINATIONS[4]	Extreme Fiber in Bending F_{bxx} — Tension Zone Stressed in Tension[5][22] psi	Extreme Fiber in Bending F_{bxx} — Compression Zone Stressed in Tension[6] psi	Compression Perpendicular to Grain $F_{c\perp xx}$[21] — Tension Face psi	Compression Perpendicular to Grain $F_{c\perp xx}$[21] — Compression Face psi	Horizontal Shear F_{vxx} psi	Modulus of Elasticity E_{xx}[21] x10^6 psi	Extreme Fiber in Bending[5][17] F_{byy} psi	Compression Perpendicular to Grain $F_{c\perp yy}$[21] psi	Horizontal Shear F_{vyy} psi	Horizontal Shear $F_{vyy'}$ psi (For members with multiple-piece laminations which are not edge glued)[20]	Modulus of Elasticity E_{yy}[21] x10^6 psi	Tension Parallel to Grain F_t psi	Compression Parallel to Grain F_c psi	Modulus of Elasticity E[21] x10^6 psi
1	2	3	4	5	6	7	8	9	10	11	12	13	14	15	16
Visually Graded Western Species															
16F-V1	DF/WW	1600	800	560[7][8]	560[7][8]	140[18][23]	1.3	950	255	130	65	1.1	675	975	1.1
16F-V2	HF/HF	1600	800	500[9]	375[9]	155	1.4	1250	375	135	70	1.3	875	1300	1.3
16F-V3	DF/DF	1600	800	560[7][8]	560	165	1.5	1450	560	145	75	1.5	950	1550	1.5
16F-V8	DFS/DFS	1600	800	650	500	165	1.2	1200	500	145	75	1.1	825	1350	1.1
The following two combinations are intended for straight or slightly cambered members for dry use and industrial appearance.[10]															
16F-V4	DF/N3WW	1600	800	650	560[7]	90[9][18]	1.5[24]	900	255	130	65	1.3[24]	650	600	1.3
16F-V5	DF/M3DF	1600	800	650	560[7]	90[12]	1.6	1000	470	135	70	1.5	750	875	1.5
The following two combinations are balanced and are intended for members continuous or cantilevered over supports and provide equal capacity in both positive and negative bending.															
16F-V6	DF/DF	1600	1600	560[7][8]	560[7]	165	1.5	1450	560	145	75	1.4	950	1550	1.5
16F-V7	HF/HF	1600	1600	375[9]	375[9]	155	1.4	1200	375	135	70	1.3	850	1350	1.3
20F-V1	DF/WW	2000	1000	650	560[7]	140[18][23]	1.4[24]	1000	255	130	65	1.2[24]	750	1000	1.2
20F-V2	HF/HF	2000	1000	500[9]	375[9]	155	1.5	1200	375	135	70	1.4	950	1350	1.4
20F-V3	DF/DF	2000	1000	650	560[7]	165	1.6	1450	560	145	75	1.5	1000	1550	1.5
20F-V4	DF/DF	2000	1000	590[7][8]	560[7]	165	1.6	1450	560	145	75	1.6	1000	1550	1.6
20F-V10	DF/HF	2000	1000	650	560	155	1.5	1300	375	135	70	1.4	950	1500	1.4
20F-V11	DFS/DFS	2000	1000	650	500	165	1.3	1400	500	145	75	1.1	900	1400	1.1
20F-V12	AC/AC	2000	1000	560	560	190	1.5	1200	470	165	80	1.4	900	1500	1.4
The following two combinations are intended for straight or slightly cambered members for dry use and industrial appearance.[10]															
20F-V5	DF/N3WW	2000	1000	650	560[7]	90[11][18]	1.6	1000	255	135	70	1.3	750	725	1.3
20F-V6	DF/M3DF	2000	1000	650	560[7]	90[12]	1.6	1000	470	135	70	1.5	775	900	1.5
The following three combinations are balanced and are intended for members continuous or cantilevered over supports and provide equal capacity in both positive and negative bending.															
20F-V7	DF/DF	2000	2000	650	650	165	1.6	1450	560	145	75	1.6	1000	1600	1.6
20F-V8	DF/DF	2000	2000	590[7][8]	590[7][8]	165	1.7	1450	560	145	75	1.6	1000	1600	1.6
20F-V9	HF/HF	2000	2000	500[9]	500[9]	155	1.5	1400	375	135	70	1.4	975	1400	1.4
22F-V1	DF/WW	2200	1100	650	560[7]	140[18]	1.6[24]	1050	255	130	65	1.3[24]	850	1100	1.3
22F-V2	HF/HF	2200	1100	500[9]	500[9]	155	1.5	1250	375	135	70	1.4	950	1350	1.4
22F-V3	DF/DF	2200	1100	650	560[9]	165	1.7	1450	560	145	75	1.6	1050	1500	1.6
22F-V4	DF/DF	2200	1100	590[7][8]	560[7]	165	1.7	1450	560	145	75	1.6	1000	1550	1.6
22F-V10	DF/DFS	2200	1100	650	560[7]	165	1.6	1600	500	145	75	1.3	1000	1400	1.3
The following two combinations are intended for straight or slightly cambered members for dry use and industrial appearance.[10]															
22F-V5	DF/N3WW	2200	1100	650	560[7]	90[11][18]	1.6[24]	1100	255	135	75	1.4[24]	800	725	1.4
22F-V6	DF/M3DF	2200	1100	650	560[7]	90[12]	1.7	1250	470	135	75	1.6	900	925	1.6

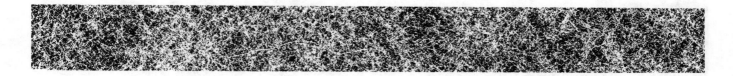

Appendix B (continued)
Allowable Unit Stresses

Members stressed principally in bending with load applied perpendicular to the wide faces of the laminations

COMBINA-TION SYMBOL[19]	SPECIES OUTER LAMINA-TIONS/ CORE LAMINA-TIONS[4]	BENDING ABOUT X-X AXIS						BENDING ABOUT Y-Y AXIS					AXIALLY LOADED		
		Extreme Fiber in Bending F_{bxx}		Compression Perpendicular to Grain $F_{c\perp xx}$[21]							Horizontal Shear F_{vyy}, psi (For members with multiple-piece laminations which are not edge glued)[20]				
		Tension Zone Stressed in Tension[5][22] psi	Compression Zone Stressed in Tension[6] psi	Tension Face psi	Compression Face psi	Horizontal Shear F_{vxx} psi	Modulus of Elasticity E_{xx}[21] x10⁶ psi	Extreme Fiber in Bending[5][17] F_{byy} psi	Compression Perpendicular to Grain $F_{c\perp yy}$[21] psi	Horizontal Shear F_{vyy} psi		Modulus of Elasticity E_{yy}[21] x10⁶ psi	Tension Parallel to Grain F_t psi	Compression Parallel to Grain F_c psi	Modulus of Elasticity E[21] x10⁶ psi
1	2	3	4	5	6	7	8	9	10	11	12	13	14	15	16
Visually Graded Western Species—(Continued)															
The following three combinations are balanced and are intended for members continuous or cantilevered over supports and provide equal capacity in both positive and negative bending.															
22F-V7	DF/DF	2200	2200	650	650	165	1.8	1450	560	145	75	1.6	1100	1650	1.6
22F-V8	DF/DF			590[7][8]	590[7][8]	165	1.7	1450	560	145	75	1.6	1050	1650	1.6
22F-V9	HF/HF			500[9]	500[9]	155	1.5	1250	375	135	70	1.4	975	1400	1.4
24F-V1	DF/WW	2400	1200	650	650	140[23]	1.7[24]	1250	255	130	70	1.4[24]	1000	1300	1.4
24F-V2	HF/HF			500[9]	500[9]	155	1.5	1250	375	135	70	1.4	950	1300	1.4
24F-V3	DF/DF			650	560[7]	165	1.8	1500	560	145	75	1.6	1100	1600	1.6
24F-V4	DF/DF			650	650	165	1.8	1500	560	145	75	1.6	1150	1650	1.6
24F-V5	DF/HF			650	650	155	1.7	1350	375	140	70	1.5	1100	1450	1.5
24F-V11	DF/DFS			650	560[7]	165	1.7	1600	500	145	75	1.4	1150	1700	1.4

The following two combinations are intended for straight or slightly cambered members for dry use and industrial appearance.[10]															
24F-V6	DF/N3WW	2400	1200	650	560[7]	90[11][18][23]	1.7[24]	1200	255	140	70	1.5[24]	950	800	1.5
24F-V7	DF/M3DF			650	560[7]	90[12]	1.7	1250	470	135	70	1.6	900	950	1.6
The following three combinations are balanced and are intended for members continuous or cantilevered over supports and provide equal capacity in both positive and negative bending.															
24F-V8	DF/DF	2400	2400	650	650	165	1.8	1450	560	145	75	1.6	1100	1650	1.6
24F-V9	HF/HF			500[9]	500[9]	155	1.5	1500	375	135	70	1.4	1000	1450	1.4
24F-V10	DF/HF			650	650	155	1.8	1400	375	140	70	1.6	1150	1600	1.6
Wet-use factors[2]		0.8	0.8	0.667	0.667	0.875	0.833	0.8	0.667	0.875	0.875	0.833	0.8	0.73	0.833

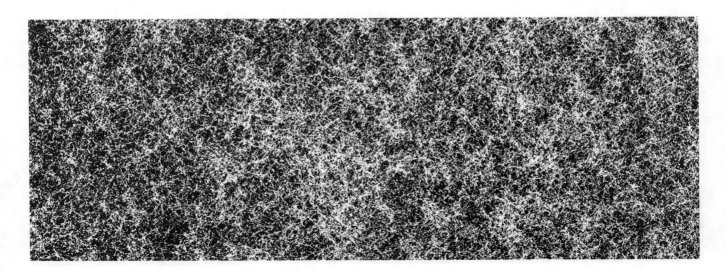

Appendix B (continued)
Allowable Unit Stresses

Members stressed principally in bending with load applied perpendicular to the wide faces of the laminations

		BENDING ABOUT X-X AXIS						BENDING ABOUT Y-Y AXIS					AXIALLY LOADED		
		Loaded Perpendicular to Wide Faces of Laminations						Loaded Parallel to Wide Faces of Laminations							
COMBINATION SYMBOL[19]	SPECIES OUTER LAMINATIONS/ CORE LAMINATIONS[4]	Extreme Fiber in Bending F_{bxx}		Compression Perpendicular to Grain $F_{c\perp xx}$[21]				Extreme Fiber in Bending[5][17] F_{byy} psi	Compression Perpendicular to Grain $F_{c\perp yy}$[21] psi	Horizontal Shear F_{vyy} psi	Horizontal Shear F_{vyy} psi (For members with multiple-piece laminations which are not edge glued)[20]	Modulus of Elasticity E_{yy}[21] x10⁶ psi	Tension Parallel to Grain F_t psi	Compression Parallel to Grain F_c psi	Modulus of Elasticity E[21] x10⁶ psi
		Tension Zone Stressed in Tension[5][22] psi	Compression Zone Stressed in Tension[6] psi	Tension Face psi	Compression Face psi	Horizontal Shear F_{vxx} psi	Modulus of Elasticity E_{xx}[21] x10⁶ psi								
1	2	3	4	5	6	7	8	9	10	11	12	13	14	15	16
Visually Graded Southern Pine															
16F-V1	SP/SP			560[7][8]	560[7]	200	1.4	1450	560	175	90	1.3	950	1450	1.3
16F-V2	SP/SP	1600	800	500[7][8]	500[7]	200	1.4	1600	560	175	90	1.4	1000	1550	1.4
16F-V3	SP/SP			650	650	200	1.4	1450	560	175	90	1.3	975	1450	1.3
The following combination is intended for straight or slightly cambered members for dry use and industrial appearance.[10]															
16F-V4	SP/SP	1600	800	560[7][8]	560[7]	90[16]	1.3	975	470	150	75	1.2	650	950	1.2
The following combination is balanced and intended for members continuous or cantilevered over supports and provides equal capacity in both positive and negative bending.															
16F-V5	SP/SP	1600	1600	560[7][8]	560[7][8]	200	1.4	1600	560	175	85	1.4	1000	1550	1.4
20F-V1	SP/SP			650	560[7]	200	1.5	1450	560	175	85	1.4	1000	1450	1.4
20F-V2	SP/SP	2000	1000	650	560[7]	200	1.6	1450	560	175	85	1.4	1050	1550	1.4
20F-V3	SP/SP			560[7][8]	560[7]	200	1.4	1600	560	175	85	1.4	1000	1500	1.4
The following combination is intended for straight or slightly cambered members for dry use and industrial appearance.[10]															
20F-V4	SP/SP	2000	1000	650	560[7]	90[16]	1.5	1100	470	150	75	1.3	725	950	1.3
The following combination is balanced and intended for members continuous or cantilevered over supports and provides equal capacity in both positive and negative bending.															
20F-V5	SP/SP	2000	2000	650	560	200	1.6	1450	650	175	85	1.4	1050	1550	1.4
22F-V1	SP/SP			650	650	200	1.6	1600	560	175	85	1.5	1050	1650	1.5
22F-V2	SP/SP	2200	1100	560[7][8]	560[7]	200	1.4	1600	560	175	85	1.4	1000	1500	1.4
22F-V3	SP/SP			650	560[7]	200	1.6	1500	560	175	85	1.4	1050	1500	1.4
The following combination is intended for straight or slightly cambered members for dry use and industrial appearance.[10]															
22F-V4	SP/SP	2200	1100	650	560[7]	90[16]	1.6	1250	470	155	75	1.4	825	1000	1.4
The following combination is balanced and intended for members continuous or cantilevered over supports and provides equal capacity in both positive and negative bending.															
22F-V5	SP/SP	2200	2200	650	650	200	1.6	1600	560	175	85	1.5	1050	1600	1.5
24F-V1	SP/SP			650	560[7]	200	1.7	1500	560	175	85	1.5	1100	1350	1.5
24F-V2	SP/SP	2400	1200	650	650	200	1.7	1600	560	175	85	1.5	1100	1600	1.5
24F-V3	SP/SP			650	650	200	1.8	1600	560	175	85	1.6	1150	1700	1.6
24F-V6	SP/SP			650	650	200	1.7	1500	560	175	90	1.5	1150	1750	1.5
The following combination is intended for straight or slightly cambered members for dry use and industrial appearance.[10]															
24F-V4	SP/SP	2400	1200	650	560[7]	90[16]	1.7	1250	470	155	75	1.4	850	1050	1.4
Visually Graded Southern Pine—(Continued)															
The following combination is balanced and intended for members continuous or cantilevered over supports and provides equal capacity in both positive and negative bending.															
24F-V5	SP/SP	2400	2400	650	650	200	1.7	1600	560	175	90	1.5	1150	1700	1.5
Wet-use factors[2]		0.8	0.8	0.667	0.667	0.875	0.833	0.8	0.667	0.875	0.875	0.833	0.8	0.73	0.833

Appendix B (continued)
Allowable Unit Stresses
FOOTNOTES

[1]The combinations in this table are applicable to members consisting of four or more laminations and are intended primarily for members stressed in bending due to loads applied perpendicular to the wide faces of the laminations. Design values are tabulated, however, for loading both perpendicular and parallel to the wide faces of the laminations. For combinations and design values applicable to members loaded primarily axially or parallel to the wide faces of the laminations, see Table No. 25-C-1, Part B. For members of two or three laminations, see Table No. 25-C-1, Part B.

[2]The tabulated design values are for dry conditions of use. To obtain wet-use design values, multiply the tabulated values by the factors shown at the end of the table.

[3]The tabulated design values are for normal duration of loading. For other durations of loading, see Section 2504 (c) 4.

[4]The symbols used for species are AC = Alaska cedar, DF = Douglas fir-larch, DFS = Douglas fir south, HF = hem-fir, WW = softwood species, SP = southern pine and ES = eastern spruce. (N3 refers to No. 3 structural joists and planks or structural light framing grade.) Softwood species (WW) and eastern spruce are included in the general category of western species although eastern spruce and some softwood species are produced in other areas.

[5]The tabulated design values in bending are applicable to members 12 inches or less in depth. For members greater than 12 inches in depth, the requirements of Section 2511 (d) 5 apply.

[6]Design values in this column are for extreme fiber stress in bending when the member is loaded such that the compression zone laminations are subjected to tensile stresses. The values in this column may be increased 200 psi where end joint spacing restrictions are applied to the compression zone when stressed in tension.

[7]Where specified, this value may be increased to 650 psi by providing in the bearing area at least one dense 2-inch nominal thickness lamination of Douglas fir-larch for western species combinations, or southern pine for southern pine combinations. These dense laminations must be backed by a medium-grain lamination of the same species.

[8]For bending members greater than 15 inches in depth, the design value for compression stress perpendicular to grain is 650 psi on the tension face.

[9]Where specified, this value may be increased by providing at least two 2-inch nominal thickness Douglas fir-larch laminations in the bearing area. The compression-perpendicular-to-grain design values for Douglas fir-larch are 560 psi for medium grain and 650 psi for dense.

[10]These combinations are for dry conditions of use only because they may contain wane. They are recommended for industrial appearance grade and for straight or slightly cambered members only. If wane is omitted these restrictions do not apply.

[11]This value may be increased to 140 psi for softwood species (WW) and to 155 psi for hem-fir when the member does not contain wane on both sides; to 115 psi for softwood species (WW) and to 130 psi for hem-fir when the member does not contain wane on one side.

[12]This value may be increased to 110 psi when the member does not contain coarse-grain material; to 140 psi when the member does not contain wane on both sides or the member does not contain coarse-grain material and wane on one side; to 165 psi when the member does not contain coarse-grain material and wane on both sides.

[13]The compression-perpendicular-to-grain design value of 255 psi is based on the lowest strength species of the western woods group. If at least one 2-inch nominal thickness lamination of E-rated hem-fir with the same E value, or E-rated Douglas fir-larch 200,000 psi higher in modulus of elasticity (E) than that specified is used in the bearing area on the face of the member subjected to the compression-perpendicular-to-grain stress, $F_c\perp$ may be increased to 375 psi. If at least two 2-inch nominal thickness laminations of E-rated hem-fir with the same E value, or E-rated Douglas fir-larch 200,000 psi higher in modulus of elasticity than that specified are used in the bearing area on the face of the member subjected to the compression-perpendicular-to-grain stress, $F_c\perp$ may be increased to 500 psi.

[14]Where specified, this value may be increased to 650 psi by providing in the bearing area at least one 2-inch nominal thickness lamination of Douglas fir-larch for western species combinations, or one 2-inch nominal thickness lamination of southern pine for southern pine combinations having a modulus of elasticity (E) value 200,000 psi higher than the E value specified.

[15]E-rated Douglas fir-larch 200,000 psi higher in modulus of elasticity may be substituted for the specified E-rated hem-fir.

[16]This value may be increased to 140 psi when the member does not contain coarse-grain material or when the member does not contain wane on both sides; to 165 psi when members do not contain coarse-grain material or wane on one side; or to 200 psi when the member does not contain both coarse-grain material and wane on both sides of the member.

[17]Footnote 5 to Table No. 25-C-1, Part B, also applies.

[18]When Douglas fir south is used in place of all of the western wood laminations required in western species combinations 16F-V1, 16F-V4, 20F-V1, 20F-V5, 22F-V1, 22F-V5, 24F-V1, 24F-V6, 16F-E1, 16F-E4, 20F-E1, 20F-E4, 22F-E3, 24F-E6 and 24F-E7, the design value for horizontal shear is the same as for combinations using all Douglas fir-larch ($F_{vxx} = 165$ psi and $F_{vyy} = 145$ psi for L3; and $F_{vxx} = 90$ psi and $F_{vyy} = 135$ psi for N3).

[19]The combination symbols relate to a specific combination of grades and species in U.B.C. Standard No. 25-11 that will provide the design values shown for the combinations. The first two numbers in the combination symbol correspond to the design value in bending shown in column 3. The letter in the combination symbol (either a "V" or an "E") indicates whether the combination is made from visually graded (V) or E-rated (E) lumber in the outer zones.

[20]These values for horizontal shear, F_{vyy} apply to members manufactured using multiple-piece laminations with unbonded edge joints. For members manufactured using single-piece laminations or using multiple-piece laminations with bonded edge joints, the horizontal shear values in column 11 apply.

[21]The duration of load modification factors given in Section 2504 (c) 4 shall not apply.

[22]The design values in bending about the x-x axis (F_{bx}) in this column for bending members shall be multiplied by 0.75 when the member is manufactured without the required special tension laminations.

[23]The following species may be used for softwood species (WW), provided the design values in horizontal shear in column 7 (F_{vx}) and in Column 11 (F_{vy}) are reduced by 10 psi and the design values in horizontal shear in Column 12 (F_{vy}) are reduced by 5 psi: Coast sitka spruce, coast species, eastern white pine (north) and western white pine.

[24]The following species may be used for softwood species (WW), provided the design values in modulus of elasticity (E_x and E_y) in Columns 8 and 13 are reduced by 100,000 psi: Western cedars, western cedars (north), white woods (western woods) and California redwood—open grain.

Reproduced from the 1988 Edition of the Uniform Building Code, copyright © 1988, with the permission of the publishers, the International Conference of Building Officials.

Appendix C
Typical Dimensions of Standard Lag Screws for Wood

[All dimensions in inches]

D = Nominal diameter.
Ds = D = Diameter of shank.
Dr = Diameter at root of thread.
W = Width of head across flats.

H = Height of head.
L = Nominal length.
S = Length of shank.
T = Length of thread.

E = Length of tapered tip.
N = Number of threads per inch.

Nominal length L in inches*	Item	Dimensions of lag screw with nominal diameter D of—												
		3/16	1/4	5/16	3/8	7/16	1/2	9/16	5/8	3/4	7/8	1	1-1/8	1-1/4
All lengths	Ds=D	0.190	0.250	0.3125	0.375	0.4375	0.500	0.5625	0.625	0.750	0.875	1.000	1.125	1.250
	Dr	0.120	0.173	0.227	0.265	0.328	0.371	0.435	0.471	0.579	0.683	0.780	0.887	1.012
	E	5/32	3/16	1/4	1/4	9/32	5/16	3/8	3/8	1/2	9/16	5/8	5/8	3/4
	H	9/64	11/64	13/64	1/4	19/64	21/64	3/8	27/64	1/2	19/32	21/32	3/4	27/32
	W	9/32	3/8	1/2	9/16	5/8	3/4	7/8	15/16	1-1/8	1-5/16	1-1/2	1-11/16	1-7/8
	N	11	10	9	7	7	6	6	5	4-1/2	4	3-1/2	3-1/4	3-1/4
1.........	S	1/4	1/4	1/4	1/4	1/4	1/4	......	......	......	......	......	......	......
	T	3/4	3/4	3/4	3/4	3/4	3/4	......	......	......	......	......	......	......
	T-E	19/32	9/16	1/2	1/2	15/32	7/16	......	......	......	......	......	......	......
1½	S	3/8	3/8	3/8	3/8	3/8	3/8	......	......	......	......	......	......	......
	T	1-1/8	1-1/8	1-1/8	1-1/8	1-1/8	1-1/8	......	......	......	......	......	......	......
	T-E	31/32	15/16	7/8	7/8	27/32	13/16	......	......	......	......	......	......	......
2.........	S	1/2	1/2	1/2	1/2	1/2	1/2	1/2	1/2	......	......	......	......	......
	T	1-1/2	1-1/2	1-1/2	1-1/2	1-1/2	1-1/2	1-1/2	1-1/2	......	......	......	......	......
	T-E	1-11/32	1-5/16	1-1/4	1-1/4	17/32	1-3/16	1-1/8	1-1/8	......	......	......	......	......
2½	S	1	1	7/8	7/8	3/4	3/4	3/4	3/4	......	......	......	......	......
	T	1-1/2	1-1/2	1-5/8	1-5/8	1-3/4	1-3/4	1-3/4	1-3/4	......	......	......	......	......
	T-E	1-11/16	1-5/16	1-3/8	1-3/8	1-15/32	1-7/16	1-3/8	1-3/8	......	......	......	......	......
3.........	S	1	1	1	1	1	1	1	1	1	1	1	......	......
	T	2	2	2	2	2	2	2	2	2	2	2	......	......
	T-E	1-27/32	1-13/16	1-3/4	1-3/4	1-23/32	1-11/16	1-5/8	1-5/8	1-9/16	1-1/2	1-7/16	......	......
4.........	S	1-1/2	1-1/2	1-1/2	1-1/2	1-1/2	1-1/2	1-1/2	1-1/2	1-1/2	1-1/2	1-1/2	1-1/2	1-1/2
	T	2-1/2	2-1/2	2-1/2	2-1/2	2-1/2	2-1/2	2-1/2	2-1/2	2-1/2	2-1/2	2-1/2	2-1/2	2-1/2
	T-E	2-11/32	2-5/16	2-1/4	2-1/4	2-7/32	2-3/16	2-1/8	2-1/8	2-1/16	2	1-15/16	1-7/8	1-3/4
5.........	S	2	2	2	2	2	2	2	2	2	2	2	2	2
	T	3	3	3	3	3	3	3	3	3	3	3	3	3
	T-E	2-27/32	2-13/16	2-3/4	2-3/4	2-23/32	2-11/16	2-5/8	2-5/8	2-9/16	2-1/2	2-7/16	2-3/8	2-1/4
6.........	S	2-1/2	2-1/2	2-1/2	2-1/2	2-1/2	2-1/2	2-1/2	2-1/2	2-1/2	2-1/2	2-1/2	2-1/2	2-1/2
	T	3-1/2	3-1/2	3-1/2	3-1/2	3-1/2	3-1/2	3-1/2	3-1/2	3-1/2	3-1/2	3-1/2	3-1/2	3-1/2
	T-E	3-11/32	3-5/16	3-1/4	3-1/4	3-7/32	3-3/16	3-1/8	3-1/8	3-1/16	3	2-15/16	2-7/8	2-3/4
7.........	S	3	3	3	3	3	3	3	3	3	3	3	3	3
	T	4	4	4	4	4	4	4	4	4	4	4	4	4
	T-E	3-27/32	3-13/16	3-3/4	3-3/4	3-23/32	3-11/16	3-5/8	3-5/8	3-9/16	3-1/2	3-7/16	3-3/8	3-1/4
8.........	S	3-1/2	3-1/2	3-1/2	3-1/2	3-1/2	3-1/2	3-1/2	3-1/2	3-1/2	3-1/2	3-1/2	3-1/2	3-1/2
	T	4-1/2	4-1/2	4-1/2	4-1/2	4-1/2	4-1/2	4-1/2	4-1/2	4-1/2	4-1/2	4-1/2	4-1/2	4-1/2
	T-E	4-11/16	4-5/16	4-1/4	4-1/4	4-7/32	4-3/16	4-1/8	4-1/8	4-1/16	4	3-15/16	3-7/8	3-3/4
9.........	S	4	4	4	4	4	4	4	4	4	4	4	4	4
	T	5	5	5	5	5	5	5	5	5	5	5	5	5
	T-E	4-27/32	4-13/16	4-3/4	4-3/4	4-23/32	4-11/16	4-5/8	4-5/8	4-9/16	4-1/2	4-7/16	4-3/8	4-1/4
10	S	4-3/4	4-3/4	4-3/4	4-3/4	4-3/4	4-3/4	4-3/4	4-3/4	4-3/4	4-3/4	4-3/4	4-3/4	4-3/4
	T	5-1/4	5-1/4	5-1/4	5-1/4	5-1/4	5-1/4	5-1/4	5-1/4	5-1/4	5-1/4	5-1/4	5-1/4	5-1/4
	T-E	5-3/32	5-1/16	5	5	4-31/32	4-15/16	4-7/8	4-7/8	4-13/16	4-3/4	4-11/16	4-5/8	4-1/2
11	S	5-1/2	5-1/2	5-1/2	5-1/2	5-1/2	5-1/2	5-1/2	5-1/2	5-1/2	5-1/2	5-1/2	5-1/2	5-1/2
	T	5-1/2	5-1/2	5-1/2	5-1/2	5-1/2	5-1/2	5-1/2	5-1/2	5-1/2	5-1/2	5-1/2	5-1/2	5-1/2
	T-E	5-11/32	5-9/32	5-1/4	5-1/4	5-7/32	5-3/16	5-1/8	5-1/8	5-1/16	5	4-15/16	4-7/8	4-3/4
12	S	6	6	6	6	6	6	6	6	6	6	6	6	6
	T	6	6	6	6	6	6	6	6	6	6	6	6	6
	T-E	5-27/32	5-13/16	5-3/4	5-3/4	5-23/32	5-11/16	5-5/8	5-5/8	5-9/16	5-1/2	5-7/16	5-3/8	5-1/4

*Length of thread T on intervening bolt lengths is the same as that of the next shorter length listed. The length of thread T on standard lag screw lengths L in excess of 12 inches is equal to 1/2 the lag screw length, L/2.

Reproduced from National Design Specification for Wood Construction, 1986 Edition, with permission from National Forest Products Association, Washington, D.C.

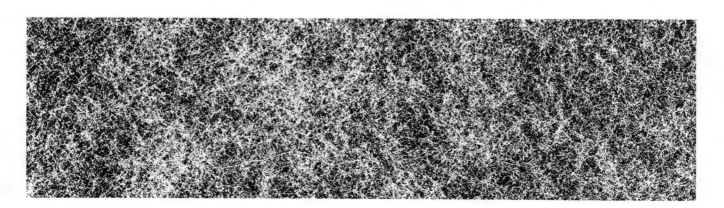

Appendix D
Typical Dimensions for Timber Connectors
Courtesy of TECO Products and Testing Corporation

SPLIT RINGS
Dimensions in inches

	2-1/2"	4"		2-1/2"	4"
Split ring:			Washers, standard:		
Inside diameter at center when closed	2.500	4.000	Round, cast or malleable iron, diameter	2-5/8	3
Thickness of metal at center	0.163	0.193	Round, wrought iron (minimum):		
Depth of metal (width of ring)	0.750	1.000	Diameter	1-3/8	2
Groove:			Thickness	3/32	5/32
Inside diameter	2.56	4.08	Square plate:		
Width	0.18	0.21	Length of side	2	3
Depth	0.375	0.50	Thickness	1/8	3/16
Bolt hole:			Projected area:		
Diameter	9/16	13/16	Portion of one ring within member, sq. in.	1.10	2.24

SHEAR PLATES
Dimensions in inches

	2-5/8"	2-5/8"	4"	4"		2-5/8"	2-5/8"	4"	4"
Shear plate:					Steel strap or shapes for use with shear plates:				
Material	Pressed steel	Light gage	Malleable iron	Malleable iron	Steel straps or shapes, for use with shear plates, shall be designed in accordance with accepted engineering practices.				
Diameter of plate	2.62	2.62	4.03	4.03					
Diameter of bolt hole	0.81	0.81	0.81	0.94					
Thickness of plate	0.172	0.12	0.20	0.20	Hole diameter in straps or				
Depth of plate	0.42	0.35	0.64	0.64	shapes for bolts	13/16	13/16	13/16	15/16

	2-5/8"	2-5/8"	4"	4"
Bolt hole—diameter in timber	13/16	13/16	13/16	15/16
Washers, standard:				
Round, cast or malleable iron, diameter	3	3	3	3-1/2
Round, wrought iron, minimum:				
Diameter	2	2	2	2-1/4
Thickness	5/32	5/32	5/32	11/64
Square plate:				
Length of side	3	3	3	3
Thickness	1/4	1/4	1/4	1/4
Projected area:				
Portion of one shear plate within member, sq. in.	1.18	1.00	2.58	2.58

Reproduced from National Design Specification for Wood Construction, 1986 Edition, with permission from National Forest Products Association, Washington, D.C.

Appendix E
Properties of Sawn Lumber and Timber

Nominal Size (in.)		Standard Dressed Size (in.) (S4S)		Area of Section A (in.^{2})	Moment of Inertia I (in.^{4})	Section Modulus S (in.^{3})	Weight[a] in Pounds per Linear Foot of Piece When Weight of Wood per Cubic Foot Equals:					
b	d	b	d				25 lb	30 lb	35 lb	40 lb	45 lb	50 lb
1 × 3		$\frac{3}{4}$ ×	$2\frac{1}{2}$	1.875	0.9766	0.7812	0.3	0.4	0.5	0.5	0.6	0.7
1 × 4		$\frac{3}{4}$ ×	$3\frac{1}{2}$	2.625	2.680	1.531	0.5	0.5	0.6	0.7	0.8	0.9
1 × 6		$\frac{3}{4}$ ×	$5\frac{1}{2}$	4.125	10.40	3.781	0.7	0.9	1.0	1.1	1.3	1.4
1 × 8		$\frac{3}{4}$ ×	$7\frac{1}{4}$	5.438	23.82	6.570	0.9	1.1	1.3	1.5	1.7	1.9
1 × 10		$\frac{3}{4}$ ×	$9\frac{1}{4}$	6.938	49.47	10.70	1.2	1.4	1.7	1.9	2.2	2.4
1 × 12		$\frac{3}{4}$ ×	$11\frac{1}{4}$	8.438	88.99	15.82	1.5	1.8	2.1	2.3	2.6	2.9
2 × 3		$1\frac{1}{2}$ ×	$2\frac{1}{2}$	3.750	1.953	1.563	0.7	0.8	0.9	1.0	1.2	1.3
2 × 4		$1\frac{1}{2}$ ×	$3\frac{1}{2}$	5.250	5.359	3.063	0.9	1.1	1.3	1.5	1.6	1.8
2 × 5		$1\frac{1}{2}$ ×	$4\frac{1}{2}$	6.750	11.39	5.063	1.2	1.4	1.6	1.9	2.1	2.3
2 × 6		$1\frac{1}{2}$ ×	$5\frac{1}{2}$	8.250	20.80	7.563	1.4	1.7	2.0	2.3	2.6	2.9
2 × 8		$1\frac{1}{2}$ ×	$7\frac{1}{4}$	10.88	47.64	13.14	1.9	2.3	2.6	3.0	3.4	3.8
2 × 10		$1\frac{1}{2}$ ×	$9\frac{1}{4}$	13.88	98.93	21.39	2.4	2.9	3.4	3.9	4.3	4.8
2 × 12		$1\frac{1}{2}$ ×	$11\frac{1}{4}$	16.88	178.0	31.64	2.9	3.5	4.1	4.7	5.3	5.9
2 × 14		$1\frac{1}{2}$ ×	$12\frac{1}{4}$	19.88	290.8	43.89	3.5	4.1	4.8	5.5	6.2	6.9
3 × 1		$2\frac{1}{2}$ ×	$\frac{3}{4}$	1.875	0.08789	0.2344	0.3	0.4	0.5	0.5	0.6	0.7
3 × 2		$2\frac{1}{2}$ ×	$1\frac{1}{2}$	3.750	0.7031	0.9375	0.7	0.8	0.9	1.0	1.2	1.3
3 × 4		$2\frac{1}{2}$ ×	$3\frac{1}{2}$	8.750	8.932	5.104	1.5	1.8	2.1	2.4	2.7	3.0
3 × 5		$2\frac{1}{2}$ ×	$4\frac{1}{2}$	11.25	18.98	8.438	2.0	2.3	2.7	3.1	3.5	3.9
3 × 6		$2\frac{1}{2}$ ×	$5\frac{1}{2}$	13.75	34.66	12.60	2.4	2.9	3.3	3.8	4.3	4.8
3 × 8		$2\frac{1}{2}$ ×	$7\frac{1}{4}$	18.12	79.39	21.90	3.1	3.8	4.4	5.0	5.7	6.3
3 × 10		$2\frac{1}{2}$ ×	$9\frac{1}{4}$	23.12	164.9	35.65	4.0	4.8	5.6	6.4	7.2	8.0
3 × 12		$2\frac{1}{2}$ ×	$11\frac{1}{4}$	28.12	296.6	52.73	4.9	5.9	6.8	7.8	8.7	9.8
3 × 14		$2\frac{1}{2}$ ×	$13\frac{1}{4}$	33.12	484.6	73.15	5.8	6.9	8.1	9.2	10.4	11.5
3 × 16		$2\frac{1}{2}$ ×	$15\frac{1}{4}$	38.12	738.9	96.90	6.6	7.9	9.3	10.6	11.9	13.2
4 × 1		$3\frac{1}{2}$ ×	$\frac{3}{4}$	2.625	0.1230	0.3281	0.5	0.5	0.6	0.7	0.8	0.9
4 × 2		$3\frac{1}{2}$ ×	$1\frac{1}{2}$	5.250	0.9844	1.313	0.9	1.1	1.3	1.5	1.6	1.8
4 × 3		$3\frac{1}{2}$ ×	$2\frac{1}{2}$	8.750	4.557	3.646	1.5	1.8	2.1	2.4	2.7	3.0
4 × 4		$3\frac{1}{2}$ ×	$3\frac{1}{2}$	12.25	12.50	7.146	2.1	2.6	3.0	3.4	3.8	4.3
4 × 5		$3\frac{1}{2}$ ×	$4\frac{1}{2}$	15.75	26.58	11.81	2.7	3.3	3.8	4.4	4.9	5.5
4 × 6		$3\frac{1}{2}$ ×	$5\frac{1}{2}$	19.25	48.53	17.65	3.3	4.0	4.7	5.3	6.0	6.7
4 × 8		$3\frac{1}{2}$ ×	$7\frac{1}{4}$	25.38	111.1	30.66	4.4	5.3	6.2	7.0	7.9	8.8
4 × 10		$3\frac{1}{2}$ ×	$9\frac{1}{4}$	32.38	230.8	49.91	5.6	6.7	7.9	8.9	10.1	12.2
4 × 12		$3\frac{1}{2}$ ×	$11\frac{1}{4}$	39.38	415.3	73.83	6.8	8.2	9.6	10.9	12.3	13.7
4 × 14		$3\frac{1}{2}$ ×	$13\frac{1}{4}$	46.38	678.5	102.4	8.0	9.7	11.3	12.9	14.5	16.1
4 × 16		$3\frac{1}{2}$ ×	$15\frac{1}{4}$	53.38	1034	135.7	9.3	11.1	13.0	14.8	16.7	18.6
5 × 2		$4\frac{1}{2}$ ×	$1\frac{1}{2}$	6.750	1.266	1.688	1.2	1.4	1.6	1.9	2.1	2.3
5 × 3		$4\frac{1}{4}$ ×	$2\frac{1}{2}$	11.25	5.859	4.688	2.0	2.3	2.7	3.1	3.5	3.9
5 × 4		$4\frac{1}{2}$ ×	$3\frac{1}{2}$	15.75	16.08	9.188	2.7	3.3	3.8	4.4	4.9	5.5
5 × 5		$4\frac{1}{2}$ ×	$4\frac{1}{2}$	20.25	34.17	15.19	3.5	4.2	4.9	5.7	6.3	7.0
6 × 1		$5\frac{1}{2}$ ×	$\frac{3}{4}$	4.125	0.1933	0.5156	0.7	0.9	1.0	1.1	1.3	1.4
6 × 2		$5\frac{1}{2}$ ×	$1\frac{1}{2}$	8.250	1.547	2.063	1.4	1.7	2.0	2.3	2.6	2.9

Used with permission from Timber Construction Manual, Third Edition, by American Institute of Timber Construction, published by John Wiley & Sons, Inc., 1985.

Appendix E (continued)
Properties of Sawn Lumber and Timber

Nominal Size (in.)		Standard Dressed Size (in.) (S4S)		Area of Section A (in.^{2})	Moment of Inertia I (in.^{4})	Section Modulus S (in.^{3})	Weight[a] in Pounds per Linear Foot of Piece When Weight of Wood per Cubic Foot Equals:					
b	d	b	d				25 lb	30 lb	35 lb	40 lb	45 lb	50 lb
6 ×	3	$5\frac{1}{2}$ ×	$2\frac{1}{2}$	13.75	7.161	5.729	2.4	2.9	3.3	3.8	4.3	4.8
6 ×	4	$5\frac{1}{2}$ ×	$3\frac{1}{2}$	19.25	19.65	11.23	3.3	4.0	4.7	5.3	6.0	6.7
6 ×	6	$5\frac{1}{2}$ ×	$5\frac{1}{2}$	30.25	76.26	27.73	5.3	6.3	7.4	8.4	9.5	10.5
6 ×	8	$5\frac{1}{2}$ ×	$7\frac{1}{2}$	41.25	193.4	51.56	7.2	8.6	10.0	11.5	12.9	14.3
6 ×	10	$5\frac{1}{2}$ ×	$9\frac{1}{2}$	52.25	393.0	82.73	9.1	10.9	12.7	14.5	16.3	18.1
6 ×	12	$5\frac{1}{2}$ ×	$11\frac{1}{2}$	63.25	697.1	121.2	11.1	13.2	15.4	17.6	19.8	22.0
6 ×	14	$5\frac{1}{2}$ ×	$13\frac{1}{2}$	74.25	1128	167.1	12.9	15.5	18.0	20.6	23.2	25.8
6 ×	16	$5\frac{1}{2}$ ×	$15\frac{1}{2}$	85.25	1707	220.2	14.8	17.8	20.7	23.7	26.6	29.6
6 ×	18	$5\frac{1}{2}$ ×	$17\frac{1}{2}$	96.25	2456	280.7	16.7	20.1	23.4	26.7	30.1	33.4
6 ×	20	$5\frac{1}{2}$ ×	$19\frac{1}{2}$	107.2	3398	348.6	18.6	22.3	26.1	29.8	33.5	37.2
6 ×	22	$5\frac{1}{2}$ ×	$21\frac{1}{2}$	118.2	4555	423.7	20.5	24.6	28.7	32.8	37.0	41.1
6 ×	24	$5\frac{1}{2}$ ×	$23\frac{1}{2}$	129.2	5948	506.2	22.4	26.9	31.4	35.9	40.4	44.9
8 ×	1	$7\frac{1}{4}$ ×	$\frac{3}{4}$	5.438	0.2549	0.6797	0.9	1.1	1.3	1.5	1.7	1.9
8 ×	2	$7\frac{1}{4}$ ×	$1\frac{1}{2}$	10.88	2.039	2.719	1.9	2.3	2.6	3.0	3.4	3.8
8 ×	3	$7\frac{1}{4}$ ×	$2\frac{1}{2}$	18.12	9.440	7.552	3.1	3.8	4.4	5.0	5.7	6.3
8 ×	4	$7\frac{1}{4}$ ×	$3\frac{1}{2}$	25.38	25.90	14.80	4.4	5.3	6.2	7.0	7.9	8.8
8 ×	6	$7\frac{1}{2}$ ×	$5\frac{1}{2}$	41.25	104.0	37.81	7.2	8.6	10.0	11.5	12.9	14.3
8 ×	8	$7\frac{1}{2}$ ×	$7\frac{1}{2}$	56.25	263.7	70.31	9.8	11.7	13.7	15.6	17.6	19.5
8 ×	10	$7\frac{1}{2}$ ×	$9\frac{1}{2}$	71.25	535.9	112.8	12.4	14.8	17.3	19.8	22.3	24.7
8 ×	12	$7\frac{1}{2}$ ×	$11\frac{1}{2}$	86.25	950.5	165.3	15.0	18.0	21.0	24.0	27.0	29.9
8 ×	14	$7\frac{1}{2}$ ×	$13\frac{1}{2}$	101.2	1538	227.8	17.6	21.1	24.6	28.1	31.6	35.2
8 ×	16	$7\frac{1}{2}$ ×	$15\frac{1}{2}$	116.2	2327	300.3	20.2	24.2	28.3	32.3	36.3	40.4
8 ×	18	$7\frac{1}{2}$ ×	$17\frac{1}{2}$	131.2	3350	382.8	22.8	27.3	31.9	36.5	41.0	45.6
8 ×	20	$7\frac{1}{2}$ ×	$19\frac{1}{2}$	146.2	4634	475.3	25.4	30.5	35.5	40.6	45.7	50.8
8 ×	22	$7\frac{1}{2}$ ×	$21\frac{1}{2}$	161.2	6211	577.8	28.0	33.6	39.2	44.8	50.4	56.0
8 ×	24	$7\frac{1}{2}$ ×	$23\frac{1}{2}$	176.2	8111	690.3	30.6	36.7	42.8	49.0	55.1	61.2
10 ×	1	$9\frac{1}{4}$ ×	$\frac{3}{4}$	6.938	0.3252	0.8672	1.2	1.4	1.7	1.9	2.2	2.4
10 ×	2	$9\frac{1}{4}$ ×	$1\frac{1}{2}$	13.88	2.602	3.469	2.4	2.9	3.4	3.9	4.3	4.8
10 ×	3	$9\frac{1}{4}$ ×	$2\frac{1}{2}$	23.12	12.04	9.635	4.0	4.8	5.6	6.4	7.2	8.0
10 ×	4	$9\frac{1}{4}$ ×	$3\frac{1}{2}$	32.38	33.05	18.88	5.6	6.7	7.9	9.0	10.1	11.2

Used with permission from Timber Construction Manual, Third Edition, by American Institute of Timber Construction, published by John Wiley & Sons, Inc., 1985.

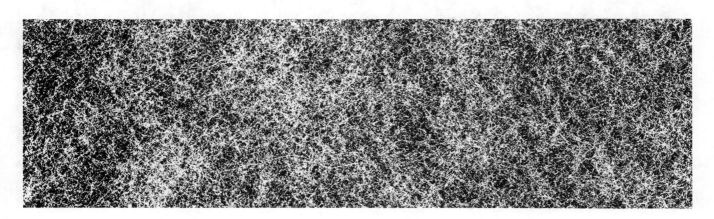

Appendix E (continued)
Properties of Sawn Lumber and Timber

Nominal Size (in.) b d	Standard Dressed Size (in.) (S4S) b d	Area of Section A (in.^{2})	Moment of Inertia I (in.^{4})	Section Modulus S (in.^{3})	Weight[a] in Pounds per Linear Foot of Piece When Weight of Wood per Cubic Foot Equals: 25 lb	30 lb	35 lb	40 lb	45 lb	50 lb
10 × 6	$9\frac{1}{2} \times 5\frac{1}{2}$	52.25	131.7	47.90	9.1	10.9	12.7	14.5	16.3	18.1
10 × 8	$9\frac{1}{2} \times 7\frac{1}{2}$	71.25	334.0	89.06	12.4	14.8	17.3	19.8	22.3	24.7
10 × 10	$9\frac{1}{2} \times 9\frac{1}{2}$	90.25	678.8	142.9	15.7	18.8	21.9	25.1	28.2	31.3
10 × 12	$9\frac{1}{2} \times 11\frac{1}{2}$	109.2	1204	209.4	19.0	22.8	26.6	30.3	34.1	37.9
10 × 14	$9\frac{1}{2} \times 13\frac{1}{2}$	128.2	1948	288.6	22.3	26.7	31.2	35.6	40.1	44.5
10 × 16	$9\frac{1}{2} \times 15\frac{1}{2}$	147.2	2948	380.4	25.6	30.7	35.8	40.9	46.0	51.1
10 × 18	$9\frac{1}{2} \times 17\frac{1}{2}$	166.2	4243	484.9	28.9	34.6	40.4	46.2	52.0	57.7
10 × 20	$9\frac{1}{2} \times 19\frac{1}{2}$	185.2	5870	602.1	32.2	38.6	45.0	51.5	57.9	64.3
10 × 22	$9\frac{1}{2} \times 21\frac{1}{2}$	204.2	7868	731.9	35.5	42.6	49.6	56.7	63.8	70.9
10 × 24	$9\frac{1}{2} \times 23\frac{1}{2}$	223.2	10,270	874.4	38.8	46.5	54.3	62.0	69.8	77.5
12 × 1	$11\frac{1}{4} \times \frac{3}{4}$	8.438	0.3955	1.055	1.5	1.8	2.1	2.3	2.6	2.9
12 × 2	$11\frac{1}{4} \times 1\frac{1}{2}$	16.88	3.164	4.219	2.9	3.5	4.1	4.7	5.3	5.9
12 × 3	$11\frac{1}{4} \times 2\frac{1}{2}$	28.12	14.65	11.72	4.9	5.9	6.8	7.8	8.8	9.8
12 × 4	$11\frac{1}{4} \times 3\frac{1}{2}$	39.38	40.20	22.97	6.8	8.2	9.6	10.9	12.3	13.7
12 × 6	$11\frac{1}{2} \times 5\frac{1}{2}$	63.25	159.4	57.98	11.0	13.2	15.4	17.6	19.8	22.0
12 × 8	$11\frac{1}{2} \times 7\frac{1}{2}$	86.25	404.3	107.8	15.0	18.0	21.0	24.0	27.0	29.9
12 × 10	$11\frac{1}{2} \times 9\frac{1}{2}$	109.2	821.7	173.0	19.0	22.8	26.6	30.3	34.1	37.9
12 × 12	$11\frac{1}{2} \times 11\frac{1}{2}$	132.2	1458	253.5	23.0	27.6	32.1	36.7	41.3	45.9
12 × 14	$11\frac{1}{2} \times 13\frac{1}{2}$	155.2	2358	349.3	27.0	32.3	37.7	43.1	48.5	53.9
12 × 16	$11\frac{1}{2} \times 15\frac{1}{2}$	178.2	3569	460.5	30.9	37.1	43.3	49.5	55.7	61.9
12 × 18	$11\frac{1}{2} \times 17\frac{1}{2}$	201.2	5136	587.0	34.9	41.9	48.9	55.9	62.9	69.9

Used with permission from Timber Construction Manual, Third Edition, by American Institute of Timber Construction, published by John Wiley & Sons, Inc., 1985.

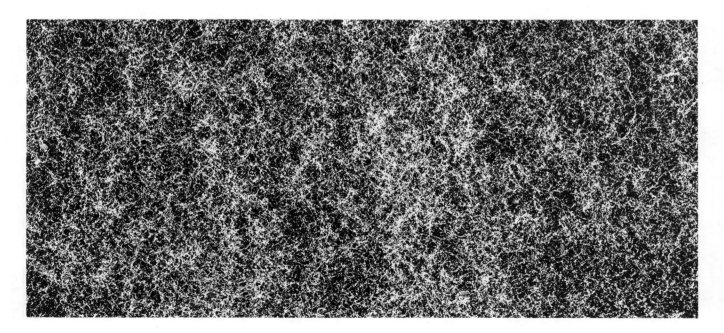

Appendix E (continued)
Properties of Sawn Lumber and Timber

Nominal Size (in.)		Standard Dressed Size (in.) (S4S)		Area of Section A (in.^{2})	Moment of Inertia I (in.^{4})	Section Modulus S (in.^{3})	Weight[a] in Pounds per Linear Foot of Piece When Weight of Wood per Cubic Foot Equals:					
b	d	b	d				25 lb	30 lb	35 lb	40 lb	45 lb	50 lb
12 × 20		11½ ×	19½	224.2	7106	728.8	38.9	46.7	54.5	62.3	70.1	77.9
12 × 22		11½ ×	21½	247.2	9524	886.0	42.9	51.5	60.1	68.7	77.3	85.9
12 × 24		11½ ×	23½	270.2	12,440	1058	46.9	56.3	65.7	75.1	84.5	93.8
14 × 2		13¼ ×	1½	19.88	3.727	4.969	3.5	4.1	4.8	5.5	6.2	6.9
14 × 3		13¼ ×	2½	33.12	17.25	13.80	5.8	6.9	8.1	9.2	10.4	11.5
14 × 4		13¼ ×	3½	46.38	47.34	27.05	8.0	9.7	11.3	12.9	14.5	16.1
14 × 6		13½ ×	5½	74.25	187.2	68.06	12.9	15.5	18.0	20.6	23.2	25.8
14 × 8		13½ ×	7½	101.2	474.6	126.6	17.6	21.1	24.6	28.1	31.6	35.2
14 × 10		13½ ×	9½	128.2	964.5	203.1	22.3	26.7	31.2	35.6	40.1	44.5
14 × 12		13½ ×	11½	155.2	1711	297.6	27.0	32.3	37.7	43.1	48.5	53.9
14 × 14		13½ ×	13½	182.2	2768	410.1	31.6	38.0	44.3	50.6	57.0	63.3
14 × 16		13½ ×	15½	209.2	4189	540.6	36.3	43.6	50.9	58.1	65.4	72.7
14 × 18		13½ ×	17½	236.2	6029	689.1	41.0	49.2	57.4	65.6	73.2	82.0
14 × 20		13½ ×	19½	263.2	8342	855.6	45.7	54.8	64.0	73.1	82.2	91.4
14 × 22		13½ ×	21½	290.2	11,180	1040	50.4	60.5	70.5	80.6	90.7	100.8
14 × 24		13½ ×	23½	317.2	14,600	1243	55.1	66.1	77.1	88.1	99.1	110.2
16 × 3		15¼ ×	2½	38.12	19.86	15.88	6.6	7.9	9.3	10.6	11.9	13.2
16 × 4		15¼ ×	3½	53.38	54.49	31.14	9.3	11.1	13.0	14.8	16.7	18.5
16 × 6		15½ ×	5½	85.25	214.9	78.15	14.8	17.8	20.7	23.7	26.6	29.6
16 × 8		15½ ×	7½	116.2	544.9	145.3	20.2	24.2	28.3	32.3	36.3	40.4
16 × 10		15½ ×	9½	147.2	1107	233.1	25.6	30.7	35.8	40.9	46.0	51.1
16 × 12		15½ ×	11½	178.2	1964	341.6	30.9	37.1	43.3	49.5	55.7	61.9
16 × 14		15½ ×	13½	209.2	3178	470.8	36.3	43.6	50.9	58.1	65.4	72.7
16 × 16		15½ ×	15½	240.2	4810	620.6	41.7	50.1	58.4	66.7	75.1	83.4
16 × 18		15½ ×	17½	271.2	6923	791.1	47.1	56.5	65.9	75.3	84.8	94.2
16 × 20		15½ ×	19½	302.2	9578	982.3	52.5	63.0	73.4	84.0	94.5	104.9
16 × 22		15½ ×	21½	333.2	12,840	1194	57.9	69.4	81.0	92.6	104.1	115.7
16 × 24		15½ ×	23½	364.2	16,760	1427	63.2	75.9	88.5	101.2	113.8	126.5
18 × 6		17½ ×	5½	96.25	242.6	88.23	16.7	20.1	23.4	26.7	30.1	33.4
18 × 8		17½ ×	7½	131.2	615.2	164.1	22.8	27.3	31.9	36.5	41.0	45.6

Used with permission from Timber Construction Manual, Third Edition, by American Institute of Timber Construction, published by John Wiley & Sons, Inc., 1985.

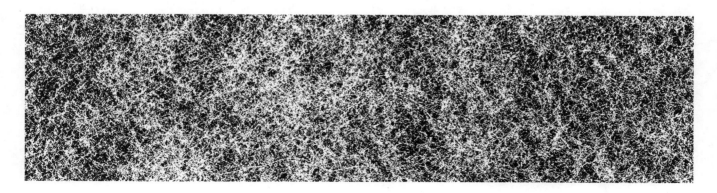

Appendix E (continued)
Properties of Sawn Lumber and Timber

Nominal Size (in.)		Standard Dressed Size (in.) (S4S)		Area of Section A (in.^{2})	Moment of Inertia I (in.^{4})	Section Modulus S (in.^{3})	Weight[a] in Pounds per Linear Foot of Piece When Weight of Wood per Cubic Foot Equals:					
b	d	b	d				25 lb	30 lb	35 lb	40 lb	45 lb	50 lb
18 × 10		17½ ×	9½	166.2	1250	263.2	28.9	34.6	40.4	46.2	52.0	57.7
18 × 12		17½ ×	11½	201.2	2218	385.7	34.9	41.9	48.9	55.9	62.9	69.9
18 × 14		17½ ×	13½	236.2	3588	531.6	41.0	49.2	57.4	65.6	73.8	82.0
18 × 16		17½ ×	15½	271.2	5431	700.7	47.1	56.5	65.9	75.3	84.8	84.2
18 × 18		17½ ×	17½	306.2	7816	893.2	53.2	63.8	74.4	85.1	95.7	106.3
18 × 20		17½ ×	19½	341.2	10,813	1109	59.2	71.1	82.9	94.8	106.6	118.5
18 × 22		17½ ×	21½	376.2	14,493	1348	65.3	78.4	91.4	104.5	117.6	130.6
18 × 24		17½ ×	23½	411.2	18,926	1611	71.4	85.7	100.0	114.2	128.5	142.8
20 × 6		19½ ×	5½	107.2	270.4	98.31	18.6	22.3	26.1	29.8	33.5	37.2
20 × 8		19½ ×	7½	146.2	685.5	182.8	25.4	30.5	35.5	40.6	45.7	50.8
20 × 10		19½ ×	9½	185.2	1393	293.3	32.2	38.6	45.0	51.5	57.9	64.3
20 × 12		19½ ×	11½	224.2	2471	429.8	38.9	46.7	54.5	62.3	70.1	77.9
20 × 14		19½ ×	13½	263.2	3998	592.3	45.7	54.8	64.0	73.1	82.3	91.4
20 × 16		19½ ×	15½	302.2	6051	780.8	52.5	63.0	73.5	84.0	94.5	104.9
20 × 18		19½ ×	17½	341.2	8709	995.3	59.2	71.1	82.9	94.8	106.6	118.5
20 × 20		19½ ×	19½	380.2	12,050	1236	66.0	79.2	92.4	105.6	118.8	132.0
20 × 22		19½ ×	21½	419.2	16,150	1502	72.8	87.3	101.9	116.5	131.0	145.6
20 × 24		19½ ×	23½	458.2	21,090	1795	79.6	95.5	111.4	127.3	143.2	159.1
22 × 6		21½ ×	5½	118.2	298.1	108.4	20.5	24.6	28.7	32.8	37.0	41.1
22 × 8		21½ ×	7½	161.2	755.9	201.6	28.0	33.6	39.2	44.8	50.4	56.0
22 × 10		21½ ×	9½	204.2	1536	323.4	35.5	42.6	49.6	56.7	63.8	70.9
22 × 12		21½ ×	11½	247.2	2725	473.9	42.9	51.5	60.1	68.7	77.3	85.9
22 × 14		21½ ×	13½	290.2	4408	653.1	50.4	60.5	70.5	80.6	90.7	100.8
22 × 16		21½ ×	15½	333.2	6672	860.9	57.9	69.4	81.0	92.6	104.1	115.7
22 × 18		21½ ×	17½	376.2	9602	1097	65.3	78.4	91.5	104.5	117.6	130.6
22 × 20		21½ ×	19½	419.2	13,280	1363	72.8	87.3	101.9	116.5	131.0	145.6
22 × 22		21½ ×	21½	462.2	17,810	1656	80.3	96.3	112.4	128.4	144.5	160.5
22 × 24		21½ ×	23½	505.2	23,250	1979	87.7	105.3	122.8	140.3	157.9	175.4
24 × 6		23½ ×	5½	129.2	325.8	118.5	22.4	26.9	31.4	35.9	40.4	44.9
24 × 8		23½ ×	7½	176.2	826.2	220.3	30.6	36.7	42.8	49.0	55.1	61.2
24 × 10		23½ ×	9½	223.2	1679	353.5	38.8	46.5	54.3	62.0	69.8	77.5
24 × 12		23½ ×	11½	270.2	2978	518.0	46.9	56.3	65.7	75.1	84.5	93.8
24 × 14		23½ ×	13½	317.2	4818	713.8	55.1	66.1	77.1	88.1	99.1	110.2
24 × 16		23½ ×	15½	364.2	7293	941.0	63.2	75.9	88.5	101.2	113.8	126.5
24 × 18		23½ ×	17½	411.2	10,500	1199	71.4	85.7	100.0	114.2	128.5	142.8
24 × 20		23½ ×	19½	458.2	14,520	1489	79.6	95.5	111.4	127.3	143.2	159.1
24 × 22		23½ ×	21½	505.2	19,460	1810	87.7	105.3	122.8	140.3	157.9	175.4
24 × 24		23½ ×	23½	552.2	25,420	2163	95.9	115.1	134.2	153.4	172.6	191.8

[a]To obtain the weight of a species of wood at a given moisture content use the following formula:

$$W = \frac{G}{1 + G(0.009)MC}\left[1 + \frac{MC}{100}\right](62.4)$$

where W = weight of wood (lb/ft^3)

   G = specific gravity of species obtained from Table 6.1

   MC = moisture content of the lumber (%).

Used with permission from Timber Construction Manual, Third Edition, by American Institute of Timber Construction, published by John Wiley & Sons, Inc., 1985.

References

American Institute of Timber Construction (AITC). *Timber Construction Manual*, 3d ed. New York: John Wiley & Sons, Inc., 1985.

American Plywood Association (APA). *Plywood Design Specification*, Tacoma, WA: American Plywood Association, 1989.

American Plywood Association (APA). *Design and Fabrication of Plywood-Lumber Beams, Supplement 2*. Tacoma, WA: American Plywood Association, 1988.

American Plywood Association (APA). *Plywood Diaphragm Construction*, Tacoma WA: American Plywood Association, 1989.

American Plywood Association (APA). *Design and Construction Guide for Concrete Forming*, Tacoma WA: American Plywood Association, 1989.

American Society for Testing and Materials (ASTM). *Annual Book of ASTM Standards, Part 22: Wood; Adhesives*. Philadelphia, PA: ASTM.

Bodig, Jozsef and Jayne, Benjamin A. *Mechanics of Wood and Wood Composites*, New York: Van Nostrand Reinhold Company, 1982.

Breyer, Donald E. *Design of Wood Structures*, 2d ed. New York: McGraw-Hill, 1988.

Diekmann, Edward F. Design of Diaphragms In *EMMSE Series*. Vol. 4. Materials Research Laboratory. University Park, PA: The Pennsylvania State University Press, 1984.

Faherty, Keith F. and Williamson, Thomas G., eds. *Wood Engineering and Construction Handbook*, New York: McGraw-Hill, 1989.

Gurfinkel, German. *Wood Engineering*, 2nd ed. Dubuque, IA: Kendall/Hunt Publishing Co., 1981.

Hoyle, Robert J., Jr. and Woeste, Frank E. *Wood Technology in the Design of Structures*, 5th ed. Ames, IA: Iowa State University Press, 1989.

Hurd M.K. *Formwork For Concrete*. American Concrete Institute, 1979.

International Conference of Building Officials (ICBO). *Uniform Building Code*, Whittier, CA: International Conference of Building Officials, 1988.

National Forest Products Association (NFPA). *National Design Specification for Wood Construction*, Washington, DC: National Forest Products Association, 1986.

Stalnaker, Judith J. and Harris, Ernest C. *Structural Design In Wood*, New York: Van Nostrand Reinhold Company, 1989.

Timber Engineering Company (TECO). *Design Manual for TECO Timber Connector Construction*, Colliers, WV: TECO Products, 1973.

Forest Products Laboratory, United States Department of Agriculture. *Wood Handbook: Wood as an Engineering Material*, rev. ed. Forest Service Agriculture Handbook No. 72. Washington, DC: U.S. Government Printing Office, New Edition: 1974.

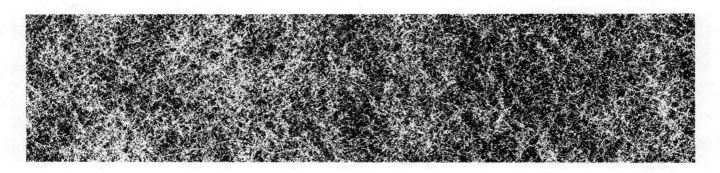

Index

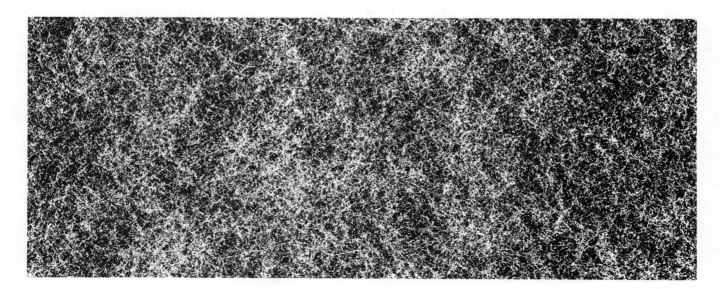